$\mathcal{F}$LOWERS CRACKING CONCRETE

Eiko & Koma's Asian/American Choreographies

ROSEMARY CANDELARIO

WESLEYAN UNIVERSITY PRESS   MIDDLETOWN, CONNECTICUT

WESLEYAN UNIVERSITY PRESS
Middletown CT 06459
www.wesleyan.edu/wespress
© 2016 Rosemary Candelario
All rights reserved
Manufactured in the United States of America
Typeset in Garamond Premier Pro
by Tseng Information Systems, Inc.

Hardcover ISBN: 978-0-8195-7647-7
Paperback ISBN: 978-0-8195-7648-4
Ebook ISBN: 978-0-8195-7649-1

Library of Congress Cataloging-in-Publication
Data available upon request

5 4 3 2 1

For Karl

CONTENTS

$\mathcal{A}$CKNOWLEDGMENTS

In the summer of 2006 I was packing up my life in Boston to move diagonally cross-country to attend graduate school at UCLA when I received an e-mail from David Gere, then chair of the World Arts and Cultures Department, announcing that Eiko & Koma would be in residence for the fall quarter. At the time I could not have predicted how that simple message would put me on a ten-year path that eventually led to this book. During my first class with Eiko & Koma, Eiko said they do not choose students, students choose them. That day, I definitely chose them. Over the course of the quarter I got to know Eiko in particular, acting as scribe for the movement class, compiling notes on each of our sessions that in retrospect represent my first attempts to put the full force of their movement into words. After the quarter ended I stayed in touch with Eiko, showing up at performances whenever possible and helping out as needed. When, at the encouragement of Susan Leigh Foster, I decided to write my dissertation about Eiko & Koma, I asked Eiko's permission. It was clear to me my research would not be possible without the full participation of the dancers. Eiko thought I was crazy to write a dissertation about Eiko & Koma, something she never failed to tell me each time we met. But she didn't stop me. And as time went on, she began introducing me to their friends, colleagues, collaborators, and family. Over the past ten years Eiko & Koma have been unfailingly generous with me, and this book simply could not exist without their participation.

Beyond Eiko & Koma, there are many people whose contributions and assistance have helped make this book a reality. Foremost among them are Angela Ahlgren and Hannah Kosstrin, who patiently read and re-read these words and gave the most generous and challenging feedback possible. This book is all the better for their input. Texas Woman's University research librarian Andy Tucker provided research assistance for chapter 2. Andrea Harris cheerfully tracked down video documentation of a 1994 panel discussion entitled "Dancing Identity: What Does It Mean to Be Asian American?," which happened as part of the yearlong Festival of Asian/Asian American Dance at the University of Wisconsin–Madison. She kindly facilitated the digitization of the video so that I could view it from afar. The always inspiring Prumsodun Ok gave me thoughtful comments on chapter 7. Rebecca Rossen kindly invited me to present an expanded version of the conclusion at the University of Texas at Austin. Sara Wolf encouraged me to be more fierce. Lydia Bell, Eiko & Koma's Retrospective Project coordinator, was a joy to work with and was unerringly helpful. Arlene Yu and numerous other librarians at the Jerome Robbins Dance Division of the New York Public Library for the Performing Arts provided invaluable research assistance, as did archivists Kirsten Tanaka at the San Francisco Museum of Performing Arts + Design and Jill Vucetich of the Walker Art Center. Debra Cash kindly shared her published reviews with me. Libby Smigel of the Dance Heritage Coalition gave me the opportunity to work in Eiko & Koma's archives. Patsy Gay taught me the ins and outs of archiving and happily tracked down stray images and bits of information for me when I could not get to New York to do it myself. Annelize Machado provided thorough and prompt assistance with citations and the bibliography. Yayoi Takeuchi introduced me to Kiko Kawamura, who proofread Japanese names and words for me. Brent Hirak provided expert assistance producing video stills. Finally, many thanks go to my anonymous readers, whose insights and guidance were invaluable.

I am particularly grateful to everyone I interviewed over the years. Whether or not their words appear directly in the book, their kindness and knowledge suffuse it. Thank-you Jeremy Alliger, Philip Bither, Donna Faye Burchfield, Caitlin Coker, Paula Lawrence, Sam Miller, Robert Mirabal, Takashi Morishita, Yoshito Ohno, Irene and Paul Oppenheim, Charles Reinhart, members of the Reyum Painting Collective, and Marcia B. Siegel. I am particularly thankful that I got the chance to meet and interview Beate Sirota Gordon (1923–2012), who produced Eiko & Koma's first official performance in the United States in 1976.

I had the opportunity to work through parts of the book at numerous conferences and with the support of various seminars and working groups. Members of the International Federation for Theatre Research Choreography and Corporeality Working Group commented on an early version of the introduction; Ramsay Burt in particular provided gentle yet sharp (and needed) critique. William Marotti generously enabled my ongoing participation in the Japan Arts and Globalization (JAG) group. I am especially grateful to have participated in the 2014 JAG works in progress retreat, where chapter 1 received a thorough reading by JAG members. I was honored to participate in the Association for Asian American Studies conference panel "Subjects in Motion: Bridging Asian American Studies and Dance Studies" with Lorenzo Perillo, Angeline Shaka, and Yutian Wong. Their camaraderie and insight on chapter 3 were invaluable. The inaugural Mellon Dance Studies Seminar, convened by Susan Manning, Janice Ross, and Rebecca Schneider, provided me with an expansive community of peers who read and commented on an early version of chapter 4. Core members of the Butoh's Corporeal Acts Working Group, formed initially for the joint conference of the Congress on Research in Dance and the American Society for Theatre Research, have been an ongoing source of information and inspiration: thank-you Tanya Calamoneri, Zack Fuller, Katherine Mezur, Megan Nicely, and Michael Sakamoto. I thank Bruce Baird in particular for his unfailing enthusiasm and collegiality.

Excerpts of chapter 4 are reprinted with permission from "Bodies, Camera, Screen: Eiko & Koma's Immersive Media Dances," *International Journal of Screendance* 4 (2014): 80–92.

I continue to be indebted to my UCLA dissertation committee, whose guidance during graduate school provided me with a firm foundation from which to write this book. Susan Leigh Foster remains a generous mentor. Her influence, along with that of Lucy Mae San Pablo Burns, Janet O'Shea, and Carol Sorgenfrei, suffuses this book.

Texas Woman's University supported this book with a Small Grant, multiple School of the Arts Faculty Scholarship Enhancement Grants, and course releases. Parts of chapters 4 and 6 were presented as part of the Faculty Spotlight Series and as a research briefing for the Department of Women's Studies. In addition, I thank Mary Williford-Shade for being the most understanding chair an assistant professor could ask for.

Ever since I took my first dance class at age four, I wanted to be a dancer. And ever since my father first showed me his bound dissertation when I was eight years old, I knew that I wanted my own name to appear on the spine of a book. What a delight it is to have those two childhood dreams come together in this book. Much of the credit goes to my mother, who drove me to all those dance classes, prioritized my education, and trusted me to make good decisions. Finally, the biggest thanks go to Karl Gossot, whose quiet support has sustained me through this book and so much more.

A NOTE ABOUT
JAPANESE NAMES AND WORDS

I follow the *Monumenta Nipponica* stylesheet with the following exceptions. I have chosen to list all Japanese names given name first, family name second. Even in Japan, where the standard is family name first, individuals with established careers outside of Japan are commonly referred to with the given name first, for example, Kazuo Ohno. Since this book primarily engages with Japanese artists through the frame of American concert dance, I employ this convention across the board to avoid confusion, unless a name appears in a direct quote, in which case I reproduce the original order. This name order is also consistent with English-language reviews, program notes, and publications. In terms of spelling, I generally eschew macrons in the case of well-established transliterations (e.g., butoh instead of butō, noh instead of nō, Ohno instead of Ōno), but keep them for less common names and words.

Furthermore, I follow Eiko & Koma's practice of writing their names with an ampersand when referring to their professional work; when I refer to them as individuals, I use Eiko and Koma.

FLOWERS CRACKING CONCRETE

Introduction

Walking into Wesleyan University's Zilkha Gallery for the launch of Eiko & Koma's Retrospective Project, I almost feel as if I am backstage at a theater rather than at the opening of an exhibition. A massive, sand-colored canvas hanging from the ceiling reinforces my perception of being behind the scenes. Upon closer inspection, the burnt surface offers me small windows through which I may catch glimpses of the gallery beyond. Students, many of them from Eiko's Delicious Movement for Forgetting, Remembering, and Uncovering class, busily rush past me, taking care of last-minute tasks. Small attentive groups, including then American Dance Festival director Charles Reinhart, Retrospective Project producer Sam Miller, and former Japan Foundation director of performing arts Paula Lawrence, gather in front of video screens behind me displaying the video compilation, *38 Works by Eiko & Koma*, which cycles through documentation of the duo's dances since they came to the United States from Japan in 1976. The energy of the crowd pulls me further down the hallway, past a table set up with a computer displaying Eiko & Koma's new Web site, and toward backdrops from *Cambodian Stories* (2006) that grace the walls. Just as the paintings by students at Reyum School of Art in Phnom Penh begin to tower over me, I notice my feet are crunching dry leaves; am I supposed to be walking here? Instead of ending at a wall, this hallway has led me into the leafy, dimly lit cave that is the set of *Breath*, Eiko & Koma's 1998 live installation at the Whitney Museum of American Art. Although I feel I could stay in this environment for hours, sounds from the main gallery draw me back toward the scorched and scarred canvas. Stepping around it, I find myself literally onstage, facing rows of empty chairs, soon to be filled by the more than one hundred attendees. I am standing on the black-feather-and straw-strewn set for *Raven* (2010), which will have a preview performance in just a few moments. Gazing around the high-ceilinged, long room, I am first struck by the media dances filling the near wall. In one, Eiko & Koma's naked bodies seem to float midair, sorrow dripping from their bodies, in *Lament* (1985), while on a nearby cracked and peeling screen, Eiko & Koma raise a white flag of surrender in documentation of *Event Fission* (1980). Opposite, the wall is all glass, providing a view of the trailer from Eiko & Koma's *Caravan Project* (1999); standing open as it did during site-specific performances all over the United States, its fiery interior is mirrored by a blanket of crimson leaves on the ground and the sun setting through bare trees. Beyond the chairs at the far end of the gallery hangs a mysterious, speckled black canvas, in front of which Eiko & Koma will end the evening with a revival of their first piece of set choreography, *White Dance* (1976). Wending its way around the perimeter of the gallery is a thread of snapshots at eye level. This literal time line is paradoxically not linear; when I reach the end, I have somehow returned to the beginning. In addition to images of well- and lesser-known works by Eiko & Koma, I spot photos of the dancers with Kazuo Ohno, Manja Chmiel, and Anna Halprin. One photo from the time line also circulates around the gallery on homemade T-shirts worn by Irene and Paul Oppenheim, the producers of Eiko & Koma's very first performance in the United States in 1976.

Time Is Not Even, Space Is Not Empty opened on November 19, 2009, and launched the three-year Retrospective Project through which Eiko & Koma aimed to examine their body of work for its continued or shifting resonances for contemporary audiences. The Retrospective gave Eiko & Koma the opportunity to rigorously examine their own practice through the collection (and sometimes production) of archival materials and the creation of new works from earlier dances. Aspects of the Retrospective included museum exhibitions of photographs, sets, and screen dances; a new living installation, *Naked* (2010); the reworking of older pieces into new dances, for example *Raven* from *Land* (1991); the revival of older works; the publication of a retrospective catalog by the Walker Art Center; and a new collaboration with Kronos Quartet, *Fragile* (2012).

For audience members, the Retrospective showcased the remarkable scope of Eiko & Koma's body of work. Since meeting at Tatsumi Hijikata's Asbestos Hall in Tokyo in 1971, Eiko & Koma have choreographed dances that for all their simplicity grapple with monumental matters: destruction and regeneration, relationships among humans and between humans and nature, and the stakes of being an artist in challenging political times. Their work is deeply informed by their participation in the 1960s Tokyo student movement; formative encounters with Hijikata and Ohno, key figures of the avant-garde postwar dance form *butoh* in Japan; relationships with Mary Wigman assistant Manja Chmiel, Jose Limón dancer Lucas Hoving, and San Francisco iconoclast Anna Halprin; and participation in the New York City arts community. These touchstones — radical politics in postwar Japan, butoh, "Neue Tanz,"[1] and downtown dance — are the foundations of Eiko & Koma's more than four-decades-long collaboration. From these influences, Eiko & Koma developed a singular performance technique and approach to choreography. Though they are considered part of a generation of American dance artists that includes David Gordon, Bebe Miller, and Ralph Lemon, their unique movement style, unrelated to modern dance or ballet; rejection of a company model; insistence upon choreographing almost exclusively on their own bodies; and do-it-yourself practices set them apart from their peers in American concert dance. The Retrospective drew attention to their impressive intersections with dance history on three continents and highlighted the skill with which they move from proscenium stages, to outdoor sites, to museum installations, and in front of and behind the camera.

Eiko & Koma's Retrospective Project also issued a vivid reminder that the two dancers have been central figures in the American concert dance scene since they moved to New York from Tokyo in 1977. But it also raised important questions, such as why so little academic research exists on Eiko & Koma, despite prestigious recognition by the MacArthur Foundation and the Doris Duke Performing Artist Award, among many others; international renown; and overwhelming critical acclaim.[2] Dance reviews constitute the largest body of writing on the pair, including early and sustained attention from noted American critics including Jack Anderson, Suzanne Carbonneau, Jennifer Dunning, Deborah Jowitt, Anna Kisselgoff, Janice Ross, Lewis Segal, and Tobi Tobias. Another important collection of writings is by Eiko herself, comprising choreographer's notes available in programs and on their Web site, and published essays.[3] Academic writing is limited to two master's theses[4] and my own published materials. A couple of books include chapters on Eiko & Koma in the form of interviews or expanded encyclopedia entries.[5]

The Walker Art Center's 2011 catalog, *Time Is Not Even, Space Is Not Empty*, is the most significant text on Eiko & Koma to date, comprising a comprehensive biography, artistic essays, and descriptions of every piece made by the pair from 1972 through 2010. Richly illustrated with photographs and including writings by some of the photographers who have worked with them for decades, the catalog is a major document. Useful appendices include information on funders, commissioners, and presenters from 1972 to 2011.[6]

Flowers Cracking Concrete: Eiko & Koma's Asian/American Choreographies does not attempt to duplicate the contributions of previous texts, but instead provides the first book-length critical analysis of the Japanese American duo's body of work, examining in detail more than half of their sixty-plus stage, outdoor, video, installation, and gallery works created over more than four decades. This long overdue study argues that Eiko & Koma's dances, like the flowers of the title, effect a gradual but profound transformation that has significant political implications. I trace the elaboration over time of the concerns that have become central to Eiko & Koma's work: the linkages between humans and nature, sustained mourning for personal and historical traumas, and the sometimes-fraught alliances among humans. My goal is to intervene in how these dances are viewed by providing historical and political contexts for the development of Eiko & Koma's choreography in Japan, Europe, and New York City. These contexts place Eiko & Koma firmly in American dance history even as they reveal the necessity of considering the duo as both Japanese and Asian American.

Adagio Activists

An extraordinary — and defining — facet of Eiko & Koma's work is the slowness with which they unfold their bodies and their dances, a pace less human and more geologic. Moving at a speed significantly decelerated from daily life, Eiko & Koma's dances shift attention to the ways that seemingly fixed elements of our world — trees, mountains, continents — are also constantly changing. The title of this book, *Flowers Cracking Concrete*,[7] signals the profound corporeal and affective work of Eiko & Koma's dances. This impossible-seeming image conveys a slow yet violent process effected through persistent and insistent micromovements and embodies the contradictions inherent in Eiko & Koma's work. Though commonly described as slow and subtle, the effect of Eiko & Koma's performances is like water eroding rock or tree roots displacing a sidewalk: the sometimes imperceptible movements of two bodies over time have a profound impact physically and emotionally on one another, their environment, and their audiences. Watching them perform, one may think that nothing in particular is happening until—gasp!—one is hit with a realization that something significant—a major shift, a rupture—has transpired. Not only have their drawn-out moving images compelled audiences to pay a different kind of attention, but they have also effected a transformation: slowly, imperceptibly, and then suddenly all at once. Although the dances do include moments of explosive movement, stuttering limbs, and sudden shifts, overall they are marked by an extraordinary insistence on taking time and an attention to the importance of the smallest of movements.

Slavoj Žižek argues persuasively that it is a political choice to do nothing, and that doing nothing is in fact still doing something.[8] For Eiko & Koma it is a striking choreographic choice. Of course Eiko & Koma do not do nothing. Even when they seem to an audience to be utterly still, for minutes or hours on end, they are always active. Eiko & Koma's appearance of doing nothing, of taking their time, of taking space to take time, results in the central mission of their dance slowly revealing itself, both over the course of one performance and over the forty-plus years of their danced collaboration. Slowness then is not just an aesthetic for the stage, but also a method of working over the long term. Moreover, in that they are often doing the same thing, it may appear as if they are doing nothing (new). And yet their stubborn persistence, their insistence upon returning again and again to the same themes and the same movements, demonstrates an extraordinary commitment to taking their time to find out what is important to them and giving that issue physical form.

What stood out to critics who first saw Eiko & Koma's choreography in the mid- and late 1970s, and continues to be the case into their fifth decade of work, is the surprising effect of their minimalist movement. Critics may have disagreed about the meaning of various performances, but they agreed on the work's impact. Unfortunately most critics have not probed the dancers' slowness further, often leaving it at the simple fact of slowness. ("Eiko and Koma Slow Time Down" and "The King and Queen of Slow Get Busy" are representative headlines.[9]) Their speed, or lack of it as it were, moreover leads some to make Orientalist associations with noh or Zen rock gardens. Many audience members assume Eiko & Koma meditate before performing, as evidenced by the regularity of questions about meditation and yoga at after-performance talk backs. Reviews often neglect to mention the moments of absurdity or outbursts of speed or violence that frequently puncture their dances, leaving unexamined the implications of taking longer than expected to start dancing, to stop mourning, and to form connections.

In order to intervene in the prevailing misreading of Eiko & Koma's aesthetic of slowness, I emphasize Eiko and Koma's backgrounds as student activists and the context of the Japanese avant-garde. As I discuss in chapter 1, Eiko and Koma each came to avant-garde performance as student activists in the early 1970s in Japan. Searching for an alternative to what they saw as the dead end of the leftist political scene, they found in dance a compelling way of acting in the world. Rather than seeing their transition from protesting in the streets to performing in galleries and theaters as a break with activism, I see it as a continuation of their critical stance in a new medium. Thinking about Eiko & Koma's choreography as a kind of activism requires a shift from focusing on what the dances signify to paying attention to what they do. I am not suggesting that Eiko & Koma's work is beyond representation or signification. Nor am I suggesting that the meaning of these dances cannot be expressed in words. On the contrary, this book challenges such beliefs, insisting instead on articulating the specific ways Eiko & Koma's choreography actually effects something in the world. Eiko & Koma do not represent mourning, I argue; they do it. They do not just represent new kinds of alliances with nature and across difference; they generate them. Very slowly.

Previously I wrote about the ways Eiko & Koma's work generated what I called "spaces apart" through the choreographed relationship among moving bodies, sites, and technologies.[10] I argued that it is in these spaces apart where alternatives to the dominant society may be rehearsed, and entrenched binaries such as nature/culture and East/West may be challenged. In this book I focus on time as a foundational concept, particularly the passage of time as conveyed through the concept of slowness. Specifically, I frame Eiko & Koma's choreography as an adagio activism. This term is inspired by Žižek's insight into what slowing down can achieve.[11] He writes,

"Do you mean we should do NOTHING? Just sit and wait?" One should gather the courage to answer: "YES, precisely that!" There are situations when the only truly "practical" thing to do is resist the temptation to engage immediately and to "wait and see" by means of a patient critical analysis.[12]

Looking back at Eiko & Koma's body of work over the past forty years, it becomes evident how they have used their dances as an opportunity to continuously analyze with their bodies the issues most important to them. In a 1986 interview, Eiko shared, "We do not want to jump into working on a dance with a concept which is just hunted. It should be some theme that slowly comes up as a concern, which we cannot help but deal with. Making the dance is one way to deal with our concern."[13] In other words, adagio activism is a decelerated, durational process compelled by a deeper searching, a patient and corporeal discernment that reveals matters of great importance. Eiko & Koma's body of work is evidence that the themes of their dances are not random but are ones with which they deeply connect, with the result that those things they choose to explore, they explore exhaustively. Moreover, their dances do not signify these matters of importance but realize them.[14] That is, dance for Eiko & Koma is not only a way to come to understand something, but a means to give it physical form, to actualize it in the world.

Slowness for Žižek, and for Eiko & Koma, is therefore not a benign aesthetic but a political intervention, like a labor slowdown when workers intentionally decrease production on an assembly line to demonstrate their centrality to the success of capitalism.[15] Slowing down enables analysis of a complicated and bewildering situation, like the function of violence, which Žižek categorizes as subjective and objective. Subjective violence includes acts committed by an individual or group of individuals that visibly disturb the status quo; crime and terror are two obvious examples. Objective violence, on the other hand, is the necessarily invisible violence — both symbolic and systemic — that sustains the very status quo from which subjective violence so graphically stands out. The urgency (Žižek calls this a "fake urgency") with which we are prompted to respond to subjective violence actually serves to mask objective violence and prevents us from comprehending how objective violence in fact begets subjective violence. Ultimately, for Žižek the most profound act is one "that violently disturbs the basic parameters of social life."[16] It is at its heart "a radical upheaval of the basic social relations"[17] that could disturb the functioning of objective violence.

Eiko & Koma's dances over the past four decades — generating connections and change over time and across borders — offer an alternative model for how art can reflect and transform society. Avant-garde art need not only cause radical breaks; it can also effectively engage in a slow, sustained process of change. Slowness as choreographic method provides the time to learn how to develop alternative ways of working in the world, including tactics that may allow one to pass outside the visibility of subjective violence, reveal the functioning of objective violence, and create alliances that could prove effective in countering objective violence. Eiko & Koma say they make work about something they need to discover, not something they already know. Their concerns, the things that they "cannot help but deal with," require repeated and careful analysis, which they conduct through their choreography.

In both Eiko & Koma's body of work and in this book, slowness is foundational without itself being the point of the dance or the analysis. It is a consistently used tool, but its results are not always the same. For example, Eiko & Koma use slowness in their dances for different ends: it may be a way to prolong mourning or to facilitate connections among humans, nature, and technology. Slowness can also draw attention to cycles of destruction and regeneration, making the long duration of cycles over lifetimes comprehensible over the course of one dance. Similarly, slowness in this book provides the foundation for viewing Eiko & Koma's work; it is a prerequisite that must be understood before the analysis can proceed. As such, aesthetics as politics is not the focus of this book, but it is the foundation. The focus instead is on the variety of ways that Eiko & Koma employ their aesthetics and to what end.

Asian/American/Dance

When I was doing research in Japan, people would say to me, "Well you know, Eiko & Koma are really American." They are simply not considered part of Japanese dance history, even though they began performing while briefly living at Hijikata's Asbestos Hall and studied with Ohno early in their careers. This view is understandable given that the dancers have had their primary residence in New York since 1977 and — not counting their experimental performances in the early 1970s—have only performed in Japan a handful of times. On the other hand, Eiko & Koma's significance in American dance history and their ongoing role in American concert dance is often elided by a popular discourse that persistently categorizes them as Asian. Rather than pointing to specific political, historical, or cultural markers that might be relevant to Eiko & Koma's work, "Asian" too often slips into an Orientalism that says far more about Asian American racialization and the legal and discursive regulation of Asian bodies in the United States than it does about the dance at hand. Moreover, these perspectives that would have the dancers be either generically American or Asian foreclose consideration of the complex personal, political, and dance historical webs that form the foundation of the work.

In this book I situate Eiko & Koma both as Japanese artists who began performing through their encounters with butoh but who have never called their work by that name, and as Asian American artists in American concert dance who have had international success. This orientation to their choreography has theoretical and methodological implications that require me to cross boundaries of dance studies, Japanese studies, and Asian American studies, and take into account theories of transnationalism, diaspora, and Asian American racial formation. In the process, I seek to expand critical understanding of the radical nature of Eiko & Koma's body of work, while also demonstrating how that work—of which the artists themselves sometimes question whether it is indeed dance or choreography—influences the field of dance studies. The book contributes to the nascent body of literature concerned with Asian American dance and expands American dance history to include the contributions of Asians and Asian Americans.

By insisting on thinking about Eiko & Koma as part of American dance history, I join Asian American scholars who examine the ways Asians have or have not been included in the idea—and state—of America. This thinking is reflected in the book's subtitle, *Eiko & Koma's Asian/American Choreographies*. I follow David Palumbo-Liu's use of the solidus to signal a simultaneous connection and separation, inclusion and exclusion, between Asian and American.[18] The addition of the slash points to the repeated exclusions of Asians from America, beginning with the Chinese Exclusion Act of 1872, even as the punctuation simultaneously resists the nationalist project of the subsumption of Asians into America, particularly as model minorities after the 1965 Immigration and Nationality Act. The slash furthermore highlights the unsettled state of both terms, acknowledging repeated and historically changing international as well as intranational contact. This is a particularly appropriate approach for Eiko & Koma, who have been permanent residents of the United States since 1979 and whose career is inextricable from American concert dance, but who maintain their Japanese citizenship.

Unlike Asian American theater and performance, Asian American dance remains woefully undertheorized.[19] Dance studies is itself a relatively new discipline, and while an analysis of race, class, and gender has been central to its formation, Asian American choreographers and dancers have remained largely invisible. I lean heavily on the work of Yutian Wong, a scholar at the forefront of Asian American dance. She is joined by scholars such as Priya Srinivasan and SanSan Kwan in developing a nascent body of literature on Asians dancing in America, the meaning of dance in diasporic communities, and the contribution of Asian Americans to American dance history.[20] As Wong established in the essay "Towards a New Asian American Dance Theory: Locating the Dancing Asian American Body" and expanded on in her book *Choreographing Asian America*, Asian American contributions have been largely erased from American dance history, despite the fact that, as she asserts, "American modern and postmodern dance forms are always already Asian American."[21] Her argument is strongly influenced by Brenda Dixon Gottschild's efforts to expose the ways that African American culture, via the presence of Africanist movement qualities, infuses American dance to the point that American dance *is* African American.[22] Wong persuasively demonstrates that Asian American bodies form an invisible foundation of American modern and postmodern dance. For example, modern dance "pioneer" Ruth St. Denis based many of her early twentieth-century Orientalist dances on work by Nautch dancers from India she met in New York, sometimes even using their bodies onstage as backdrops to her solos.[23] Merce Cunningham famously began employing the *I Ching* in the 1950s in his chance operations, which separated dance making from narrative and even the express intent of the choreographer. Steve Paxton later drew heavily from aikido, among other movement forms, in his development of contact improvisation in the early 1970s. In each of these cases, the unacknowledged appropriation of Asian bodies and concepts is regarded as the product of individual (white, American) genius.

It is not a matter, however, of simply inserting "forgotten" dancers back into the dance history canon. As Wong deftly demonstrates with the case of Michio Ito, a Japanese dancer who enjoyed enormous success in the United States before being deported to Japan during World War II, repeated revivals and retrospectives of his work have never quite remedied his absence from the canon.[24] An examination of American legal, political, and popular discourses reveals that the pattern in dance history of alternately emphasizing or erasing Asian Americans is in fact a fundamental condition of American national identity formation. Karen Shimakawa explicates this condition as a process of abjection—à la Julia Kristeva—in which Asian Americans are both "constituent element *and* radical other"[25] of the nation. In other words, "America" is defined through the (ongoing) exclusion of Asian (American)s, who nonetheless constitute an essential part of that same identity. It is important to note that the abject is always internal to the deject, even as it is excluded. This ambiguity or contradiction is reflected in the literal, material, legal, and symbolic abjection of Asian Americans. For example, Japanese internment excluded Japanese Americans from "America" by drawing them further in. Another example is the alternation between legal exclusion and model minority status. Abjection is, after all, an unstable process, requiring continuous reinforcement.

Asian American studies has proven invaluable for teasing out the complex forces that impact Asian American dancers in general and Eiko & Koma in particular. This book asserts that what Eiko & Koma do onstage—their choreographic decisions—can be productively analyzed as Asian American cultural critique. In addition to guiding my orientation to the dancers' body of work as a whole, the discipline is also a source of scholarship on mourning, melancholia, reparation, intercultural performance, and multiculturalism that helps me analyze Eiko & Koma's predominant themes. However, I must acknowledge that the discipline's focus on art as a source of legible stories of immigration, oppression, and resistance has meant that text-based productions like literature and theater have been favored, while body-based or abstract work runs the risk of not being visible as Asian American. This is not unique to Eiko & Koma, but is a larger issue faced by many Asian American performers. Wong discusses the same phenomenon in relation to work by Sue Li-Jue and Denise Uyehara, noting that pieces lacking an explicit Asian American critique become "unidentifiable in terms of inhabiting a thematic Asian American niche."[26] In other words, content rather than form is where politics becomes comprehensible within the field.

This book takes as a given that choreography is inherently political, that aesthetic choices reflect political investments, and that dancing bodies are formed within regimes of discipline and viewed by their audiences in the context of the politics of representation. Though these statements may seem self-evident, this kind of thinking about dance only became possible with the rise of dance studies scholarship beginning in the mid-1980s and has not fully made its way into other disciplines.[27] In bringing together dance and Asian American studies I, like Wong, seek to racialize and politicize aesthetics. In particular, I aim to demonstrate how the US Orientalism inherent in American modern dance has obscured the politics of Eiko & Koma's dances, even while awarding those dances the highest honors. At the same time, I argue for the choreography itself as Asian American critique; in doing so, I assert that dance is not merely a vehicle for telling stories, but more important, is a way of enacting a particular politics.

Methodology

My goal to elucidate the politics of Eiko & Koma's choreography is best achieved through choreographic analysis, through which I critically unpack the dances to demonstrate what these unique works effect in the world. My primary sources, then, are the dances themselves. I draw on extensive observation of Eiko & Koma's performances, rehearsals, and workshops. Live performances I was not able to see in person I watched through video documentation and studied through photographs, promotional materials, newspaper previews and reviews, and program notes available in Eiko & Koma's personal archives and in collections at The Jerome Robbins Dance Division of The New York Public Library and the San Francisco Museum of Performance + Design. Media dances created specifically for film or video I have watched on my computer, on gallery walls, and in university and museum screening rooms.

Eiko & Koma's dances challenge an easy separation between choreography and performance. Because they are both choreographers and usually the only performers of their dances, it can be difficult to separate Eiko & Koma's movement style and choreography from their individual bodies. Furthermore, the vocabulary often appears deceptively simple: small, subtle, continuous movements that contain none of the virtuosity or proscenium-oriented, presentational qualities of many other dance forms. Nonetheless it is possible to construct a choreographic analysis based on the following questions: What choices have the choreographers made in the creation of each piece, including the title? What is the site of the dance? How do the bodies move through time and space? What is the quality of their movement? Where are they in space? Are there other bodies in addition to Eiko & Koma? What is the relationship between the bodies onstage? How do the costumes, music, and sets relate to the moving bodies? What meanings accrete to this series of decisions? The writing of Thomas DeFrantz in *Dancing Revelations* is a particular influence in this sense.[28] His richly descriptive prose paints a detailed picture of each dance, including movement vocabulary and quality, music, structure, and spacing. In each paragraph DeFrantz shows his readers what is happening in the dance and then, based on the evidence he presents, tells them what the choreography means; his analysis of many of Alvin Ailey's eighty works forms his arguments, rather than merely supporting them. DeFrantz's specific and evocative writing style employs the very same Africanist aesthetics that he detects in Ailey's choreography, which pushes me to elaborate the aesthetic principles that undergird Eiko & Koma's movement vocabulary, such as slowness.

Even as I foreground the process of choreographic analysis, I must acknowledge that my analysis could not have developed without an embodied perspective based on my experiences studying with Eiko & Koma, whom I first met in 2006 when I was a graduate student at the University of California, Los Angeles. Indeed, Susan Leigh Foster asserts in *Reading Dancing: Bodies and Subjects in Contemporary American Dance* — arguably the first text to outline choreographic analysis as a methodology — that developing a visual, aural, and kinesthetic knowledge of movement is a prerequisite to discerning a dance's codes and conventions.[29] In addition to taking Eiko & Koma's movement class, Making Dance as an Offering, I also worked with Eiko to produce a written record of that class and served as an unofficial teaching assistant for her undergraduate seminar, Delicious Movement for Forgetting, Remembering, and Uncovering. Although I had seen one or two of their dances prior to meeting them, it was only through dancing with them twice a week, seeing how they contextualized their work with other artists and thinkers, and talking to them in their temporary office that I came to appreciate the full force of the choreography. At the same time I began to notice how Eiko & Koma's dances were frequently misread as foreign and mystical: a type of meditation, or something akin to the process of tending a Zen Buddhist rock garden. I puzzled over the lack of critical and scholarly writing about their significant body of work that dared probe beneath the slow-moving surface. Why were their acclaim and success, both richly deserved, accompanied by such a superficial consideration of their choreography rather than a deep engagement with what the movement was actually doing? Through my experience working closely with Eiko & Koma, I became compelled to develop the kind of analysis I felt was lacking. As the daughter of a Filipino American father, I have a personal stake in challenging the way Asian bodies in the United States are rewarded as exceptional but at the same time are never quite allowed to be "American."

Although this book is not an ethnography of Eiko & Koma, I did employ the ethnographic method of participant observation to continuously deepen my knowledge of the movement I analyze. Since 2006 I have spent many hours with Eiko and Koma at their home in New York City and have traveled to their performances, workshops, exhibitions, and residencies across the United States and in Japan and Taiwan. I have also participated to varying degrees in their work. For example, in addition to participating in numerous Delicious Movement workshops, I have done a range of tasks, including stage managing performances, mending props, assisting backstage, handing out programs, and more. In 2012 I worked as a Mellon Archive Fellow with the Dance Heritage Coalition to inventory, assess, and organize Eiko & Koma's personal archives, alongside Eiko and Patsy Gay, a specialist in archival methods. I also worked with Eiko to help her conceptualize their Archive Project, consistent with their artistic vision and practices. This hands-on approach to research has given me enormous insight into individual choreographic projects as well as the entire span of Eiko & Koma's career.

In addition to analyzing Eiko & Koma's choreography, it is important to pay close attention to how Eiko and Koma's early years in Japan, their time performing in Western Europe, and their decision to settle in New York influenced both their movement style and concerns. This contextual information is not always available from the dances themselves and must be acquired through supplemental historical and archival research and interviews with people who were there and can give first-hand reports. I have interviewed Eiko & Koma numerous times in addition to spending hours simply hanging out and chatting. My relationship with the artists has given me access to their longtime friends, collaborators, presenters, and critics, who have generously shared their thoughts, memories, and materials with me through formal interviews and casual conversations. These interviews provide vital background information and form part of the evidence to support my argument about Eiko & Koma's choreography.

I furthermore examine archival materials about Eiko & Koma to ascertain the extent to which changing discourses of race, multiculturalism, and identity in the United States have impacted how their choreography is viewed. How was contemporary Japanese performance received in the mid-1970s in the wake of the Vietnam War and in the midst of a nascent Asian American political movement? What does it mean that butoh performances by Kazuo Ohno and Dairakudakan proliferated alongside performances by New York–based Japanese artists Eiko & Koma and Kei Takei at precisely the moment that the Japanese American redress movement, which sought reparations and an official government apology for the internment of Japanese Americans during World War II, gained traction in the 1980s? How have Eiko & Koma benefited from multicultural policies and practices of the 1990s? Have those same multicultural policies and practices also obscured the force of Eiko & Koma's dances? Furthermore, what does it mean during this time period to be performing "modern" Japan in the form of an avant-garde movement practice and yet to be read in Orientalist terms, which generally tie the "Orient" to traditions fixed firmly in the past?

Some of the same questions I ask of the archive can also be asked of Eiko & Koma, presenters, dance critics, and the dancers' artistic collaborators through interviews. For example, Beate Sirota Gordon, the former performing arts director of the Japan Society and the Asia Society and the first presenter of Eiko & Koma's work in the United States in 1976, has provided me with invaluable information about the cultural contexts in which Eiko & Koma began to perform in the United States.[30] At that time, Gordon's programming decisions in New York City played a large role in determining what "Japanese" meant in America, as artists she booked for shows at the Japan Society often subsequently toured all across the country. Similarly, presenters such as Charles Reinhart of the American Dance Festival and Jeremy Alliger of the now defunct Boston-based Dance Umbrella played a large role in defining Eiko & Koma's work through the contexts in which their dances appeared, establishing the choreography (often commissioned as well as presented by these agencies) as American in the former case and as part of a cutting-edge Japanese dance community in the latter. These brief examples are illustrative of the ways presenters, critics, and collaborators have participated in the construction of Eiko & Koma's work before it is choreographed, as it is performed, and after the performance is over. Conducting interviews allowed me to get the details and nuances of this information, often not available in archives and not evident in the dances themselves.

The result, I hope, is that my engagement with Eiko & Koma and their choreography mirrors their own engagement with their work. Like them, I do not want to approach their work "with a concept that is just hunted," but I want the analysis to develop out of a sustained engagement with the dances themselves. My goal is to employ their choreographic method in my analysis in order to offer readers a more complex and slowed-down experience of Eiko & Koma and their work. Taken together, these varied experiences, along with analytical, archival, and ethnographic methods, suggest the major themes, or concerns, of Eiko & Koma's body of work.

Overview of Chapters

Flowers Cracking Concrete places Eiko & Koma's dances in their political, dance historical, and cultural contexts and analyzes those dances for their individual and collective impact. The first two chapters pay particular attention to establishing Eiko & Koma's influences and early history in order to intervene in the Orientalist discourse that too often defines them as singular and timeless. It is true that their work is unique, but it developed through particular life and artistic decisions and encounters, not through some inherent cultural or national essence. The examination of Eiko & Koma's early career in chapters 1 and 2, for example, provides an alternative view of three crucially important periods of dance history, but from the perspective of marginal participants in these moments. What was it like to study with the key figures of butoh for short periods of time in the early 1970s, but not be in the inner circle of disciples who worked with Hijikata and Ohno for years to develop their unique butoh expressions? What did it mean to study dance in Germany with Chmiel at a time when her Wigman-influenced style was out of favor, but *Tanz Theater* had yet to predominate? How was it possible to be integrated into the New York downtown dance scene as newcomers to the United States whose performance style differed from the predominant white abstract and pedestrian postmodern dance? And how did each of these encounters shape Eiko & Koma's body of work?

Chapter 1, "From Utter Darkness to *White Dance*," traces the development of Eiko & Koma's political commitments, aesthetics, and dance style from their time growing up in postwar Japan through their early "cabaret" performances in Japan and their initial dances in Europe and the United States. The chapter focuses particularly on the years 1971 to 1976, during which the pair moved from the "utter darkness" of not only their *ankoku butoh* teachers but also the political situation in Japan to the premiere in New York of what they call their first piece of set choreography, *White Dance* (1976). I argue that for Eiko & Koma choices about how, where, and at what pace to move have from the beginning always been both choreographic and political decisions.

After their American debut, Eiko & Koma returned briefly to Japan before moving to the United States permanently in 1977, where they immersed themselves in the New York downtown dance scene, creating one new piece each year and establishing themselves as critically acclaimed mainstays of American avant-garde dance. Chapter 2, "'Good Things Under 14th Street," considers Eiko & Koma's experimental choreography—*Fur Seal* (1977), *Before the Cock Crows* (1978), *Fluttering Black* (1979), *Trilogy* (1979–1981), and *Nurse's Song* (1981)—in relationship with their new home in New York City, placing the duo's work in the larger contexts of American postmodern dance, the downtown dance scene, and 1970s politics. From this point on, I claim, Eiko & Koma's work was deeply engaged with participating in and responding to American—and particularly New York City—influences. My analysis of these early dances shows that despite a sometimes radical change in style from piece to piece, Eiko & Koma demonstrate a consistent commitment to choreographing oppositional politics. This consistency notwithstanding, I suggest the dances that were most successful with critics were those that employed slowness as a choreographic method.

Chapter 3, "Japanese/American," shifts the perspective from the contexts in which Eiko & Koma began to make dances to the discursive contexts that impacted the reception of their work. Specifically, the chapter examines a change that took place between the early 1980s and the mid-1990s in how Eiko & Koma's work was represented and understood by producers and critics. At precisely the time when Eiko & Koma's work was becoming more integrated into American dance, the pair—initially called "avant-garde" and "postmodern"—became increasingly presented as "Japanese" and "Asian," particularly after Japanese butoh companies began to appear on American stages in the early 1980s. Through an analysis of dance reviews in the *New York Times* and other New York papers covering dance, I argue that Eiko & Koma have not been legible to US audiences as Asian American, or even American, because discourses that interpellate them as Japanese or Asian have been too dominant. I discuss multiple discourses that impact Eiko & Koma's work, including what Barbara Thornbury has called a "kabuki discourse," something I have identified as a nuclear discourse that is particularly entwined with the American reception of butoh, and an Asian American discourse.

Having discussed in chapters 1 through 3 the cultural, dance historical, and discursive contexts of Eiko & Koma's early work, in chapters 4 through 7 I abandon chronology in favor of analyzing recurrent choreographic and kinesthetic themes evident in dances from across Eiko & Koma's body of work, including nature, mourning, and intercultural alliances. These chapters individually and as a whole demonstrate how the duo's artistic concerns cycle throughout their repertoire, extending over long periods of time and sometimes overlapping with other themes. Just as Eiko & Koma's choreography and career constantly return to earlier projects to mine them for further significance, my analysis, too, cycles through temporalities to get at what the dance is about and what it does. Individual works cannot be discussed in isolation, but must be understood in relation to other dances that grapple with the same ideas or produce the same effects. For example, when analyzing a particular cycle within Eiko & Koma's body of work, I focus first on one dance in particular, then compare and contrast that dance with others that precede and follow it in order to articulate what remains constant over the decades and what changes, to what effect. Moreover, these cycles do not necessarily take place in a defined span of time and then give way to another theme. Rather, Eiko & Koma may return to an earlier concern years later. Chapters 4 through 7 thus overlap in terms of chronology. Furthermore, no one theoretical approach could account for all of the cycles. Each theme calls for its own unique frame of analysis.

Chapter 4, "Dancing-with Site and Screen," explores the prominence of human-nature relationships in Eiko & Koma's body of work, as exemplified in *River* (1995) and as seen in stage pieces like *Grain* (1983) and *Night Tide* (1984), site dances like *The Caravan Project* (1999), screen dances such as *Husk* (1987), and the living installation *Breath* (1998). Specifically, I home in on the relationships choreographed in these pieces between nature and culture, bodies and technology, that are not based in binaries or mutual exclusion but in interconnection, or what I call interface. I argue that Eiko & Koma practice in these dances a choreographic methodology of "dancing-with" nature and technology that enables the generation of interfaces through a slow and concerted process in which all active participants, including potentially the audience, are altered. This body of work is a recurring reminder of the potential for creating alternate ways of being in the world, in which the relationship between nature and technology has many complex possibilities beyond an either/or binary.

Chapter 5, "Sustained *Mourning*," examines Eiko & Koma's decades-long investigation of mourning as a choreographic practice. Here slowness refers not only to the movement in a particular dance, but also to Eiko & Koma's long-term focus. In works including *Elegy* (1984), *Lament* (1985), *Wind* (1993), *Duet* (2003), and *Mourning* (2009), the duo prolongs mourning such that it acts as a stubborn, even resistive melancholia. I draw on psychoanalysis, Asian American studies, and art analysis to provide a context for my theorization of the labor of Eiko & Koma's prolonged mourning and its effects. I argue that this group of dances theorizes mourning as not merely a private, individual process, but a societal, public melancholia that highlights issues and events that can never be resolved but must nonetheless be grappled with. Their choreography, I suggest, accomplishes this with performances of a sustained mourning through which Eiko & Koma evidence the ability to dwell in a space of heightened emotion without necessarily effecting a trans-formation of those strong feelings, both over the course of one dance and throughout the decades of their work. Grief in this case becomes a physical labor—sometimes even a battle—on endless repeat. This cor-poreal theorization of mourning is a crucial reworking of the concept that rejects the beginning-middle-end ideology of Freudian psychology in favor of a postwar temporality in which such a linear resolution is no longer possible.

Chapter 6, "Ground Zeroes," demonstrates how Eiko & Koma's post-9/11 dance, *Offering* (2002), drew on their long-term engagement with sustained mourning. Together with other dances, including *Event Fis-sion* (1980), *Land* (1991), *Raven* (2010), and *Fragile* (2012), *Offering* calls attention across time and continents to a shared history in Trinity, New Mexico, Hiroshima and Nagasaki, and New York City. I argue that this collection of Eiko & Koma's dances generates a critical transtemporal and transnational space in which divisions between here and there, now and then, us and them are called into question. I further suggest that these pieces differ from the melancholic choreography of the previous chapter, in that they transform rather than sustain mourning. These dances dis-play a process of metamorphosis that occurs over the course of a piece, in which the bodies become something new through interacting with the other elements in the piece. I understand this transformation of mourn-ing through the notion of reparation, a concept derived from psycho-analysis and adapted by Asian American studies scholars, that offers the possibility of creative action to productively address crisis and loss.

Chapter 7, "'Take Me to Your Heart': Intercultural Alliances," cen-ters on a group of dances beginning with *Cambodian Stories* (2006) that points to an important attention to intercultural alliances in Eiko & Koma's work. Made in collaboration with young painters from the Reyum Art School in Phnom Penh, Cambodia, these intergenerational and interdisciplinary works among Asians and Asian Americans—including *Cambodian Stories Revisited* (2007), *Quartet* (2007), the re-vival of *Grain* (1983/2007), and *Hunger* (2008)—were presaged by the duo's collaboration with Anna Halprin in *Be With* (2000). In particu-lar, this chapter engages with the history of intercultural performance to demonstrate how Eiko & Koma's work, focused on what I call choreo-graphing intercultural alliances, differs from other noted intercultural

collaborations that often remain mired in Orientalist discourses or uneven power structures. Unlike the interfaces of chapter 4, intercultural
alliances do not attempt to create a new entity, but instead seek to enact
strategic ways of working together, undoing in the process assumptions
that separate East and West, modernity and tradition.

The concluding chapter, "In Lieu of a Conclusion: 'Step Back and
Forward, and Be There'"[31] takes a long view of Eiko & Koma's body
of work through the lens of their Retrospective Project (2009–2012)
and ongoing Archive Project. I discuss the live installation *Naked* (2010)
as an emblematic work of the Retrospective and Archive Projects that
explicitly engages Eiko & Koma's core choreographic practices of site-
adaptivity and (re)cycling, which extend their concerns across time and
space. In this way I demonstrate that Eiko & Koma's archival practices
are in fact a continuation of their choreography. I then review current
debates about performance archives in order to highlight Eiko & Koma's
intervention in the understanding of what it means to archive. I argue
that Eiko & Koma's ongoing engagement with their own choreography—in the form of continually revisiting ideas and recycling movement, costumes, and sets—challenges the future-orientation of archives
and interrupts the body-documents binary that has developed between
those favoring the body as an archival site and those advocating for the
document-as-performance. In contrast, Eiko & Koma's site-adaptive and
cyclic choreographic practices show that archiving is an ongoing activity
that generates connections among bodies, objects, and sites.

CHAPTER 1

ℱROM UTTER DARKNESS
TO *WHITE DANCE*

Eiko & Koma had their New York premiere with *White Dance* at Japan Society's Japan House on May 6, 1976. The delicate yet tension-suffused dance featured periods of extended stillness punctuated by moments of absurdity: a slap, a cry, a cascade of potatoes. Although only a one-night engagement, the performance enabled a six-month sojourn in the United States, including subsequent performances at The Cubiculo, The Performing Garage assisted by Dance Theater Workshop, and the New York Public Library at Lincoln Center (the latter under the title *The White Moth*). Prominent dance critics at *The Village Voice*, *Dance Magazine*, and *Soho News* called the work "shocking in some way I can't articulate"[1] and "profoundly exciting,"[2] in part for the way it "coheres and engages our interest because we watch Eiko and Komo [*sic*] repeatedly enter, inhabit, and leave the inextricably linked states of fragility and determination."[3] How is it that two Japanese student activists turned dancers were able to create such a stir in New York, both uptown at the venerable Japan Society and NYPL and downtown at venues known for producing avant-garde and postmodern performance? Where did this dance come from? What was it about their dance that left dance critics unable to articulate meaning yet captivated nonetheless?

This chapter examines the development of Eiko & Koma's political and aesthetic commitments during their early years in Japan and their initial forays into dance performance in Japan, Germany, the Netherlands, and the United States. I contend that their choreography evidences from the very beginning an oppositional stance that although devoid of explicit activist messages nonetheless proposes ways of being in the world that challenge structures of power. It is also during this time that Eiko & Koma can be observed making decisions about what is important to them and how to incorporate it into their dancing. As Eiko said in a 1988 interview, "The question is: How shall I continue? What do I preserve and what do I not take in? What do I fight against in consideration of keeping something that I care about?"[4] I open with an introduction to Eiko and Koma's background growing up in postwar Japan and coming-of-age as activists in late 1960s and early 1970s Tokyo.[5] The focus then turns to their formation as dancers and dance makers from 1971 to 1976, first in Japan with the key figures of butoh, Tatsumi Hijikata and Kazuo Ohno, then through more than two years of performance and study in Europe, including with Mary Wigman dancer Manja Chmiel, and ending with their first performances in the United States. This period of movement from one continent to another parallels the pair's movement away from the "utter darkness" of their ankoku butoh teachers toward their own *White Dance*. At the same time, their trajectory provides the opportunity to retrace some of the paths of twentieth-century modern dance history.

The Dance of Utter Darkness

In a time line Eiko & Koma created for their Retrospective Project, the dancers constructed a chronological representation of their lives and career.[6] With this document, the pair situated their body of work historically, culturally, and politically, including not only notable moments from their career, but also significant events such as the Beatles' first concert in Tokyo, the beginning of the Vietnam War, and their own participation in Jimmy Carter's 1980 presidential campaign. Notably, the time line begins not with Koma's birth in provincial Niigata on Japan's northwestern coast in 1948 and Eiko's in Tokyo in 1952, but with the defeat of Japan in 1945. By marking their own beginnings with this decisive ending, an act of aggression and destruction unparalleled in human history, they acknowledge this moment as a major rupture, a turning point after which nothing can be the same. With this deliberate staging of their relationship to history, Eiko & Koma demonstrate how their sense of time extends beyond what we normally think of as beginnings and endings, a quality that has become characteristic of the sense of time in their work. The time line also places the dancers' births in the context of the end of the US occupation of Japan and the duration of the Korean War, and therefore subject to and implicated in geopolitical entities and events well beyond the local.

Though this act of staging their relationship to history is a recent one, there is no doubt that aftershocks of war and occupation resonated in both of their lives. Eiko and Koma were small children during the period of reconstruction after the intense destruction of World War II. Hiroshima and Nagasaki of course were devastated by the atomic bombings, but many other cities, including Tokyo, were firebombed and had to be rebuilt. Evidence of the war lingered, through broken infrastructure, the visible evidence of wounded war veterans, and US military occupation. Even after occupation officially ended in 1952, US military bases in Japan served as supply stations for the Korean War and later for the war in Vietnam, keeping armed conflict in the forefront of people's minds, even as Korean residents of Japan were relocated to North and South Korea.

Takashi Koma Yamada's parents split up when he was still small.[7] His father, reportedly haunted by the war, took Koma's brother, while Koma remained with his mother. Their life together in the often snow-covered port city of Niigata was modest. Koma talked in a movement workshop about how his mother would split an egg with him during his childhood, giving him the yolk to eat with his rice, taking only the white for herself.[8] In contrast, Eiko Otake was the only child of a banker and homemaker. Though based in Tokyo, her family spent a number of years living in Tochigi Prefecture in rural central Japan for her father's job, which gave Eiko an early appreciation for nature. In the midst of this solid middle-class foundation, arts and politics were also strong currents in the Otake household. Both of Eiko's grandmothers were geishas (indeed, Eiko has worn one of her grandmother's silk kimonos as a costume for years), and her grandfather was an artist. And despite her father's profession, he was also a communist.[9] In this politically active and creative environment, Eiko took three years of modern dance classes as a child and played the piano, but reportedly did not have an affinity for either.

The mid-1950s through the early 1970s in Japan was a time of intense change, including rapid industrialization and urbanization coupled with enormous economic growth. These developments were not disconnected from postwar US involvement in the country, a relationship concentrated in (but not limited to) the US-Japan Mutual Cooperation and Security Treaty, referred to in Japan as "Anpo." The treaty came up for renewal in 1960 and 1970 and in both cases was driven through by the ruling party and riot police, despite massive protests against it. In the wake of the treaty's renewal, the government promoted what William Marotti calls "a depoliticized everyday world of high growth and consumption and a dehistoricized national image"[10] in order to defuse the opposition. By the time of the 1964 Tokyo Olympics, this strategy appeared to be successful. All evidence of postwar destruction was gone, and in its place was a modern, regulated, thriving version of Japan for the world to see.

In the midst of such radical changes, many Japanese struggled with how to negotiate and express their relationship to those changes. As Marotti eloquently states, "Artists in Japan discovered hidden forms of domination in the everyday world and imagined ways in which their own practices might reveal, or even transform, such systems at their point of articulation in people's daily existence."[11] In other words, even as structural and societal changes were implemented, a vibrant avant-garde was on the rise, eager to develop and implement contestatory and interventionist practices that could impact the new status quo, both during the Anpo protests and in the deflated aftermath of the security treaty's passage. The Neo Dada Organizers, for example, were a group of nine artists including Genpei Akasegawa, Ushio Shinohara, and Masunobu Yoshimura who came together for anti-Anpo protests and a series of three exhibitions in 1960. In both protest and art (or more precisely, anti-art), they favored physical and sometimes violent action with everyday objects and rubbish: throwing stones at the Diet, slashing canvases, karate chopping chairs. Akasegawa then went on to found Hi Red Center (Hai Reddo Sentā, active 1962–1964) with Natsuyuki Nakanishi and Jirō Takamatsu. That group created public events that commented on and critiqued the sanitizing of Tokyo even as they conspicuously participated in it. Their event, HRC *shutoken seisō seiri sokushin undō ni sanka shiyō!* (Let's participate in the HRC campaign to promote cleanup and orderliness of the metropolitan area!, 1964), featured Hi Red Center members in white lab coats and surgical masks sweeping and scrubbing sidewalks in the Ginza neighborhood of Tokyo shortly before international attendees of the Olympic games arrived. These artists took the changes in society, politics, and the city and performed them to their extreme and absurd, if logical, conclusions.[12]

Not all artists of the avant-garde were interested in direct action, however. In the midst of pervasive anxiety about urbanization and industrialization, there were also frequent attempts to reconnect to or re-create tradition. This instinct sprang at least partially from the reality of rural to urban migration and the sense that rural traditions were being lost. The reach for tradition was, however, more connected to a modernist interest in indigenous art, rather than a form with which rural folks would have identified. In this case, rather than being an opportunity for an encounter with the strange and foreign, as with European surrealism, the turn was to Japan's own indigenous and folk practices. For many Japanese artists, including architect Kenzō Tange, visual artist Tarō Okamoto, and designer Kiyoshi Awazu, this was evident through their turn to the prehistoric Jōmon period for figurative and conceptual inspiration. This served two ends. First, as Michio Hayashi so elegantly put it: "The primitive cultural force is summoned as the dialectical other vis-à-vis modern technology."[13] Second, the turn to the indigenous and the folk gestured to a people unsullied by the consequences of the nationalist-modernist ideology that drove the state for almost a century. The idea of a prenational Japan provided an alternative model to both Japanese empire and industrialization in the midst of midcentury upheaval and restructuring.[14]

Eiko and Koma, like many young people in Japan, confronted the fundamental changes in society by joining the vibrant student protest movement that swept Japan, and much of the world, in the 1960s. Although aware of the dynamic spirit of avant-garde experimentation, Eiko says, "We were too busy with anti-government and anti-Vietnam War demonstrations to pursue art seriously."[15] Koma joined the movement when he arrived in Tokyo as a political science student at Waseda University in 1967. Eiko, following her family's example, had been involved in activism from an early age and even led the first strike by Japanese high school students in 1969. When she entered the law department at Chuo University in 1970, her activism continued.

The 1960s Japanese student movement had its roots in the postwar years. The 1947 Constitution, though drafted by an American team led by General Douglas MacArthur, concentrated Japanese optimism about liberal changes in Japanese society, including individual rights, a democratic government, and a commitment to international peace.[16] Many people, however, felt betrayed by the Japanese government's military relationship with the United States as concentrated in Anpo, which they felt contradicted Article 9's renunciation of war.[17] By 1968, the resurgent New Left student protest movement had expanded its concerns to include Vietnam, Okinawa (which remained under US control until 1972), and the very nature of universities and education. Noting the relation-ship between the Japanese government and higher education, students resisted indoctrination into state ideology, which they linked to capi-talism and militarism. The groups Zengakuren (the All Japan Federa-tion of Students' Autonomous Bodies, founded in 1948) and Zenkyoto (Joint Struggle Committee, 1968–1970) were at the center of this un-rest, a mass movement employing direct action, riots, strikes, and occu-pations. By the early 1970s a lack of effective unity at the time of the 1970 renegotiation of Anpo as well as police suppression and violence led to splintering of the movement into factions. Finally, the public and bloody United Red Army fiasco in 1972, in which a revolutionary armed group killed some of its own members and engaged in a drawn-out standoff with police, signaled the end of the student movement.

In 1971 both Eiko and Koma had begun to feel the effects of the dog-matic and increasingly violent student movement, and they began to seek other outlets for their oppositional beliefs. Eiko explains the transi-tion in this way:

> While numerous political theorists—none standing out any more than the others—presented us with logic, idealism, and tactical thinking, somehow these things led us to despair. By contrast, [art-ists such as filmmaker Oshima Nagisa, playwright/theater director Kara Juro, artist Kudo Tetsumi, and designer/artist Yokoo Tada-nori, as well as European filmmakers such as Jean-Luc Godard and Federico Fellini] showed us how they built their lives upon their confusion and frustration. In their works, we sensed that the means and the end are inseparable, that being revolutionary means being radical, and that the body is our vessel and foundation for explo-ration, experimentation, and expression.[18]

For Eiko and Koma, then, the move from the barricades to the dance studio was not about abandoning their political ideals but about finding a new, sustainable way to practice them.

Given the close associations between art and protest in 1960s Japan, Eiko and Koma's transition from one movement to the other is not so unusual. Marotti notes that members of the new avant-garde made "an attempt to conduct politics directly out of artistic performance, neither as an adjunct to protest nor through the conventional forms of agitprop but rather through the political potential of their practice itself."[19] Though the methods of protest were different, the goals were often aligned. For example, the policy statement of the 1969 conference of the student body of Waseda University declared: "We start from individuals . . . There should exist neither sectarian nor bureaucratic logic. We must start speaking with 'words' from inside of ourselves. . . . Let us found a radical struggle based on self-reliance and individualistic conceptions."[20] This call for individual determination as opposed to dependence on institutions or ideology echoed the turn to personal, immediate experience already present in the new avant-garde, particularly through performance, installation, and even painting that evidences the involvement of an active body. These practices were especially evident in the Gutai Art Association, including Kazuo Shiraga's *Challenging Mud* performance (1955) and his method of painting with his feet; Shōzō Shiramoto's paintings made by hurling glass bottles full of paint; and Saburō Murakami's *Passing Through* (1956), in which he propelled himself through twenty-one paper screens.[21]

For Koma, leaving the student protest movement and New Left politics meant leaving behind the entrenched hierarchies and leader-follower roles of the old society.[22] For both Eiko and Koma, withdrawing from the student movement was about opposition to dogmatism and violence. Throughout their work in the 1970s, they repeatedly rejected the black and red flags of their movement days in favor of the white flag of surrender. One could also see their rejection of a single meaning in their work as an ongoing reaction against dogmatism. And yet, they also seem to be perpetually working through these early experiences. The themes of joint struggle and interpersonal violence, for example, repeat over and over across their body of work as part of a cycle of violence, remorse, mourning, and new beginnings.

As Eiko and Koma each made the transition from activist to artist, each dove into the thriving Tokyo avant-garde art scene. They did not have far to go. The Shinjuku area of the city was home to both Waseda University and underground theaters. It was there that they each came upon performances by Tatsumi Hijikata's dancers. By this time, the "new" avant-garde had been active for over fifteen years (in fact, some would say it ended by 1970). Dance and performance were integral parts of the Japanese avant-garde, significantly through Hijikata's dance experiments that pushed the boundaries of the form.[23] Hijikata was born in 1928 in Akita prefecture in northern Japan, where he studied modern dance with Katsuko Masumura, a student of Takaya Eguchi, one of Japan's modern dance pioneers who had traveled to Germany in the 1920s to learn from Mary Wigman. Upon settling in Tokyo, Hijikata studied ballet, jazz, and modern dance with Mitsuko Andō, where he became acquainted with Kazuo Ohno, who along with Hijikata would become a major figure in butoh. The two performed together in Andō's dances while working on other projects. In 1959 Hijikata had his formal choreographic debut with *Kinjiki* (*Forbidden Colors*), which he performed with Ohno's son, Yoshito.[24] Taking its title from a Yukio Mishima novel, the dance caused a stir with its shocking homoerotics and violence. Reaction to the dance prompted Hijikata, his wife Akiko Motofuji, and the elder Ohno, among others, to split from the mainstream All Japan Art Dance Association, which had presented Hijikata's dance. At the same time, the notoriety that the piece attracted led to Hijikata being introduced into the avant-garde arts scene by Mishima himself. From then on, Hijikata's work took place not in the context of modern dance but in the avant-garde arts community.

His experiments were known at first by the English term "experience," then ankoku butoh 暗黒舞踏, and later simply as butoh. The word butoh (from bu 舞 "to dance" and toh 踏 "to step, to tread") originally meant "stamping dance," but that sense had long fallen out of use. Instead it appeared more commonly as butohkai 舞踏會, meaning a Western social dance ball. In the early 1960s the term ankoku buyo 暗黒舞踊 ("dance of utter darkness") was coined to refer to Hijikata's dance experiments, but was soon switched to ankoku butoh. Some people point to the word butoh's signification of Western dance as a gesture to the intercultural influences on the dance, but I follow Baird's suggestion that the sense of "foreign" implied by the term was employed not to reference specific dances, but rather to signal that this was something entirely unfamiliar, something that had not been seen before.[25] The use of butoh rather than buyo allowed the group to clearly delineate themselves from Japanese dance (buyo), just as they had already drawn a clear line between their work and modern dance by leaving the All Japan Art Dance Association. As dancers such as Ohno, Akira Kasai, Akaji Maro, and others struck out on their own, they continued to call their work butoh, but the "utter darkness" qualifier was dropped along the way.[26] Eventually the word came to encompass all the iterations and adaptations of the form developed by Hijikata and Ohno.

There is a tendency in the West to connect the "utter darkness" of butoh to the atomic bombs dropped on Hiroshima and Nagasaki in August 1945, effectively ending World War II, but this link is simply not evident in the work of Hijikata and Ohno.[27] Eiko & Koma do directly connect themselves to this moment, although this connection came explicitly many years later, only after Eiko witnessed the fall of the Twin Towers from their apartment window.[28] Although the "utter darkness" of ankoku butoh was not in explicit reference to larger societal conditions, it may be useful to think of the postwar period broadly as one of utter darkness. While there are certainly aspects of this time unique to Japan, including a massive epistemological shift from understanding the emperor as divine to his being merely human, there are many ways this period in Japan is analogous to what was happening around the world. It was a time in which societies and economies were being rapidly transformed through large-scale industrialization and urbanization, the arts were being deeply questioned in part for their association with fascist ideologies, and radical politics spilled into the streets.

In its first decade, butoh's search was for what could be expressed through the body and how. Marotti points out that from the start ankoku butoh lacked a recognizable style precisely because of its antiformalist nature.[29] Throughout the 1960s Hijikata experimented with how to fundamentally alter the uses, techniques, and significations of the body, often through collaborating with other artists.[30] In a series of "Hijikata Tatsumi DANCE EXPERIENCE Gatherings," he shared the stage with dancers, writers, and artists, including Masunobu Yoshimura, Isao Mizutani, Shūzō Takiguchi, Tatsuhiko Shibusawa, Tadanori Yokoo, and Mishima. In the publicity materials, the programs, and the gatherings themselves, movement was but one aspect of the multilayered and multivalent productions, which drew heavily on surrealism and neo-Dada. Miryam Sas argues that intermedial practices like this not only led to unprecedented cross-genre collaboration and borrowing, but also "reconceived relationships among art, technology, and environment."[31] This kind of relationship is evident throughout Eiko & Koma's body of work, particularly in the way they bring together their moving bodies with natural and built environments, video, musicians, and other elements.

Despite butoh's resistance to explanation and interpretation, identified by Baird,[32] there have been countless attempts to define the form by describing its aesthetic elements, categorizing major themes, or outlining creative processes or methodologies. Nanako Kurihara, who wrote one of the first in-depth examinations of butoh in the United States, defines the dance, in typical fashion, as a "contemporary dance form. . . . Typically performed in white makeup, with shaved heads, ragged costumes, slow movements and crouching postures." She goes on to say that "butoh portrays dark emotions—suffering, fear, rage—often by employing violence, shocking actions and mask-like facial expressions that transform instantly from one extreme of emotion to another."[33] Her description of the form is a common one, but while it is frequently associated with the "original" butoh, I contend that these descriptions stem from later works, particularly those by Sankai Juku, an idea I expand on in chapter 3.

Eiko and Koma found their way separately in 1971 to Hijikata's Asbestos Hall in the Meguro neighborhood of Tokyo. Koma says that Hijikata "had a big house and free groceries. I had nowhere to stay and no money. I was lucky and Mr. Hijikata said, 'Okay, tomorrow you can come to my house.' Sometimes very nice things start from coincidence, not your own determination. Three months after I moved into his house, Eiko, whom I had never met before, came into that same house for food and lodging."[34]

Hijikata's wife Motofuji established Asbestos Hall in 1950 as a live/work space with a bright, high-ceilinged studio and plenty of room for other dancers and students to stay. In 1974 the studio was transformed into a theater space, but until then it was used primarily for training and rehearsals. In exchange for room and board, Eiko and Koma and others trained with Hijikata and performed with other students in cabarets and theaters one, two, and even three times a night. Since 1959 Hijikata and Motofuji had been producing cabaret shows as a source of income that also provided financial support for Hijikata's "real" dance work. These lucrative shows featured scantily clad men and women performing "artsy" dances for American GIs and Japanese men.

At this point, twelve years after his groundbreaking 1959 performance, Hijikata was a well-known and even notorious member of the Tokyo avant-garde arts scene. As such, it is no surprise that he would

have attracted student activists and questioning young people, drawn to his daring acts and wild charisma. And yet 1971 was a peculiar time to be with Hijikata. His dance experiments throughout the 1960s, fueled by close collaborations with other avant-garde artists, had culminated in the 1968 performance *Hijikata Tatsumi to Nihonjin: Nikutai no Hanran* (*Tatsumi Hijikata and the Japanese: Rebellion of the Body*).[35] That solo represented a major shift in his choreography, with its constantly transforming personas from a weary and diseased old man to thrusting, large golden cock-wearing virility, to young girl enthusiasm, but it was not yet the style for which Hijikata remains best known. That technique, a tightly choreographed and specific method of layering images to produce a movement vocabulary, announced with 1972's epic *Great Dance Mirror of Burnt Sacrifice—Performance to Commemorate the Second Unity of the School of the Dance of Utter Darkness—Twenty-seven Nights for Four Seasons*, had not yet congealed. Some of the dancers who had been with Hijikata since the 1960s, such as Ko Murobushi and Bishop Yamada, were leaving to start their own projects. There is also a sense that women like Yoko Ashikawa were becoming more important in Hijikata's work at that time, whereas his dances in the early and mid-1960s had been quite male centered. Although Hijikata's dancers continued to perform between 1968 and 1972, both in "high art" venues and cabarets, this period is often overlooked by Hijikata scholars, in part because in retrospect *Twenty-seven Nights* overwhelms what came before it, and in part because Hijikata's cabaret dances have for the most part not been taken seriously by scholars.[36]

Bruce Baird suggests that changes over time in Hijikata's cabaret, in which his high and low art performances more and more came to resemble one another, can be attributed to a competitive cabaret marketplace. In that context, his shows got a reputation for being a kind of "weird, funky cabaret" in which female nudity appeared along with surrealist and Dadaist images. For example, Hijikata borrowed ideas from works such as Marcel Duchamp's *The Bride Stripped Bare by Her Bachelors, Even (The Large Glass)* (1915–1923), with its iconographic, geometric figures and accompanying mythic writings. Baird also attributes the growing similarities between the cabaret and stage works to Hijikata's choreographic push to be two things at once, for example beauty and ugliness.[37] In this context, it is not odd to think about avant-garde butoh and commercial cabaret in the same bodies. And while these performances remained dependent on women's bodies being on display and still attracted older Japanese men wanting nothing more than to ogle young, nearly naked women, they also attracted young radicals like Eiko and Koma, who were interested in art that was challenging the political and social status quo. Both Eiko and Koma ended up at Asbestos Hall after having seen a performance at Shinjuku Art Village, one of the numerous underground theaters that populated the Shinjuku neighborhood of Tokyo at the time. Eiko in particular mentions being impressed by the way the women performers were willing to make themselves look ugly. This rejection of Japanese standards for female appearance and comportment likely presented an exciting alternative for someone already committed to challenging the status quo.

From all accounts, Asbestos Hall was an open and fluid environment at the time, where no one was turned away. In addition to apprentices who were committed to working with Hijikata for the long term, like noted dancers Yoko Ashikawa and Saga Kobayashi, there was a steady stream of students, radicals, and young artists coming and going at any given time. According to butoh scholar Caitlin Coker, "People would somehow get introduced to Hijikata, or they would just find the studio and show up."[38] There they would have an interview, or more likely a conversation with Hijikata, who would at the end of the talk tell them to come to *keiko* (training) the next day. At a time when frequent student strikes meant no school, young people needed something to do with their free time or something to help them recover from the intensity of the barricades. Moreover, the good economy meant that many young people could afford to float around from place to place without worrying too much about how they would eat or where they would stay.[39] In a climate in which many young people were unsettled and searching for an alternative way of life, Asbestos Hall provided a viable, and likely exciting, short- or long-term option.

When Eiko arrived at Asbestos Hall, Koma had already been there for three months. They started working together after they were assigned to dance what was called an "adagio" at a cabaret. Neither Eiko nor Koma had studied dance seriously growing up, so they acquired dance and performance training on the fly. From all indications, this was a completely typical experience. According to multiple sources, people who showed up at Asbestos Hall were typically sent out to dance cabaret right away, sometimes even their first night at the studio. They would be given simple instructions, often by fellow performers, such as "hold this position," or "move slowly," or "if something goes wrong, take off your shirt very slowly."[40] As the performers gained more experience and improved their performance, they would be given more complicated choreography.

Asbestos Hall residents would dance in both cabarets and more "artistic" performances in small theaters like the Shinjuku Art Village, where they would typically wear a small thong-like garment with white makeup covering the body. Photographs taken by Tadao Nakatani in 1971 show a small stage with what looks like white sheets casually hung up at the back and stage right.[41] The photos show frequent partner work, with a couple of patterns. In the first, one partner is on hands and knees while another partner sits atop the first. In a variation of this position, four dancers kneel side by side, flanks touching, to provide a base for a fifth dancer to recline, head thrown back, abdomen tensed, feet floating in the air. Other partner work took place in the vertical plane, as a man standing tall and straight held a woman with her legs wrapped around his neck, facing him, his face obscured by her pelvis. Another photograph shows a person laid back, rear lower ribs balancing on the supporting partner's shoulder as the legs arc forward and toward the floor. Although the photos show static poses, one can imagine the performers slowly morphing from one position to the next, as Eiko & Koma do in their 1983 work *Beam*. Other photographs show slides projected onto Ashikawa and Kobayashi's near-naked bodies as they kneel downstage center, calling to mind later work by photographer Eikoh Hosoe (Ukiyo-e projections, 2002–2003, and *Butterfly Dream* with Kazuo Ohno, 2006) as well Eiko & Koma's 1976 *White Dance*, in which a drawing of a moth is projected onto and over Eiko.

After the late-night cabaret shows were over, the night was not yet at an end. Motofuji talks about everyone going to a local bathhouse to wash off the makeup, before rushing to catch the train home for a few hours of rehearsal before bed (see figure 1.1).[42] Some people recall they were not given enough food to eat. And while the cabaret shows were quite profitable—payments averaged 10,000 yen per performance—the dancers turned over all their earnings to Motofuji and received only 500 yen back.[43]

FIGURE 1.1 *Late night rehearsal at Asbestos Hall, Tokyo, 1972.*
Photo: Makoto Onozuka.

Eiko has described the studio as a temporary hideout from the chaos
on campus and in the streets that characterized Japan, like much of the
world, at the time. Three months after meeting, Eiko and Koma decided
together to leave the autocratic environment under Hijikata to pursue
their own projects. If as part of the student movements they were trying to challenge power, why would they stay with a man with a singular
power? Although their time with Hijikata was brief, it is clear that Eiko
and Koma absorbed his basic approaches to performance, the foremost
being that it was possible to make a living dancing cabaret. Baird goes so
far as to call cabaret, rather than a high art approach, constitutive in the
development and spread of butoh and butoh-related movement beyond
Hijikata, in that "acquisition of a kind of fundamental cabaret style is an

important avenue" for dancers to make a name, and a living, for themselves.⁴⁴ Certainly the experience dancing cabaret with Hijikata gave Eiko and Koma and other dancers like Ko Murobushi, Carlotta Ikeda, and Yumiko Yoshioka a way to market and support themselves when they first went to Germany in 1972 and France in 1977, respectively.⁴⁵

Even though Eiko and Koma had less than a year's training between the two of them, they were clearly excited by the possibilities performance offered and felt empowered to make their own dances. They put together a cabaret show under the name Night Shockers to make money to fund a trip abroad. At the same time, they put together "artistic" shows for which they created their own sets and costumes. The pair gave their first performance of original work at Waseda University in 1972, an event captured through four extant black-and-white photographs.⁴⁶ All four images show Eiko, naked or perhaps wearing a small thong, her skin covered in clumped and flaking white makeup or rice flour. Koma is only present in two of the images. In one he wears a dark, knee-length kimono, and his skin is also covered in the white, flaking substance; in the other, he is in a side lunge, all in shadow, while she is captured mid-movement, head in profile, torso forward, the light from a projected image of a still life spilling over her skin. In these images, Koma is low to the ground, his kimono blending with the shadows and dark floor, whereas Eiko is upright, frontal, and often splayed open to the audience. Even when she kneels, she towers over Koma's curled form. Though her skin appears to be peeling off her body, and her joints, ribs, and hip bones protrude, she is no fragile creature, but a concrete and rooted body, confronting her audience with a barely contained urgency.

In these images, elements from Hijikata's cabaret shows are evident. For example, white body makeup and using the body as a screen for projections were common in Hijikata's dances at Shinjuku Art Village at the time. On the other hand, the use of a kimono as a costume (which became a frequent element of Eiko & Koma's performances) seems unrelated to Hijikata. Although he does wear a kimono in *Rebellion of the Body*, its specificity as a white bridal kimono suggests he is using it to play with gender, an idea furthered by the fact that he dons it backwards. In contrast, Koma never uses a kimono to cross-dress, and though gender is often obscured or blurred in Eiko & Koma's body of work, this is often effected through nakedness, rather than clothing. Nor does Koma's way of wearing the kimono resonate with the way Hijikata playfully misuses *geta* sandals in *History of Smallpox*. Instead, the kimono is simply something to wear that is easy to move in. Some of the kimonos that Eiko has worn over the years from her geisha grandmothers are markers of cultural context. They are worn simply and loosely (and sometimes backwards), without the conventional undergarments and belts.

At the same time that Eiko and Koma worked in cabarets as Night Shockers to save money to travel abroad, they started to make artistic work as Eiko & Koma, and took a twice-a-week improvisation class with Kazuo Ohno. Whereas the atmosphere under Hijikata was highly controlled—from what one should do onstage, to what one earned and ate offstage—the scene at Ohno's home studio, high on a hill in the Kamohoshikawa suburb of Yokohama, could not have been more different than the urban Asbestos Hall. Ohno never told students what to do or how to dance, and in fact he often claimed that he had nothing to teach. He did not lead movement exercises or phrases, but rather talked about metaphysical concepts, art and artists, and dancers he had seen. From these inspirational words and image prompts meant to inspire movement, students were expected to find their own dance.

As a young man in the late 1920s and early 1930s, Ohno saw dancers such as La Argentina and Harald Kreutzberg perform, experiences he returned to again and again over the course of his life, including through the dance that made him world famous at age seventy-three, *Admiring La Argentina* (1977).[47] However, it was not these experiences that prompted him to start taking modern dance classes; rather, it was his lifelong job as a physical education teacher at a Christian girls' school that led him to study with the founders of Japanese modern dance, Baku Ishii, Takaya Eguchi, and Misako Miya, the latter two of whom had studied with Mary Wigman in Germany. Ohno had only just started to perform with Eguchi and Miya when he was called up for military service; he served for eight years, including one year as a prisoner of war. Upon his return to Japan in 1946 he resumed performing, and in 1949 he had his solo choreographic premiere. That same year he opened the Kazuo Ohno Dance Studio. For the next ten years, he made his own dances while participating in other people's works. While dancing for Mitsuko Andō, Ohno met Hijikata. For most of the 1960s, Ohno stopped choreographing his own dances in favor of participating in Hijikata's dance experi-

FIGURE 1.2
*Eiko & Koma
with Kazuo Ohno
after a performance
in Tokyo.
Photo: Courtesy
of Eiko & Koma.*

ences. By the time Eiko and Koma met Ohno in 1971, he was performing live only occasionally and was making a series of experimental films with filmmaker Chiaki Nagano.[48]

Even though Hijikata and Ohno had long collaborated, leaving one to study with the other was still an unusual move, even in the avant-garde world of butoh. Given Eiko and Koma's political background and the general antiauthoritarian atmosphere among student protestors and young avant-garde artists, the attraction to someone who says, "I cannot tell you what to do, you have to figure that out for yourself," must have been undeniable. Still, it was not easy work. Eiko remembers the trek from Sagami-Ohno, where she lived with her parents, out to Yokohama for Ohno's twice-weekly class: the train ride followed by a walk up the hill, and the extra effort it took when it was cold. One night she arrived to find she was the only student. She describes the sweet awkwardness of receiving his full attention. He taught her how to bloom and wilt, placing his hand behind hers. She never forgot this first (and last) experience of Ohno's one-on-one coaching.[49]

But even this self-driven, more open environment was not enough to keep Eiko and Koma rooted. Though they openly and lovingly credit Ohno as a teacher and had frequent contact with him until his death (see figure 1.2), they acknowledge that they were not among the disciples who worked intimately with him for years, if not for decades. Indeed, some of Ohno's closest disciples became his caregivers and constant companions through his death at age 103 in 2010. Eiko and Koma's early political activism instilled in them a fierce independence and an insistence on a "do it yourself," or DIY, approach to art making, which made them bristle at the idea of being someone's disciples. (Nor have they ever wanted to have their own disciples, thus their resistance to codifying a technique or transferring their repertoire to other dancers.) So, after studying with Ohno for less than half a year, Eiko and Koma left Japan together. Having already left school, they had a drive to do their own thing and felt that they needed to get far away in order to have the space to do that. Eiko once suggested to me that extended proximity to greatness results in just serving that greatness. Obviously they would not be who they are or be making the work that they do without the formative experiences living at Asbestos Hall or training with Ohno, however briefly. But they also craved experiences beyond the islands of Japan, and in late 1972 Eiko and Koma set off to continue their movement research elsewhere.

White Dances

The early 1970s was a period of major departures for Eiko and Koma, who were at that point on their way to becoming Eiko & Koma. They left school, two major figures of avant-garde dance, and finally even their country. Suzanne Carbonneau emphasizes that Eiko & Koma were not traveling in order to perform. "Performing was, rather, a strategy for discovering the world . . . while they 'researched [their] lives.'"[50] Although she seems to mean this quite literally — dance was a means for the pair to see the world and travel beyond Japan — her phrasing quite nicely points to the way that Eiko & Koma have since used their dance to understand their relationship to time, history, humans, and nonhumans. In a manner prescient of their future movement style, in which a specific beginning or end is less important than noticing and participating in the ever-evolving moment, the pair embarked on a slow journey whose destination was not entirely clear at the outset, departing Japan on a boat bound for the Soviet Union. The one thing they knew for certain was that they had made a conscious decision not to go to the United States. On the one hand, their opposition to the Vietnam War precluded the United States as a destination; going there, they felt would signal an implicit acceptance of the government's actions. On the other hand, they had a sense that everyone was going to the United States at that point, and indeed a number of Japanese avant-garde artists, including Yoko Ono and Yayoi

Kusama, had been welcomed into the New York art scene in the 1960s. Spain was one possible destination—Eiko remembers studying Spanish on the ship—however, they ultimately rejected that option because of their political opposition to Francisco Franco's fascist dictatorship. After their ship docked, the pair then took a train to Moscow. Somewhere along the way they decided to go to Germany, and in Moscow they boarded a plane to Vienna, where finally they took a short train ride to Munich.

Ending up in Germany was not random, however. In a discussion about this period of their lives, Koma pointed to the long history of artistic exchange between Japan and Germany, and in particular to the links between their teacher, Ohno, and Mary Wigman's modern dance style.[51] Cultural exchanges among Japan and European countries had in fact been commonplace since the Meiji Restoration in 1868, when the Japanese began a concerted effort to show their country, policies, and products to be on a par with those of the Western powers, often through the adoption or adaptation of Western practices and conventions. At the same time, all things Japanese enjoyed an enormous popularity in the United States and Europe, prompting artists there to themselves adopt or adapt Japanese techniques. For example, the aesthetics of noh circulated to Europe and were incorporated into the practices of playwrights and theater directors such as W. B. Yeats, Jerzy Grotowski, and Samuel Beckett; in turn, Japanese theater practitioners of the 1960s and 1970s were themselves influenced by some of these same European artists.[52] It was not unusual then that the Japanese pioneers of modern dance studied in Europe in the 1920s, some with Mary Wigman herself, and introduced German "new" dance to Japan. Koma remembers Ohno talking to them about Kreutzberg and Wigman. Koma and Eiko themselves discovered pictures of Dore Hoyer in the Music Library at the Tokyo Bunka Kaikan 東京文化会館. Of these German dancers Eiko says, "They were like kind of romantic figures for our soul. We couldn't romanticize our own teacher because we were too rebel [*sic*] ourselves. We were always questioning; and there was some senior students who look at Hijikata and Ohno like this [looking at them as if they were god]. . . . I just couldn't get involved in that because we were always questioning. But those photos became instead my kind of romantic . . . where my romantic idea can go forth."[53]

There was something in these dancers, whom they only knew through photos and stories, which resonated with the political focus on the individual, that contributed to Eiko & Koma's worldview. They had seen Martha Graham and had read about Merce Cunningham, which gave them the sense that they knew what was happening in American modern dance. But at that point, Wigman's style was out of favor and even disappearing, and Koma says that in that context they were interested in searching out the roots of what was by then called *Ausdruckstanz*.[54]

Arriving in Munich soon after the 1972 Olympics, the city had a vibrant young people's culture that attracted the dancers. Almost immediately, they self-produced a two-month, late-night run at a small theater called ProT, while also continuing to support themselves with cabaret shows.[55] Upon arriving in Germany, Eiko had written to Mary Wigman about the possibility of studying with her and had received her response that she was too ill to teach.[56] At their performances they distributed a flyer asking for leads to where they could study Wigman's technique. One day an audience member suggested that they contact Manja Chmiel in Hannover. Chmiel, a longtime assistant to Mary Wigman, had developed her own career as a solo dancer and had a school there. Eiko wrote to her immediately, and when they received a letter in return inviting them to Hannover, they packed up the old car they had acquired and moved north.

Upon meeting, Chmiel asked them to dance for her. Eiko reports, "Whether she liked it or not, I don't know, but she did say immediately after that that we shouldn't be learning about choreography from her."[57] Despite this recent statement, Eiko said in a 1998 interview with Deborah Jowitt that Chmiel gave them feedback that helped them "maximize the visual and emotional impacts" of their dances by paying attention to lighting and paring down their movements.[58] In addition, Chmiel "encouraged them to train their bodies for expansion and life so that they could transmit movement on a larger scale."[59] She arranged for the dancers to take ballet classes for free at the Stadthaus in the mornings and to take her modern classes in the evenings. In the afternoons, she gave them access to her studio to rehearse for their regular late-night cabarets and for occasional campus and museum performances at the Studentenheim and the Kunstverein.

According to Eiko & Koma, however, the most important thing

FIGURE 1.3

White Dance, *Young Choreographer's Competition, Cologne Opera, Germany, 1973.*
Photo: A. Loffler.

Chmiel taught them was not dance technique, but their power as a team;
until that point they had viewed their partnership as merely a tool for
survival and a step to becoming solo dance artists. She gave the duo the
time and space to develop their work and pushed them to take their partnership seriously by entering them in a noted competition (alternately
referred to in materials by and about Eiko & Koma as the Kölner Preis,
the Young Choreographers' Competition, and the Cologne Choreographers' Competition), with Kurt Jooss as one of the judges. Eiko & Koma
were among the three finalists in the competition and were invited to
perform at the Cologne Opera (see figure 1.3).

That show, like all of their performances in Europe, was called *White
Dance.*[60] The title acts as an expression of independence from their first
dance teachers, Hijikata and Ohno. Eiko & Koma's dance, the title suggests, is specifically not the "utter darkness" of their butoh teachers, nor
that of the failed student movement. The color white moreover provided

a powerful contrast to the black and red flags of various political movements. In Eiko and Koma's activist histories, as well as in the times in which the piece was made, there was a significant resonance of political allegiance with the color white, especially in opposition to black (anarchism) or red (communism). White also calls to mind the act of surrender, death, and ritual. Suzanne Carbonneau suggests that in "embracing whiteness as an antidote to the black uniforms of anarchism they had worn in the student movement, they meant whiteness to signal their decision to leave their pasts behind in order to create anew."[61] The choreographers explicitly took up the white flag of surrender almost a decade later in *Event Fission* (1980), an act that calls to mind John Lennon and Yoko Ono's 1973 declaration of the conceptual country, Nutopia, with its white flag of surrender to peace. While calling their dance "white" implied a strong sense of rejection, it also provided continuity, for example through the white makeup used in both traditional Japanese performance and butoh. In this way, the literal whiteness of their dance provides a connection, like that sought by some other avant-gardists, reaching back beyond recent history. Indeed, one of the few books the dancers took on the road was Zeami's late fourteenth- to early fifteenth-century treatise on noh, the *Kadensho*.[62]

The movement in these *White Dance*s was not set, although Eiko & Koma did have a loose score of movements to draw from and an order of the movements agreed upon in advance. According to Joan Rothfuss, "The events combined moves they had learned from their various dance teachers — Kazuo Ohno, Tatsumi Hijikata, and others — with such Dadaesque actions as cutting their hair, throwing raw eggs, cooking fish, dragging a bundle of carrots, and painting their bodies with dough."[63] In Koma's words, "We were just trying to do something strange."[64] Remnants of these dances remain in photographs from performances in theaters and museums in Germany and the Netherlands, and in a recently discovered twelve-minute color film — minus sound track — made in Amsterdam circa 1973, which is the earliest known footage of Eiko & Koma (see figure 1.4). The film alternates between performances and scenes of Eiko and Koma in their kitchen, revealing the closeness of their communal relationship in life as well as in dance. While their words are lost, their dancing includes movements strikingly similar to Hijikata's early 1970s choreography for Ashikawa and Kobayashi as well as origi-

FIGURE 1.4
*Still from first known video footage of
Eiko & Koma, Amsterdam, circa 1973.
Courtesy of Eiko & Koma.*

nal vocabulary that would later appear in Eiko & Koma's *White Dance*
(1976) and *Fur Seal* (1977).

Despite Koma's seeming dismissal—"just trying to do something
strange"—in fact they were clearly doing something radical and shocking, and even profound, with their bodies, evidenced in the enthusiastic
reception that greeted them in Europe and North Africa from 1972 to
1974. Those performances moved easily among late-night theaters, opera
houses, museums, and performance festivals, echoing the way that Hijikata's radical dances could also read to multiple audiences, both high art
and bawdy at the same time. Certainly in Europe there was an added layer
of Orientalism impacting the reception of their work, in the sense that
"Oriental" read as high culture. Eiko concedes that "the fact we grew up in
postwar Japan remains significant and essential in the ways we think and
work, more so than the fact we studied and worked in Germany briefly.
You know, sometimes you are reminded of what you have absorbed early
on when you are away from where you grew up. But we were not cultural
exports and we didn't play for exoticism. I think we are careful not to."[65]

In negotiating their cultural and national differences through dance,
the pair found themselves having to work with and against being received
as the Other, no matter where they were. In any case, their singularity as
Japanese dancers in Germany in the early 1970s, drawing from an as-yet-
unseen-outside-Japan movement style, helped them stand out to audiences and mentors alike.

Their high-profile performance at the Cologne Opera resulted in
other artists seeking them out and led to further performance and teaching opportunities beyond Hannover. For example, Lucas Hoving saw
Eiko & Koma perform in Amsterdam and invited them to teach a mas-

ter class at the Rotterdam Dance Academy, where he was then a director. Hoving, famous for his years spent dancing with José Limón, strongly suggested that they go to New York. At the time Eiko & Koma were not even sure they would continue to dance beyond their time in Europe, due in part to Eiko's persistent ankle injury. Hoving, however, convinced them not to give up dancing until they had been to New York. Though the time with Chmiel and Hoving was brief, their influence, like that of Hijikata and Ohno, would continue to resonate throughout Eiko & Koma's career.

During their time in Europe, Eiko & Koma were constantly on the move. They had a cheap car, and as soon as they heard about a new opportunity, they would head off. After spending some time in the Netherlands and forming the Linden Gracht Dance Laboratory with Mitsutaka Ishii, the pair toured in France, Switzerland, and Tunisia. In Tunisia one of their audience members urged the pair to perform in New York and suggested they contact her cousin, who turned out to be Beate Sirota Gordon, then performing arts director at the Japan Society. Gordon is a significant figure in US-Japanese relations.[66] At age twenty-two, Gordon participated in the drafting, translating, and negotiating of the Japanese constitution and was instrumental in enshrining equal rights for women in that document. In addition to the Japan Society, Gordon also served as performing arts director at the Asia Society. In her role at the Japan Society beginning in the 1950s, Gordon was responsible for introducing both traditional and contemporary performing artists from all over Asia to American audiences. Both the cousin and Eiko wrote to Gordon, who was hesitant to present performers whom she had not seen and chosen herself. Despite her reservations, she decided to proceed with booking Eiko & Koma based on her cousin's recommendation, provided they had round-trip tickets and money deposited in an American bank account for living expenses.[67] The dancers agreed, then returned to Japan to work, raise the required money, and deal with Eiko's ankle injury. During that time, they studied again with Ohno and began to work on a piece to perform in the United States the following year.

White Dance

Eiko & Koma arrived in the United States in April 1976, ready to premiere *White Dance*.[68] By this time the Vietnam War had ended, and the pair were no longer conflicted about entering the country. Although the dance they made for their American premiere shared a name with their European performances, the dancers consider the 1976 piece their first set choreography. They felt that a high-profile venue like the Japan Society called for "a little more choreographic effort," which included "actually deciding on music, costumes and program notes."[69] The dancers spent their time in Tokyo processing the movement, choreography, and expression lessons learned during their years in Europe, both through formal instruction and through their extensive performance experiences. Premiering five years after the pair met at Asbestos Hall, *White Dance* was the culmination of the duo's first period of movement and life research.

A sense of momentous transition between their first five years working together and their arrival in America was captured in a version of their biography frequently used in programs in their first few years in the United States:

> EIKO & KOMA began working together in 1971 while members of Hijikata's company in Tokyo. After a Tokyo debut they traveled to Hannover, Germany, in 1972 where they met and studied with Manja Chmiel, a disciple of Mary Wigman. For the next three years EIKO & KOMA performed throughout Europe and Tunisia. A year's added study in Yokohama with Ohno Kazuo prepared them to continue their dance in America.[70]

Indeed, the teachers and mentors enumerated in this biography remained consistent from this point forward in Eiko & Koma's career, although mentions of Hijikata did diminish over the years, a fact Eiko explains by noting that their relationships with Chmiel, Ohno, and even Hoving were ongoing, while the one with Hijikata ended when they left Asbestos Hall. They never saw him or were in touch with him again.[71] While the pair would continue their choreographic experimentation through the early 1980s, a process discussed in detail in chapter 2, their arrival in the United States was a major turning point in their work.

Two years of performing around Europe had taught them valuable lessons about how to generate opportunities for themselves. Before departing Japan, Eiko sent letters to all the *Dance Magazine* correspondents across the United States, letting them know of the duo's impending visit and asking if anyone would help them set up a performance.

Irene Oppenheim, then a West Coast reviewer for *Dance Magazine* and a critic for local Bay Area papers, responded, inviting the pair to contact her once they arrived, so they arranged a layover in San Francisco on their way to New York. Oppenheim recalls trying to figure out what their work was like during that first meeting: "I would ask them, 'does it use kimonos?' And they would say, 'Yes, but it's not traditional.'" The critic was quite taken by them, despite the dancers' halting English, remembering, "They were very young and very charming and very beautiful."[72] By the end of the meeting, Oppenheim agreed to arrange an invitation-only performance in a former garage of a small private school the coming weekend in order to accommodate Eiko & Koma's New York schedule. In addition to securing the venue and recruiting her friends and acquaintances to attend, she recalls being given the peculiar task of purchasing two hundred pounds of potatoes for use in the performance. Did the dancers really like to eat potatoes?

As a transitional piece in Eiko & Koma's career, *White Dance* reflects the style that characterized the experimental dances they performed in Europe while introducing new choreographic elements. The dance also represents their efforts to connect with an entirely new audience whose context for what they were seeing was different than that of audiences in Japan or Europe. "When they first came [to the US] they really were pioneers," says Oppenheim.[73] Indeed, the pair arrived in the United States, and even Europe, before butoh or any similar movement practices were known outside of Japan, with the exception of a handful of photographs in William Klein's 1964 book, *Tokyo*. For American audiences, the context for Eiko & Koma would have been Japanese performance artists like Yoko Ono, or American avant-garde performance, such as what Oppenheim talked about seeing in San Francisco at theaters such as the Theater of Man.[74] Others found a context for what they saw in the "early moderns." Janice Ross, for example, in a review of Eiko & Koma a year and a half after their San Francisco debut, describes their work as "an honest and forceful amalgam of the raw beauty and violence of Mary Wigman's expressionistic theater and the metaphorical density and fragility of Asian art."[75] This view was likely shaped by press releases for the pair that described their work "as avant-garde dance in the Japanese manner, [showing] the influence both of Japanese traditional and German modern dance."[76] Whatever the context of the individual viewer, Oppenheim says, "I think that a lot of their appeal, at least in the early days, was that they were so exotic to us."[77] At that time, there was still a strong division between "ethnic dance" and "modern dance"; as Japanese people performing avant-garde dance, Eiko & Koma were perceived as a rarity.

Like their embrace of the political meanings of "white," Eiko & Koma incorporate other gestures of opposition as part of their attempt to figure out how to further their own political questioning through dance. The US premiere of *White Dance* was supplemented by the appearance of a loose adaptation of Mitsuharu Kaneko's uncredited 1948 poem *Ga* 蛾 (Moths) in the program. Written during the American occupation of Japan and postwar reconstruction, the poem speaks to glimpses of beauty and determination amid the overwhelming inevitability of death. Eiko's adapted translation reads in part:

> To live is to be fragile
> So is it a fault to nurture a dream?
> Oh moth! what is life to you?
> You've been exhausted ever since you lost your cozy pupa,
> You've carried the weight of time upon your back
> And gasped for breath
> While taking a rest
> After such a short journey,
> Then started on another voyage
> Into an unknown future.[78]

Kaneko (1895–1975) is noted as the only Japanese poet to write antiwar poetry during World War II, including "Bald," an account of his attempts to help his son fail his draft physical. Kaneko is also considered an outsider in Japanese society, due not only to his extensive travels abroad, but also to his writings, which eschew and outright reject societal conventions. Taking up these words, in English translation, over a quarter of a century later, Eiko & Koma signal their own desire to "nurture a dream" with their dance, even as they acknowledge the ongoing violence and absurdity of life at the end of the Vietnam War.

Absurdity and opposition are both evident in *White Dance*'s opening scene. A version of the madrigal "The Agincourt Carol" plays as Eiko sits slumped forward in a printed casual kimono center stage, and Koma strikes a flouncy pose upstage left.[79] No one moves for what seems an eternity, and then Koma begins to carefully pick his way around and across the stage, stepping lightly on his toes and occasionally flicking his foot back with a flourish to reveal his bare buttocks through a slit in the back of his bright red short kimono, worn backwards. Satisfied with his trip around the stage, he exits purposefully, having never acknowledged Eiko's presence. In Kaneko's poem, "Opposition" (not quoted in the program), the poet lists all the things to which he is opposed, including school, work, and "the Japanese spirit." "I'm against any government anywhere / And show my bum to authors' and artists' circles," he writes.[80] For those familiar with Kaneko's poetry, Koma's mischievous reveal of his own bare bottom in *White Dance* recalls the poet's desire to challenge every element of society. This cheeky behavior is furthered in publicity materials and programs for the dance. A photograph of Eiko shows her suspended midair, leaping yet posed almost as if she is seated in a chair. Her torso is bent all the way forward, feet flexed, knees bent, her whitened buttocks and legs revealed by her kimono as it floats above her body. Another frequently reprinted photo shows Koma facing away from the camera, his butt sticking out from a slit in his mid-calf-length kimono donned backwards, legs in wide parallel.[81] This "showing of the bum" resonates with Eiko & Koma's days as student activists, but here it is more playful than militant, more sassy than offensive.

But *White Dance* was not limited to absurd and cheeky moments. Eiko's slow-moving solo, which makes up the middle section of the dance, ushers in a contemplative mood. Balancing on her tailbone, she reclines midstage, allowing her four limbs to billow around her until it seems there is nothing else happening in the world except this small dance. Eiko developed this solo when she was suffering from her ankle injury, so the movement was initially functional. The solo, however, demonstrates the value of rootedness in their work, not only as a visual anchor, but also in terms of duration of time. Even when she eventually rises to the vertical plane, allowing projections of photos of medieval Japanese patterns to suffuse her and her surroundings, her sustained movement-in-stillness is captivating.[82]

In contrast to Eiko's intense, grounded presence in the center of the stage, Koma often bounds across the space. When the two are reunited onstage, they move not in unison but rather in tension with one another.

Their taut muscles bristle even as their joints bend in unexpected angles, only to rebend in other configurations again and again. A kick or a slap explodes out of stillness. Then, near the end of *White Dance*, it suddenly becomes clear why Oppenheim had to buy all those potatoes. Koma rushes onstage, a huge sack over his shoulder, as potatoes cascade to the ground in a series of rolling thumps, kicking up small clouds of dust as they fall. The tubers have scarcely rolled to a stop, scattering across the stage, when Koma scurries back with another sack over his shoulder, repeating the dramatic potato drop once, twice, before throwing the canvas sack in a wide arc toward the wings and careening into the back wall. Meanwhile, Eiko holds the center of the stage, her deep stance rooting her in place as she pulls her hands into fists at her hips, elbows jutting backwards, as if ready to fight. Robert A. Fredericks, reviewing the Japan Society debut performance for *Dance Magazine*, wrote of the potatoes: "After recovering from the initial shock, I found it profoundly exciting. Not only the sight of those potatoes rolling around and spilling over the edge of the stage but the dust that flew from them, the sounds they made as they slipped from the bags and thudded on the wooden floor, all contributed to the effect."[83] The multisensory engagement demanded by the potatoes — how they looked, sounded, smelled — draws attention to Eiko & Koma's neo-Dada-style use of these everyday objects.

Even as it revels in the nonsensical — "Why potatoes? What have they got to do with moths?"[84] — *White Dance* also signals an attention to cycles of living and dying and the attendant violence thereof that later became a central concern for the choreographers. Deborah Jowitt saw struggle and combat in the dance: "But their work isn't pretty or sentimental; it's pervaded with horror, studded with moments of violence."[85] Fredericks noted how Koma "swatted [Eiko], and not gently."[86] Oppenheim saw a violence in the piece that was less shocking than it was moving. For her *White Dance* evoked a deep sadness that felt linked to Vietnam, a war that had ended only the year before.[87]

Perhaps more significantly, the work shows Eiko & Koma trying to determine what their choreographic project will be. The piece stages modern dance influences such as Koma's enthusiastic leaps and Eiko's striking side attitude alongside a startling cascade of potatoes and alternately meditative and disturbing minimalist movements. Shoko Letton suggests that the "ugly" movements can be traced to Hijikata and the "beautiful" ones to Ohno;[88] this binary interpretation is in line with many analyses that contrast Ohno's "angelic" works with Hijikata's "demonic" ones. Rather than staying with this dichotomous view, Kaneko's "Opposition" offers another way to approach these contradictions. Kaneko writes: "[T]o oppose / Is the only fine thing in life. / To oppose is to live. / To oppose is to get a grip on the very self."[89] In this way we can see the oppositions in *White Dance*—the ugly and the beautiful, the sublime and the absurd, the meditative and the explosive all together in this one piece—as not merely an amalgamation of previous influences, but rather a way of coming to understand Eiko & Koma.

By the time Eiko & Koma ended their trip to the United States, they were no longer just using dance to see the world, but were making a concerted decision to become artists. Their bodily research had led them beyond experimenting with Hijikata and Ohno's movement approaches to finding their own unique combination of extended stillness with moments of absurdity that unfold over time into a profound engagement with existential matters. Their experiences in New York in particular led them to see a place for themselves in that city's experimental downtown dance scene, a possibility they had not seen for themselves in Tokyo. When they returned to Japan, it was to arrange cultural exchange visas, with Gordon's help, for their return to New York, where they settled in 1977. The following chapter examines Eiko & Koma's first five years as residents of New York City, with a focus on the dances they created during that time, one new piece each year, and the various artistic influences they absorbed.

CHAPTER 2

"GOOD THINGS UNDER 14TH STREET"

_____

When Eiko & Koma settled in New York, the city, like many other major US cities, was experiencing what was referred to as an "urban crisis." So-called white flight to the suburbs, coupled with systematic economic disinvestment and government neglect, had left abandoned swaths through cities like New York, and particularly neighborhoods like the Lower East Side, which had traditionally been working class and immigrant communities. As landlords abandoned and even destroyed their buildings, and residents fought to stabilize their neighborhoods, artist subcultures were able to take root and flourish downtown thanks to low or no rent on commercial and residential spaces.[1] According to Christopher Mele, "Downtown described not only a place but an aesthetic or genre of music, dance, fashion, hairstyle, art, and performance."[2] In particular, Mele claims, the downtown scene was defined in opposition to "uptown," which was epitomized by the famous nightclub Studio 54. While uptown stood for wealth, excess, commercialism, celebrity, and privilege, downtown stood for alternative, experimental, radical, underground, and weird. The economic opportunity to live and create work inexpensively downtown allowed clubs, galleries, and performance spaces to develop as crucibles for a new art scene in which punk music, visual arts, film, and performance intersected.

Koma's description of the contradictions of mid-1970s New York paints a vivid picture of what he and Eiko encountered when they landed in the city:

When we arrived here [in New York] in 1976, we had the feeling that somehow we missed a very important art movement. Already, Judson [Dance Theater] was over. We could see that Soho was developing into artists' lofts by then. We couldn't find Yayoi Kusama [she lived in New York from 1956 to 1973, when she returned to

Japan] or Allen Ginsberg—though we did find Ginsberg later. And the city was bankrupt. Garbage was everywhere. People were lying down everywhere on the street. It was a weird time.[3]

Despite the feeling of having missed an era, Eiko & Koma in fact arrived in New York in the middle of a major boom in American postmodern dance, often referred to as the downtown dance scene.

In remarks made at a 2012 event sponsored by the Lower Manhattan Cultural Council, Koma recounted his memories of being told that nothing good was happening above 14th Street. "So I tried to look for good things under 14th street," he says. "I visited Meredith Monk, the experimental composer and vocalist. She was performing at her loft. And after that we played baseball together in a vacant lot. I remember Tricia Brown performing at her loft. David Gordon was also performing at his loft. Nobody had money. Lucinda Childs was performing her solo piece without any music at Danspace."[4]

As Koma's narrative indicates, downtown Eiko & Koma found themselves immersed in an active group of artists who, like the pair of new New Yorkers, were using their art to imagine new ways of being in society. Even when a specific political message was absent from the work—and it often was—the act of identifying with "downtown" was not just a geographic orientation, but a fundamentally political one. During this time, Eiko & Koma began experimenting with a variety of movement vocabularies, novel themes, and interdisciplinary collaborations with their new artist friends. Their pieces infused the then predominant mode of "dance for dance's sake" with uncommon qualities such as extended stillness and overt expressivity. Moreover, Eiko & Koma's combination of recognizable postmodernist characteristics such as nonlinearity and juxtaposition with novel (to the United States) ways of moving their bodies led to the pair quickly becoming critically acclaimed mainstays of the New York avant-garde.

I argue that the dances Eiko & Koma made in their first years in New York—*Fur Seal* (1977), *Before the Cock Crows* (1978), *Fluttering Black* (1979), *Trilogy* (1979–1981), and *Nurse's Song* (1981)—participated in the inherent social critique that characterized much of the late 1970s downtown arts scene. Although these works sometimes employed radically different styles (belly dance, punk, hippie), reviewers nonetheless came to expect a particular kind of quality of movement from Eiko & Koma and did not hesitate to critique dances that did not live up to their expectations. It is not my intention here to say the reviews were right or wrong, but to point out how a misunderstanding of Eiko & Koma's choreography was beginning to accrue even around these early works. As I show in chapter 3, this misunderstanding had a major impact on their dances being seen as Asian rather than Asian American. The danger of reading Eiko & Koma's choreographic preference for slowness and stillness as a culturally determined aesthetic attribute rather than the bodily articulation of a fundamental oppositional politics is that dances deviating from a particular style are then rejected on that basis, without a consideration of how they might be attempting to politically achieve the same thing as previous dances, simply through different means.

This experimental period in Eiko & Koma's choreography coincides precisely with a transitional period in American experimental dance observed by critic Marcia B. Siegel. In the introduction to *The Tail of the Dragon: New Dance, 1976–1982*, Siegel argues that the changes that took place in the dance scene between 1976 to 1982 were not the result of a specific and visible revolt, as had been the case with Judson Dance Theater a generation earlier,[5] but their effects nonetheless resulted in a visible and distinct change in American experimental dance. According to Siegel, social and cultural changes in the United States produced dancers who were concerned with dance itself, expressive not abstract, aggressively physical not pedestrian.[6] Her description of how the height of arts funding in the 1970s (before the beginning of the Reagan era) enabled the wider circulation of experimental dance while also requiring it to become standardized is particularly worth noting, especially since this is the precise climate in which Eiko & Koma began performing in the United States and during which they made a name for themselves. Siegel notes, "Subsidies underwrote dance performance and dance touring across a spectrum of taste wide enough to encompass experimental artists. . . . In some ways the experimental companies were better prepared to reach a wide audience than traditional groups. They were committed to flexibility, not wedded to proscenium spaces or rigid programming; they could dance in parks or schools, they could include local performers, improvise, and adapt to the conditions they found. But little by little, the diversity, the unpredictability, the strangeness that was so much a part of experimental dance was tamed and toned down."[7] She points out how the exigencies of these increased touring opportunities produced a need for set repertory pieces that fit into allotted time slots and could be billed as either well-reviewed hits or exclusive premieres.

Eiko observes that the kinds of needs described by Siegel had a specific impact on their choreography. Rather than presenting a full evening, as they had done on the European festival circuit and as they did in their first dances in the United States, Eiko & Koma began making shorter works. "Here, for the first time we were asked to make a piece and it doesn't have to be a full evening, which allowed us to think differently. And I think that's a choreographer's thinking, and that's why I feel like at that point we are also are very much a part of American modern dance."[8] This chapter focuses on the transitional period of Eiko & Koma's first five years in New York to demonstrate how their work during this time was both impacted by and incorporated into the larger contexts of American postmodern dance, avant-garde arts and music, and late 1970s politics.

Fur Seal

When Eiko & Koma returned to the United States from Japan in late spring 1977, a little over a half a year after their first trip ended, they brought with them an entirely new dance, *Fur Seal*. In this piece, the dancers playfully alternate between embodying seals—lying on the ground, upper body raised forward and up, hands working like flippers—and exploring the full use of their human legs through walks, runs, jumps, balances, and lifts that they may have picked up during their time studying with Manja Chmiel a few years earlier. The sixty-minute performance is accompanied by whale songs, Schubert, and "I Am the Walrus" by the Beatles, punctuated by frequent silence. An encore was performed to Bob Dylan's "One More Cup of Coffee." The dance is representative of the experimental, high energy, and sometimes absurdist work of Eiko & Koma's first years and at the same time foreshadows the pair's abiding concern with nonhumans and nature, particularly American landscapes. A 1976 trip to see harbor seals mating on the beaches of northern California impressed Eiko & Koma and inspired them to work on this new dance in Tokyo with the express intention of premiering it in New York.

Fur Seal marked a crucial break from Eiko & Koma's long-term work

with *White Dance*. The new theme spurred them to expand their movement vocabulary and explore new ways of staging their work. At the
same time that they broke new choreographic ground, the use of another
Mitsuharu Kaneko poem (from which they took their title) and reference to a nonhuman subject provided some continuity with their previous piece. In the case of *Fur Seal*, however, seals were not the metaphorical inspiration that the moths had been for *White Dance*, but a real-world
one. The experience of seeing and smelling the seals in California must
have resonated strongly with Kaneko's evocative stanzas:

> The sunlight beats down like sleet
> Today is their wedding feast
> Today is their big holiday
>
> All day long they wallow in the mud
> Ceaselessly bowing and curtseying
> Rubbing their fins together
> And rolling their bodies like carrels
>
> Fur Seal
> How foul-smelling is your breath
> How slimy is your back
> Clammy as the abysmal depth of an open grave
> Your body is ponderous as sand-bags
> How mediocre, how banal you are
>
> Your somber elastic shape
> Your dolorous lumps of rubber
> Bob and sink in the sea
> In the sorrowful rays of the evening twilight[9]

The poem focuses on seals at the time in their life cycle when they
leave the water, through which they easily glide, for an awkward and lum-
bering sojourn on land spent mating and gestating. Despite the sunshine
and celebratory air Kaneko lends the seal mating, his repugnance toward
the creatures is palpable. His aversion to them reveals a sort of existential
horror; he seems to ask, "Is this all we are?"

Whereas Kaneko encountered the seals as a disdainful observer, Eiko
& Koma approached the creatures with a sense of bodily curiosity. Eiko
described the seals in a newspaper preview of their dance: "We saw how
they moved. They don't need their feet very much, but move with their
whole bodies. They are such lazy things, but they are always looking at
you. And they are recreative. They know just enough of life; I think we
know too much. We have so much information, we don't know what to
do with it. They know. We were interested in the way the seals eat, too.
They don't spend their whole time finding food—just a little. Then they
are free to play and move. That's where our dance came from."[10] What
would it require to embody the seals? How could the dancers wallow,
bow, curtsy, roll, bob, and sink on the seals' "recreative" terms? After the
fragility of moths, the ponderous, fleshy substance of seals must have
presented a tempting challenge. Eiko & Koma roll, scooch, contract, and
undulate, all without the use of their hands, arms, or legs.[11] Eiko & Koma
become all trunk, like the set piece hanging downstage left: a tree trunk
stripped of all branches, leaves, and roots.[12] Land-bound locomotion for
both the seals and these seal-dancers is an awkward struggle, expending
maximum effort for minimal forward motion.

Fur Seal had its premiere at the Riverside Dance Festival in New York
City in June 1977. The festival program included the Sophie Maslow
Dance Company, the Isadora Duncan Centenary Dance Company, the
Rudy Perez Dance Company, guest choreographer Hanya Holm, and
many others. In a bill that heavily featured modern dance, and particularly early modern dance, Eiko & Koma must have stood out as strikingly
unfamiliar.

Upon first seeing *Fur Seal*, Jennifer Dunning wrote, "You watch,
unable to look away," adding, "There is no one like these two dancer-
choreographers. Theirs is the intensity of strong, white light, exhausting but beautiful."[13] These sentences from a short two-paragraph *Dance
Magazine* review (part of a much longer piece addressing a number of
concerts) were used extensively in Eiko & Koma's publicity materials for
the next several years and came to define the pair's early work in the press,
framing their work as singular, something to which one is inextricably
drawn.

For many audience members, the opening section concentrated the
kind of experience Dunning described. When lights come up, the stage

remains only dimly lit. One can discern two figures, one reclining, and one upright next to the tree trunk that hangs in the space. Dark costumes and a dark stage blend together, against which exposed fragments of bodies — lower legs, a torso, an elbow — pop out. And then nothing happens. Nothing at all. Like the seals Kaneko accuses of wallowing and laziness, Eiko & Koma seem to be doing nothing but existing on the stage for minutes at a time. Eventually it becomes evident that they are not still, but rather their movement is infinitesimal, proceeding at an unhurried pace. Beginning curled up on her left side, Eiko takes all the time in the world to transition to her stomach, arms tucked under, lower legs pointing up, face out to the audience. I cannot call what she does rolling, because that suggests momentum and gravity and a certain inevitability that cannot be assumed in this case. She then drops her feet to the left, millimeter by millimeter, eventually bringing them back up, then repeating the process on the other side. During the whole time, silence reigns. Still Koma stands, perhaps a foot away but in another world. He seems to lean on the tree trunk, eventually taking it off its axis and revealing its suspension. Finally, gravity takes over in both cases: the trunk swings back and Koma begins to play with it, even as the weight of Eiko's lower legs finally takes over, provoking a response from the rest of her body. From this point, approximately five minutes into the dance, the pace picks up, but the experience of suspended time, of watching with bated breath, suffuses the rest of the performance, imbuing even periods of whimsy and hyperactivity such as the seal-waltz Eiko & Koma perform to the Beatles' "I am the Walrus," with a feeling of intensity and microcontrol. More than anything, Eiko & Koma's masterful stillness, their commitment to "doing nothing" onstage, grabbed audiences' attention and immediately characterized their work for critics.

The dancers, once sped up to a recognizable pace, neutralize Kaneko's poetic distaste for the seals with a bodily exploration of seal free time. What might they do during their "big holiday"? (See figure 2.1.) Koma spends his solo recreative seal time fully exploring the stage space. Everything he does is bigger and more accelerated than anything he has done before. He propels himself into the air and falls loudly, only to spiral immediately back up to standing. He circles the stage, a full-legged walk developing into deep lunges, his arms held above his head in an overcurve that seems to extend his trunk upward. He sinks to the ground. Jumps.

FIGURE 2.1 *Flyer for 1977 concert at Theater of Man, San Francisco. Courtesy of Eiko & Koma.*

Collapses into the floor. This time as he tries to rise back up, everything is superheavy: legs, torso, all of it. *I am the walrus GOO GOO GOO JOOB*, indeed.

When late in the piece, Eiko reenters the stage wearing a furry shift, Koma skitters toward her and past her off stage. Her seal playtime is taken up with light, controlled, almost waltzy steps. If Koma's games were big and heavy, Eiko's are full of suspension and extension. She bounces and then twists slowly forward. *Whooooooo!* She waltzes with herself and then arrests her momentum. Ending eventually at the bare trunk, she is rejoined by a now fur-clad Koma, a big flower stuck behind his ear. The absurdity begins to build. They both assume positions around the hanging trunk, feet wide and knees deeply bent. As they begin to locomote from this position, weight shifting side to side, their trunks feel heavy, as if they have to grunt with exertion each time they lift a leg. Coming back to the tree trunk, Eiko beats it rhythmically and ritually first with one bent arm, then the next. Finally, they come together in an awkward embrace that appears frequently in their body of work, arms over each other's backs, rocking back and forth from one side to another. *Ho ho ho, he he he, ha ha ha!* Eiko jumps on Koma, her legs around his neck, and flips back over. As he drags her across the stage, she spits a flower, Koma's erstwhile hair ornament, from her mouth. These *expert texpert choking smokers* stomp around the stage, arms bent at elbows, upper arms level with shoulders, lower arms pointing straight up. They hiss. They shout. They stagger. They bow. It's over.

Whereas the 1984 media dance based on *Fur Seal*, *Wallow*, attempts a more thorough, and sober, embodiment of seals, the 1977 dance makes no claim to verisimilitude, favoring instead a postmodern collage sensibility.[14] Whale sounds, a popular song ostensibly about a walrus, a poem about fur seals, harbor seal behavior, a tree trunk — all of these are equally valued in the dance, no matter their actual relevance to fur seals. The black satin costumes worn for most of the piece make the dancers look human, though ironically their movement is more seal-like while in the satin costumes and more human-like in the fur ones. Nonetheless, the human-animal morphing ventured in this dance is an important initial experiment that later became a hallmark of Eiko & Koma's work.

Not all reviewers embraced Eiko & Koma's second work. One review ("'Fur Seal' boring, but intriguing") goes so far as to suggest that adding video of actual fur seals to the performance would help audiences under-stand the dance better and would go a long way to prevent people walk-ing out of the performance, as the author witnessed. The author clari-fies the problem as one of unfamiliarity: "Avant garde dancers with their roots in the traditional Japanese style, the two are not only presenting a subject that is basically alien to American audiences, but using an alien theatrical language as well."[15] For others, this "alienness" elicited an Ori-entalist deference, if not understanding; it was a performance, as one re-viewer put it, "to respect and in some ways to enjoy for its originality and sense of integrity."[16] This sentiment calls to mind Bonnie Sue Stein's later writing about butoh: "The work of these Japanese artists is so thorough and so 'Japanese' that Westerners sense a searing honesty.... [S]pectators who may not like it . . . still respect the experimentation and the perfor-mance skills required."[17] Couched in these remarks by both authors is an assumption that one cannot understand the performance because it, like the performers themselves, is so "other." It is assumed to be incom-prehensible, but still has something to admire. While this Orientalist re-sponse to the work was not the attitude of the majority of critics, it did represent a growing trend, one I track through this chapter and examine in detail in chapter 3. By and large, however, critical response to *Fur Seal* was overwhelmingly positive, and Eiko & Koma were welcomed into the New York dance scene as singular avant-garde artists. Anna Kissel-goff, for example, wrote, "At root, their method is as old as Aesop. But their message has the same resonance of post-Sartre and post-Beckett drama."[18] Their next work mined precisely this tension between fable and postmodern performance.

Before the Cock Crows

Eiko & Koma's first dance created entirely in the United States, *Before the Cock Crows, Thou Shalt Deny Me Thrice*, premiered at the San Fran-cisco Museum of Modern Art in summer 1978.[19] As the name suggests, the sixty-minute dance tells a story of betrayal, though it has perhaps more resonance with Delilah's Old Testament seduction and betrayal of Samson than with Peter's New Testament fear-based denial.[20] Featur-ing the most specific story line of all Eiko & Koma's dances, *Before the Cock Crows* is also the most specifically gendered. Eiko owns the birch-branch-delimited stage, spiraling and snaking seductively past Koma before shooting him in the back with her childhood playtime finger guns. Immediately remorseful, she mourns excessively even as Koma comes back to life. Abruptly, Eiko becomes a chicken herself, the cock that has crowed throughout the dance, pecking and scratching, oblivious to the preceding events or the spellbound audience watching her. Accompanied by a Romanian folk song, music by "Belly Dance King" George Abdo and his Flames of Araby Orchestra, and rooster sounds, the dance ends with Koma sinking beneath the weight of a birch branch contraption borne on his back—part oversized crown, part cross—as Eiko herself (no longer a chicken) is bowed by the weight of her own actions. Unlike their two previous works, in this dance it is eminently clear that Eiko & Koma are humans playing characters, at least until Eiko becomes a chicken.[21] Seen retrospectively in the context of Eiko & Koma's larger body of work, *Before the Cock Crows* is an early iteration of the pair's oft-repeated mating ritual and a precursor of their attention to cycles of mass violence in the most intimate of settings, a theme explored in detail in chapter 5. For critics, this dance also opened up the possibility of comparing and contrasting Eiko & Koma's work with modern and postmodern dances.

Like *Fur Seal*, *Before the Cock Crows* opens with a period of extended stillness, which had by that point become a marker of Eiko & Koma's dances in the United States. Although reviews and video documentation reveal distinct variations in the opening[22]—sometimes Eiko is onstage braiding her hair when the audience enters, sometimes both are there when the lights come up, sometimes Koma comes crashing in later— the lack of discernible movement remains a constant. A cock crows. For minutes, a pulsing track with Middle Eastern instrumentation, perhaps meant to evoke biblical lands, fills the space. The dancers do not respond; impassive, Eiko kneels upstage center while Koma stands downstage right, his left arm raised. They are both draped in folds of material: she in red, he in tan. The stage is inexplicably outlined with long, thin birch branches. By the time the music ends, Eiko has microscopically shifted her head forward, her torso twisting ever so slightly in response. In silence and decreasing light, Koma raises his head and lets his hand descend slowly to his side. This seems to be a signal to speed up to a tortoise-like pace. The protracted openings for which Eiko & Koma were becoming known seemed designed to grab the audience's attention and keep them there, holding their breath (a number of reviews use this as metaphor), until they are absolutely sure that the audience is with them, at which point they slowly begin to unfold their movement. The dancers recognized the necessity of shifting their audience into an alternate time space and rooting them there for the duration of the piece.

While today that same stillness, combined with layered images and curious juxtapositions, might be seen as butoh or butoh-like, it is important to remember that butoh was not yet known in the United States and was only just being introduced to France. Moreover, Eiko & Koma have never used that term for their work. Instead, at the time Eiko & Koma were embraced and understood as avant-garde or postmodern. Shoko Letton sees a connection between Eiko & Koma's movement style and American postmodern dance, which she identifies as "a minimalist philosophy of simple means, repetitions, everyday movements and objects, and the manipulation of time."[23] At the same time, Letton continues, "Eiko and Koma's slowness was considered to be a part of their cultural performative tradition."[24] In other words, audiences assumed that what they were seeing was in some way inherently and traditionally Japanese because the dancers themselves were Japanese. Just enough information about Japanese arts and practices had circulated popularly in the United States that audiences felt they could identify things like Zen and noh in Eiko & Koma's dances, even though the dancers had little experience with either.

In fact what Eiko & Koma were doing at the time was actively exploring and absorbing new influences. For example, Eiko took belly-dancing lessons while they were making *Before the Cock Crows*; that experience is particularly evident in the dance's Middle Eastern sound track and in a solo watched by Koma and the audience alike. Eiko's willowy arms slowly wave above her head like two snakes, only they are the ones doing the charming. As her hips swivel, taking their time, her dress emphasizes the spirals in her body. Her gaze appears internal, but she keeps her body facing the audience and occasionally even glances its way as her arms and torso continue their side-to-side body waves. Employing the arched back, cocked hip, and spirals of belly dancing, she seduces the audience and Koma both without ever exposing her belly.

While Eiko holds down the center of the stage with her serpent-like arms and torso, Koma circles and criss-crosses the stage, drawn to her, but also trying to draw some attention of his own. Despite largely appearing to be in their own worlds — each with his or her own movement vocabulary and swaths of stage space — the two dancers are clearly, though inexplicably, drawn to one another. They follow each other, approach and then retreat. After one such retreat Eiko hides her face and turns her back to Koma, yet a slight turn of her head indicates that she is still paying close attention. Is she being coy, drawing him in? In other dances in which the pair less clearly represents human characters, this choreographic pattern is described as a mating ritual. Here it is better described as seduction, with Eiko clearly seducing Koma, and the audience in the process (see figure 2.2).

In the next section, the type of submerged violence that critic Janice Ross previously identified in *Fur Seal* surfaces.[25] Koma curls forward almost in a yoga child's pose far downstage, close enough to touch audience members in the first row of the black box theater. As before, Eiko follows him. This time, however, she does not retreat but instead comes up directly behind him. Just when the audience might expect consummation, suddenly she yells, "Bang! Bang! Bang!" her hands held in loose "guns," the utterances accompanied by sharp torso movements. "Bang!" The combination of their proximity to the audience, her unexpected vocalization, the absurdity of her child's play gestures, and the deadly seriousness of her intent are shocking, as is her immediate remorse. Or rather it is not her remorse that shocks so much as the excess of emotion on display. A Sicilian mourning song comes on, and Eiko embodies the sorrowful guitar and sobbing male voice. She sharply strikes her own solar plexus, lashes out with clawed hands, and falls to the ground, draping her wracked body over Koma's. She rolls him, drags him, sinks to the ground again. She keens, collapses, not even noticing that he is now rolling by his own volition.

In the late 1970s this kind of overt and even excessive emotion in dance had long been out of style. Letton astutely observes, "Most postmodernists' performative modalities used consciously developed *in*expressive performance techniques. . . . In stark contrast, however, Eiko and Koma developed their gestural movements in a highly expressive way."[26] And yet, she argues, their dance did not present a unity among gesture, bodily comportment, and facial expression; rather, it included complex and perhaps contradictory layers that opened up possibilities for the meaning of that expression beyond a single emotional response.

dance
New York Premier
**BEFORE
THE COCK CROWS**

OCT. 26, 27 & 28 – 8pm
29 (Mat.) 3pm
AMERICAN THEATRE LAB.
219 W. 19 St., N.Y.C.
924-0077
$3.50 OR TDF

AFTER THEIR EXTENSIVE PERFORMANCES IN JAPAN, EUROPE AND AFRICA, EIKO AND KOMA ARE
KNOWN HERE FOR THEIR PREVIOUS WORKS <u>WHITE DANCE</u> AND <u>FUR SEAL</u>.

SUNDAY WORKSHOPS:

Nov. 5, 12, 19, 26 -- 2:00-4:00 p.m.
$5.00 per class -- Can be taken individually or as a series.
FOR INFORMATION AND REGISTRATION, WRITE OR CALL:

NEW ARTS MANAGEMENT
47 W. 9th Street
New York, N.Y. 10011
691-5434

FIGURE 2.2 *Flyer for the New York City premiere of*
Before the Cock Crows *at American Theatre Lab.*
Courtesy of Eiko & Koma.

Those contradictory layers provided a postmodern choreographic context for the expressionist vocabulary.

For example, even though *Before the Cock Crows* is the most strongly narrative of Eiko & Koma's works, the narrative is not only *not* sequential, but in fact serves to disrupt what came before.[27] Following the over-the-top mourning scene and a tentative détente between Eiko and the reanimated Koma, chicken sounds suddenly fill the space, and Eiko's movement inexplicably shifts. Another cock crows, and Eiko is now herself a chicken. Low to the ground, she pecks with her nose, chin to the floor, butt in the air, index fingers pecking, poking, occasionally pointing at herself. She pecks on, beleaguered. Meanwhile Koma begins to make his way across the stage, burdened with a triangular contraption of branches on his back. Is this a sort of cross? Finally he cannot go any further, the weight of the branches forcing him to sink slowly to the ground. In fact, everything sinks in unison with Koma: the sound, lights; even the formerly erect Eiko is pushed down by the weight of what she has done, arms straight out to the side, knees bending forward in parallel. As the final lights fade, Koma is trapped on the floor under his contraption, and Eiko is only inches from the floor: feet together, knees bent, head forward, arms parallel to the floor. Each is crucified in his or her own way.

Marilyn Tucker noted of the piece, "The movement is so elastic, so suggested and dreamlike, that anyone else present in the large and appreciative audience probably might have interpreted things differently."[28] And indeed, New York and California critics offered a number of possible narratives. Some tracked it quite closely to the biblical story of Jesus, Peter, and Judas. Others saw the stages of a male-female relationship being worked through. More important than the various interpretations offered by the critics are the ways they used *Before the Cock Crows* to work through Eiko & Koma's place in American modern and postmodern dance. Tucker calls them "a force in the avant garde to be reckoned with,"[29] while Lewis Segal writes that in their work "minimalism gained unexpected virtuosity."[30] Jean Nuchtern makes an extended comparison of Eiko & Koma's methods of creating narrative and expressing emotion to Martha Graham's, finding that Eiko & Koma maintain an inward focus while Graham's dancers react to the forces around them. She goes on to observe, "What [Eiko & Koma] leave out structurally is the notion of cause and effect. They are, they exist and can be looked at as both object (their actions symbolize something else) and subject (the performers reveal what's happening to them.) Where Graham presents emotions experienced in sequential time, Eiko and Koma present emotional archetypes frozen in time."[31] Only twenty-six and twenty-nine years old at the time, Eiko & Koma were already being taken quite seriously by American dance presenters and critics.

Fluttering Black

If *Before the Cock Crows* referenced biblical narratives and evoked the elsewhere of the Near East, Eiko & Koma's next dance, *Fluttering Black* (1979), could not have been more specific to the time and place of its creation.[32] The duo described *Fluttering Black*, presented at the downtown venue The Performing Garage, as "a work that acknowledges the last summer of the seventies."[33] Suzanne Carbonneau agrees that "as a metaphor for the end of an era of hope for radical political change, the dance was painfully potent."[34] Backed by a large black banner, the performance enacted the experimental, anticommodity ethos of the late 1970s New York downtown scene. Like *Fur Seal* and *Before the Cock Crows*, *Fluttering Black* was the result of Eiko & Koma's encounter with new people, styles, and situations; unlike the previous two pieces, however, *Fluttering Black*'s politics was more explicit. In a preview in the *Village Voice*, Burt Supree calls *Fluttering Black* "anarchic, cosmopolitan chaos." He quotes Eiko & Koma — "'without any color, without any decoration'" — and adds, "without any systematic structure."[35] Supree's reference to anarchy, while perhaps offhand, was nonetheless relevant. The titular black banner calls to mind the anarchist symbol of the black flag, which signals the absence of nation-states. Contrary to the white flag of surrender sometimes employed by Eiko & Koma, the black flag signals opposition and defiance. While the symbol represented the mind-set of the downtown scene, it also harkened back to Eiko & Koma's student activist days in Tokyo, when black flags, among many others, flew on campuses and in the streets.

Fluttering Black was a collaboration with musician Glenn Branca. Eiko met Branca through his girlfriend, with whom Eiko waitressed at Magoo in Tribeca. Branca, then an up-and-coming no wave musician, now an iconic noise composer, wrote "The Spectacular Commodity" for the choreographers and accompanied the performances live with his trio,

The Static, who were billed as "No Wave rock on stage."[36] No wave was a short-lived but influential movement of underground music, film, and art in New York City in the late 1970s and early 1980s that came out of the punk subculture. An explicit rejection of the then-popular new wave, no wave music in particular can be characterized as abrasive and atonal, with driving rhythms that reflected the bleak and nihilistic late 1970s outlook. Listening to the music today, in the wake of the broad critical success of bands like Sonic Youth, who use alternate tunings, "The Spectacular Commodity" no longer sounds grating.[37] But at the time, when atonal music and alternate guitar tunings were only beginning to be explored, the music must have been shocking.

"The Spectacular Commodity" references Guy Debord's 1967 text, *The Society of the Spectacle*, which argues that the commodity is no longer the product of labor but is now, as spectacle, the object of consumption. In *Fluttering Black*, the performers signal their refusal to be subjected to the spectacle, or even to participate in creating one, through a forceful elimination of any connection between sound and movement. They cover their eyes with blindfolds and stuff wads of cotton in their ears, which are then covered with duct tape for good measure. Audience members, too, were offered wads of cotton to stuff in their ears should the music be too loud, or if they wanted to experience the same dulled senses as the performers. Eiko & Koma sought each other blindly in the space — Supree observes them "bumble together, shoving and bumping"[38] — only able to feel the vibrations of the music. The musicians, too, were meant to not hear each other; unable to coordinate, their music intentionally lost coherence. Only a thin line of water marking the boundary of the stage kept the dancers' "off-balance, grotesquely cramped gestures" and "frantic gyrations"[39] contained. Throughout the performance, they are decidedly themselves, neither characters as in *Before the Cock Crows*, nor nonhuman creatures as in *Fur Seal*. Though Eiko & Koma credit Mura Dehn, the noted jazz dancer and chronicler of African American social dance, in the program, their movement in *Fluttering Black* seems to have less to do with jazz technique than with punk and performance art.[40] In photos, Eiko displays more than a passing resemblance to punk pioneer Siouxie Sioux.

For the only time I can think of in their entire body of work, the physical effort of their dance is clearly evident. Their bodies appear heavy, ex-

FIGURE 2.3 Fluttering Black *at The Performing Garage,*
New York City, 1979. Unknown photographer.
Courtesy of Eiko & Koma.

hausted. By the end, blindfolds removed, Eiko's hair sticks to her face,
and holes in Koma's black long-sleeve shirt are visible. Whereas the pair
normally seems utterly in control of their bodies down to the smallest
muscle fiber, here their bodies seem about to explode or collapse. It is
completely unpredictable (see figure 2.3). All we know for sure is that
they have pushed themselves all the way to the edge. And perhaps they
really were exhausted. Eiko & Koma performed three August weekends

in a row, dancing *Before the Cock Crows* in Program A at 8:00 pm, then a shortened version of *Fur Seal* followed by the premiere of *Fluttering Black* in Program B at 10:00 pm.[41]

Immediately following the three-week run at The Performing Garage, Eiko & Koma performed an untitled piece based on *Fluttering Black* at the San Francisco Museum of Modern Art. The dance was performed twice within the "Variable Landscape" created by Isamu Noguchi as part of his retrospective exhibition.[42] Photos documenting performances at the San Francisco Museum of Modern Art make the dancers seem more like protesters than punks. Gone is the live band in the intimate, alternative downtown performance space, as well as the sense of being members of a subculture with a coherent if abrasive vision. Here Eiko & Koma dance in the midst of the Noguchi show, although most of the exhibition is blocked from view by a massive white banner reading "NO WAVE" in black, block lettering. Maybe the banner was their way of trying to include the absent band, whose music was heard only on recording. It was also a tactic to inject the underground sensibility of the no wave movement into a premiere arts institution, giving the impression of the dancers as young, rebellious upstarts protesting the establishment. One photo by Marilyn Gray shows Eiko, mouth open in a big "O," right arm looking like it is ready to take a decisive backswing at someone or something. Another photo, also by Gray, shows the pair standing, separated by almost the length of the banner, looking more like art students dressed in black tops and pants; Koma has streaks of flour across his pant legs and sleeves that look more like the result of white paint artfully applied rather than a confrontation with his surroundings.

Reviews of both versions of the dance show that critics were puzzled by it. Tobias calls it "flimsy and theatrically contrived."[43] Supree says, "Eiko and Koma seem to have chosen a ground of deliberate confusion and deprivation to work in. And it's too shallow for them."[44] An unnamed writer in *Artweek* adds that the dance was "more contrived and deliberately striving for effect"[45] than any of their previous works. The critique in *Artweek* is revealing, noting that Eiko & Koma "broke the continuity of their action too many times for spectators to become absorbed in it."[46] Though these reviewers do not explicitly say so, the quality of stillness framing the action that had worked so well in previous dances was missing from this piece. As a result, moments that might have been profound given increased time and space felt forced.

It is also true that for admirers of the duo's previous dances, *Fluttering Black*'s punk aesthetic must have felt incongruous. Eiko explains, "Living in the US brought us many excitements. The first few years, we got so excited about having this new way of communication, meeting interesting talented people who were all pretty much anti-authority. We went into punk rock, and this and that, but some of these excitements faded quickly."[47] Just as they had experimented with belly dancing in *Before the Cock Crows* only to leave it behind soon after, so too did they try out—and abandon—no wave. Nonetheless, it is instructive to consider this and other early pieces, not only as part of a developmental period during which Eiko & Koma clarified for themselves and their audiences their signature style, but also as evidence of the consistency of their central concerns. While they never again used punk music, subsequent dances show them still challenging societal conventions and resisting normative behavior.

Trilogy

After a brief foray into punk and the color black, Eiko & Koma returned to the color white with *Trilogy*. Choreographed over the course of three years, the dance includes three sections, "Cell" (1980), "Fission" (1979), and "Entropy" (1981). Each had its own separate premiere before the premiere of *Trilogy* in New York in 1981. In an interview with a dance critic, Eiko & Koma shared their research process for *Trilogy*, saying that they had "studied lots of science . . . the lifespan of amoebas, astronomy, Einstein, how time changes, entropy." They also looked "at cells . . . into the body, so it becomes kind of formless . . . so that the inside of the body goes beyond the skin."[48] As the quote suggests, Eiko & Koma did not look at human cells to celebrate the human, but to move beyond it. Though the differences between a single-cell life-form and a solar system are vast, the dancers' bodily attention is such that they are able to reveal both the vastness of the minute and the patterns and details of something normally too large to grasp. "Their apparent calm is illusory," observes a program note, calling attention to how the pair's seeming stillness is in fact constituted through constant micromovements, just as a view of the stars or the skin does not reveal the roiling activity of cosmic bodies or cells. A press release described the piece as a "mediation between infinitely large and infinitesimally small energies" in which Eiko & Koma "dance toward the point where our distinctions between animal, vegetable and mineral blur."[49] While Eiko & Koma claimed in newspaper articles that their intention was not to make a polemical dance, the word "fission" implied more than simple cell division to audiences at a time when the escalating American-Soviet nuclear arms race dominated the nightly news. In this context, audiences saw *Trilogy*, and especially "Fission," as a warning from a postnuclear future.

At the beginning of "Cell," the performance space stands empty except for a white mat at the center of the stage and piles of flour around its perimeter. In response to an insistent knock at the stage door, Koma careens through the space and opens the door, to reveal Eiko and a large industrial dolly cart. Covered in layers of wheat paste, white material, and gauze, and wearing spiky black wigs, Eiko & Koma might be bandaged humans or exoskeletal creatures. Their appearance calls to mind their earliest performances in Tokyo, when their bodies were also covered in globs of lumped and cracking flour paste. Then, however, they were nearly naked; now they are bound in layers and layers of material, gauze, and paste. The costumes depersonalize them and make them look almost indistinguishable. They are cellular twins, crusty amoebas. Even their faces are coated with paste so thick that their eyes appear to be closed or missing. Describing their unsettling appearance, Jack Anderson writes, "Their faces are chalk white and blank. They scarcely have faces at all."[50] The primary occupation of "Cell" is the slow-motion journey from the doorway to the mat center stage, accompanied inexplicably by Andean flutes: Eiko sinks onto the dolly; Koma rolls her across the space and upon arrival uses his own torso to maneuver her onto the mat. Once there, they crawl and roll, though their locomotion does not get them anywhere in particular, just more flour covered and entwined. They wrap themselves around each other so that they seem to literally be in bondage with one another, cells that attempt to reverse their division, or perhaps victims of a nuclear accident whose limbs have been rearranged and fused with one another's bodies: head to foot, all legs, torsos only.

If "Cell" is concerned with microlocomotion, "Fission" is primarily about the struggle to stand.[51] No sooner do the twinned performers rise to their feet than they topple, over and over again. Their efforts sometimes become combative, as one seems momentarily to dominate the other: Eiko climbs on his back; Koma sits on her folded body; Eiko's legs clamber up Koma's upright torso and find their way around his neck. But these moments never last long before the next collapse sends them both tumbling to the ground, left to sort out their limbs and attempt to rise once again. Despite their precarity, they pass through a number of moments of striking solidity, such as when they stand facing the audience, their gaze unusually direct, right fists raised above their heads in a pose strikingly similar to protestors raising the black power salute. Later they tilt forward in a cross between a back attitude and a yogic dancer's pose. Their right arms balance out the lifted left foot, and yet the impact of the image is as if they are attacking the viewer, their forward momentum and coiled energy evident, even as they stand still. Their bodies seem to be vessels of, if not rage, then some kind of dangerous energy. They crouch, but appear ready to spring. They frequently hold their hands in fists. Sometimes they move like dolls or robots, their stiff exoskeletons or artificial limbs hampering nuanced movement. They grunt and grimace.

After finally gaining their feet and stomping around, they tumble in opposite directions and then matter-of-factly walk upstage to don red shoes and red bibs over their peeling skin. The term "entropy" suggests a degree of disorder or randomness in a thermodynamic system, and the final section of *Trilogy* certainly delivers on that idea. While "Cell" functions as a prelude to "Fission," "Entropy" has the performers singing Japanese children's songs while dancing a sort of child's-play ballet. Are the children of "Entropy" the next stage of development for these formerly cellular creatures? How else to understand their orthogonal behavior? Or is their entropy — lost energy that cannot be converted to work — a form of sly resistance? Considered in relationship with *Nurse's Song*, which premiered eight months later, this section seems a precursor to the latter dance's ideas about children's play as intervention into oppressive structures of society.

Eiko & Koma's appearance as damaged creatures performing under the title "Fission" in the midst of an escalating Cold War and a growing anti-nuclear movement led to powerful associations for the audience between their dance and Hiroshima and Nagasaki. Reviews were full of words like catastrophe, nightmare, devastation, shattering, and survival. Deborah Jowitt's description represents the typical response: "You can imagine them as the victims of Hiroshima, as terribly damaged people; you can imagine them as life itself disintegrating."[52] One article even declared in its headline, "Dancer's Performance at UB Is Drama on Nuclear Anxieties."[53] Beyond the title, imagery, and choreography, the fact that Eiko & Koma were themselves postwar Japanese nationals certainly underscored any perceived links to nuclear weapons.[54] Eiko & Koma addressed this issue in an interview with a dance critic. It is worth quoting them in full to understand how they saw their work:

> Politically speaking, especially because the title of the second section is "Fission," people might imagine this to be related to Hiroshima, but when we made that piece we had no intention. We knew that we were giving that kind of message to the people, but we tried not to emphasize that part too much, because if a person is receiving that message, there is no way we can do anything stronger. I mean, to imagine what had happened after Hiroshima is enough. We don't have to deliver some message, we don't want to conclude that message, we leave that up to the audience. We don't know any more than you do already about the dangers of nuclear things, and aren't in a position to say "Look . . . enough of this." But we know that it can be—and it's perfectly fine with me. In fact if someone is taking that message seriously I'm glad to have had a part in it, but that's not where the dance lies on.[55]

This desire to leave interpretation of their work open rather than convey a particular message is consistent across Eiko & Koma's career. This is congruent with their rejection of the dogmatism of the Tokyo student protest movement and resonates with the larger trend toward postmodernist thinking that rejected unitary meaning. Nonetheless, it does not mean that Eiko & Koma's works, including *Trilogy*, do not have a political impact, nor that their own politics do not somehow suffuse their choreography. In fact, despite their disclaimer, Eiko & Koma performed "Fission" as part of a number of benefits, including Dancers for Disarmament and the Anti-Nuclear Dance Benefit Concert, put on by the People's Anti-Nuclear Information & Cultural Committee.[56] Clearly they were supportive of the anti-nuke movement and were willing for their work, and this dance in particular, to be used in its service.

It is important to note that this association between *Trilogy*, and in particular, "Fission," and the nuclear bombing of Hiroshima and Nagasaki and more generally nuclear holocaust predates the introduction of butoh to the United States. Butoh as a form is often anecdotally perceived and described in the United States and Europe as being inspired by and evoking the imagery of the nuclear bombing of Japan. This is entirely a Western interpretation of the form with no connection to its history, technique, or practice. Nonetheless, the interpretation is persistent and often is reported as fact. Clearly there was something useful there for American audiences in terms of butoh playing the role of a reminder of national culpability, a sort of symbol of "never forget." And yet reading this association onto the form places the responsibility on Japanese bodies to represent and remind, fixing them as representations of a past atrocity and discounting their ability to participate in contemporary discourses. I explore these ideas in depth in chapter 3.

The period in which *Trilogy* was choreographed was the most overtly politically engaged of Eiko & Koma's career. A two-page spread in the fall 1981 issue of *Contact Quarterly* entitled "Dirt News 1" outlines the duo's plans for Dirt Shop, "a floating coalition of performing artists and audience who work for a positive community, world survival (including us as artists) and an information exchange on cultural and political matters." The impetus for Dirt Shop comes from their desire to no longer "be depressed and repressed by the insanity of the political world."[57] Across the two pages, Eiko & Koma model the networking and information sharing they hope to cultivate by writing about venues, festivals, and benefits where they have recently performed. They mention interactions with the American Indian Movement (AIM) and anti-nuclear events as examples of the types of things other performing artists could engage with, but also as an opening for similar groups to invite them to participate. Even more than *Trilogy*, their next piece, *Nurse's Song*, embodied the spirit of Dirt Shop.

Nurse's Song

After the bleakness and isolation of *Fluttering Black* and the damaged yet persistent bodies of *Trilogy*, *Nurse's Song* seems to attempt to recapture a period of innocence, depicted here as childhood but also gesturing to the by then ending hippie generation. The fifteen-minute-long dance ran on a program with *Trilogy* for four nights at The Kitchen in late November 1981. Like *Fluttering Black*, *Nurse's Song* continued Eiko & Koma's practice of initiating interdisciplinary collaborations with other artists in order to make friends and continue relationships. Though originally planned as the first part of a full-length work, *Songs of Innocence*, slated for an August 1982 premiere at PS122, along with "a comprehensive retrospective of their work,"[58] the project was abandoned when *Nurse's Song*, like *Fluttering Black*, was panned by critics who had largely praised the choreographers' prior works.

At the opening of this chapter I quoted Koma talking about looking for Allen Ginsberg when they first arrived in New York. They finally met him during a summer residency at the Naropa Institute in Boulder, Colorado, in 1981. Ginsberg had been closely associated with the arts- and psychology-focused Buddhist institution (now an accredited university) since its founding in 1974. At Naropa, Eiko & Koma taught a five-week workshop described as "Dance Sequences and New Repertory directed towards performance."[59] A letter from Ivan Sygoda, Eiko & Koma's longtime manager at Pentacle, to Barbara Dilley[60] at the Naropa dance department offers course descriptions for their classes. Of particular interest is the description of the repertory class, which explains that the pair "will collaborate with participants on the re-creation, from their powerful and original repertory, of a work called 'Rebellion,' originally made in 1980."[61] No record remains of this 1980 piece, but it is interesting to think of the pair working with students on a dance called "Rebellion" ten years after they themselves left school as young activists and began dancing. This idea fits right in with both *Fluttering Black* and *Trilogy*.

Even as they worked with students, Eiko & Koma also spent time with Ginsberg and saw him and his partner, poet Peter Orlovsky, give poetry readings. They were particularly impressed with how the pair often concluded their readings by singing Ginsberg's original composition of William Blake's "Nurse's Song."[62] The idyllic, innocent tune would seem to stand in stark contrast to the idea of rebellion and anarchy:

> When voices of children are heard on the green,
> And laughing is heard on the hill,
> My heart is at rest within my breast,
> And everything else is still.

"Then come home, my children, the sun is gone down,
And the dews of night arise;
Come, come, leave off play, and let us away,
Till the morning appears in the skies."

"No, no, let us play, for it is yet day,
And we cannot go to sleep;
Besides, in the sky the little birds fly,
And the hills are all covered with sheep."

"Well, well, go and play till the light fades away,
And then go home to bed."
The little ones leaped, and shouted, and laughed,
And all the hills echoed.[63]

For Blake, the *Songs of Innocence* about the uncorrupted state of childhood provided a contrast to his *Songs of Experience*, which detail the repressions and restrictions of adulthood. It is easy to see Ginsberg's attraction to the resistance to normalized morality and oppressive societal structures inherent in Blake's *Songs*, and by extension Eiko & Koma's attraction to Ginsberg as a counterculture icon. As they were working on a new piece at Naropa, Eiko & Koma asked Ginsberg if they might use some of his songs in a dance; he agreed. The premiere, and only, performances of *Nurse's Song* were dedicated to "Allen and Peter."

Eiko & Koma invited Bob Carroll (1941–1988) to sing "Nurse's Song" and play the part of the Nursemaid to Eiko & Koma's children. Carroll was a solo performer and comic whom Eiko & Koma met through artist Sandra Lerner.[64] Eiko says, "Bob really was a vagabond performing artist. He was in Europe a lot and he was kind of a traveling artist, doing his own thing, managing himself. Very political . . . . We saw in him this sacredness, like a real serious beauty as a performer."[65] Though he is largely absent from performance history, in the late 1970s and early 1980s Carroll was a hit on the alternative theater festival circuit in the United States and Europe and was known for his unique brand of radical political comedy. To Eiko & Koma, Carroll was far more than a collaborator; he was a close friend who introduced the pair to avant-garde artists like Iowa Theatre Lab founder Ric Zank and cellist/performance artist Charlotte Moorman, which led to Eiko & Koma's participation in fund-raisers for Moorman's Annual Avant Garde Festival of New York. He also was the one who first took Eiko & Koma out to the Catskills (where the Iowa Theatre Lab had recently relocated). Jennifer Dunning described Carroll as "an endearingly mad poet of a performance artist,"[66] and in the program he is listed as the organizer of a 1982 Radical Humor Conference at New York University. Singing the part of the Nurse-maid, Carroll was accompanied by a three-member band and a volunteer chorus who performed in exchange for food and drink.[67]

When the lights come up on *Nurse's Song*, a four-sided, bright yellow, silk curtain encompasses the stage. From behind the curtain, Eiko & Koma count off: "*ichi, ni, san,* GO!" They count in Japanese one through three, but skip four, making a pun out of the Japanese word for "five." When the curtain drops at their exhortation, Eiko & Koma are in the center of the stage, dressed in what Dunning called "South Seas Island garb."[68] Their hair is done up in ponytails, and Koma wears a necklace made of chili peppers. Carroll is sitting on the floor in a corner singing, surrounded by the musicians and other singers. Eiko & Koma skip and crawl and play hopscotch. Eiko mounts Koma's back and plays horsey, slapping his butt and holding one ponytail in each hand. Whether they are tiptoeing across the space or conducting the band, everything they do is exaggerated. They are adults playing at being children playing (see figure 2.4). At the end, they curl up in Carroll's lap, as the repeating refrain "all the hills echo-ed" fades.

Though they could not seem more different, *Nurse's Song* is actually an apt companion to *Fluttering Black*; it, too, is a document of the end of the 1970s. In stark contrast to that piece, however, there is no alienation here, no decay, only the simple pleasures of children at play. For Blake, and for Ginsberg, this innocence was itself a resistive state. But almost fifteen years after the Summer of Love, that kind of protest evidently no longer felt relevant to viewers, at least not to audiences in New York, as evidenced by their reported reticence to sing along to the repeating last line. Perhaps that is also why the piece felt so false to critics; in 1981, in the recessed economy of Reagan's America, how was such innocence possible? It felt like the remnant of another era that did not fit comfortably in the early 1980s. Reviewers found it "contrived"[69] and the choreographers "pretenders."[70] Unsure if the work was sentimental or ironic,

FIGURE 2.4 Nurse's Song, *1981 (studio shot).*
David A. Fullard, PhD, photographer. All rights reserved.

they found that the dance "doesn't completely squash bite and wit under the weight of good cheer, but it doesn't give those qualities clear passage either."[71] A number of reviewers simply complained that Eiko & Koma's movements looked nothing like those of actual children. Dunning even accused the work of displaying "shades of *Blue Lagoon*,"[72] referencing the 1980 Brooke Shields movie about two children shipwrecked alone on a South Pacific island, a movie that even to my then ten-year-old mind was embarrassingly naïve.

Other than the feeling that the dance did not fit in its time, reviews also show that *Nurse's Song* did not match expectations for Eiko & Koma's work, which had already solidified within five years of their arrival in New York. By this time they were permanent residents of the United States and had already accumulated an impressive list of major grants, including a Creative Artists Public Service Grant and a Choreography Fellowship from the National Endowment for the Arts, and were part of the NEA Dance Touring Program. Audiences expected from their work a certain amount of seriousness and transformation — of their bodies, time, and space. Deborah Jowitt's review provides a particularly insightful window into those expectations and how *Nurse's Song* missed the mark. For her, Eiko & Koma's dances up until this point "presented ideas we all comprehend, even though there are mysterious crannies in them that we can attribute to Japanese traditions we know little of."[73] *Nurse's Song*, however, did not contain any "crannies of tradition," at least not the American expectation of Japanese tradition, with the result that the audience felt somehow robbed of the Orientalist pleasure they looked for in the duo's work. I explore this theme in depth in the following chapter.

According to Eiko, *Nurse's Song* "was a failure in many ways. We were so engrossed in trying new things, being new New Yorkers, and making friends. *Nurse's Song* was essentially about us with our friends Bob Carroll and Allen Ginsberg."[74] Though those relationships may have been stimulating for the artists, the product did not result in work that was equally satisfying for audiences. The critical reaction to *Nurse's Song* was a wake-up call for the duo. Eiko said, "We weren't as much as hurt as we thought, it's not worth it."[75] Rather than continuing with *Songs of Innocence* and Dirt Shop, Eiko & Koma began to take stock of where they were in their work and how they wanted to move forward. Koma reflected, "I learned a lot from those experiments. Yes, everything is possible. If we can make a dance on the beach, we can make anything."[76] Yet at the same time they felt they had reached an end of what they could do in New York City. "I remember thinking it was time to go," says Eiko. "Then [Ronald] Reagan had that landslide win [in the 1980 presidential election]. We had to wonder what to do philosophically, politically, culturally in the long run."[77] An evaluation of their work was in order.

In 1982 Eiko & Koma purchased an old farmhouse and a plot of land in the Catskills and retreated there for two years. Eiko often says of their work that their interests and vocabularies are not broad, but they go deeply into them. This narrowing and deepening began in earnest when they left New York City for the Catskills. As Eiko observed, "What remains important is what one really cares to explore over a long period of time. . . . So, our focus shifted from youthful adventure to being professionals — a huge shift from being young artist wannabes."[78] The work they produced there signaled the concentration of their signature style and the clarification of their central concerns of mourning, human relationships with nature, and relationships with other humans previously hinted at in *Fur Seal, Before the Cock Crows*, and *Fission*.

Whereas this chapter detailed the second five years of Eiko & Koma's work together as a time for them to absorb and experiment with new influences from their lives in the United States, chapter 3 looks at how producers and critics represented Eiko & Koma during the same period and how this shifted over time, to show how larger discourses about Japanese performance began to obscure the force of Eiko & Koma's work.

CHAPTER 3

${\cal J}$APANESE/AMERICAN

The summer 1978 issue of *Bridge: An Asian American Perspective* included a special dance section featuring nine short articles over twenty-four pages (see figure 3.1). In the opening essay, dancer/choreographer and guest editor Reynaldo Alejandro describes the 1970s American dance boom and asks, "What share of this prolific expansion of the dance experience has been the result of Asian American contribution and participation? Does the trend of an increasing role for Asian Americans in dance reflect the fact [that] collectively, we as Asians are fast becoming the most numerous immigrant group, or does it reflect an increase in public interest and demand for our creative skills?" He further notes that "an increasing number of Asian and Asian American performers are appearing in theaters all over the United States; the works of Asian and Asian American choreographers are in increasing demand; and American dancers and choreographers themselves are investigating various Asian dance forms to be performed and researched."[1]

The special section includes features on both Asian American and Euro American artists performing "traditional" Asian dance, as well as two essays in which choreographers Eleanor Yung and Yen Lu Wong describe the development of original contemporary works. This combination of subjects—Asian dancers in America, traditional Asian dance, and new works by Asian American choreographers about the Asian American experience—demonstrates that dance was one of the ways Asian American identity was being worked out in the 1970s. Were Asian Americans simply Asians in America, a diverse group of people who had in common their location in the United States? Were Asian Americans defined by their diasporic cultural practices or by immigrant experiences and encounters with processes of US racial formation? The *Bridge* dance section raises all these questions.

A year later, a 1979 *New York Times* Arts and Leisure feature article by

AN ASIAN AMERICAN PERSPECTIVE

BRIDGE

VOL. 6 NO. 2 SUMMER 1978 $1.50

ASIAN
AMERICAN
DANCE

THE
ASIAN
AMERICAN
ASSEMBLY
CONFERENCE

AAMHRC
SECTION

FIGURE 3.1 *Cover of* Bridge Magazine *6, no. 2 (Summer 1978).*
Museum of Chinese in America, Bridge Magazine *Collection.*

Gwen Chin also noted the increasing presence of Asian American performers in American modern dance companies, asking more specifically, "Japanese Dancers in America: What Draws Them?" The article begins with a listing of single (and presumably singular) Japanese dancers in American dance companies and a discussion of how and why they stand out. Tellingly, there is no indication that any of these dancers may be American, although one is specified as "half-Japanese." The author goes on to call modern dance "antithetical to traditional Japanese dance" even as she rehearses assumptions, supported by various "experts," about restrictive tradition in Japan, and in contrast, the possibility of freedom of bodily expression in the United States.[2]

Eiko & Koma make an appearance at the end of both publications. In the *New York Times* article they are mentioned — and pictured — as choreographers of postmodern works. In the *Bridge* special section they are included in a "Roundtable Discussion with Asian American Dance Choreographers" along with Sun Ock Lee, Saeko Ichinohe, and Reynaldo Alejandro. In response to the interviewer's first question, "Why have you chosen to choreograph in the modern dance idiom rather than in a traditional Asian dance form?"[3] Eiko and Koma clarify that they never practiced any traditional dance form. At that point, Eiko & Koma disappeared abruptly and without explanation from the rest of the roundtable, as if not including "traditional" dance in their influences or work somehow rendered them invisible, even to other Asian Americans at the time. This would suggest that at the time a connection to "tradition" was a fundamental qualifier of Asian American status, even among choreographers making original modern dance works.

I take this literal disappearance from the page as the point of departure for this chapter, which examines the absenting of Eiko & Koma as Asian American subjects. I suggest this absenting is due not only to their apparent inability to fit into concepts of what it means to be Asian American, and specifically Japanese American, but also to discourses that increasingly represented them as Japanese or Asian, even as their work became more and more influenced — and supported — by their lives in the United States. I begin by putting Eiko & Koma's early performances in the United States in the context of competing discourses of the Asian American movement and what Barbara Thornbury calls "America's Japan," which she asserts was formed through reception of kabuki per-

formances in New York, particularly through reporting about these performances in major New York newspapers and magazines.[4] I then discuss
how dance presenters and critics represented Eiko & Koma when they
first arrived in the United States in the late 1970s and compare these
representations with those from the 1980s and early 1990s to note how
perceptions of them changed during that period. In particular, I show
how the international circulation of butoh led to a new discourse about
Japanese performance that I call a "nuclear discourse," which linked the
avant-garde performance with the aftermath of the American nuclear
bombing of Hiroshima and Nagasaki. I argue that the discourses of
kabuki-Japan and "the bomb" impacted the reception of Eiko & Koma's
work, preventing a reading of the work as Asian American and glossing
over the ways their work is fundamentally shaped by their lives in the
United States. These twin discourses obscure the meaning of the work
and in the process limit our understanding of what it means to be Asian
American.

Asian America and "America's Japan"

The *Bridge* and *New York Times* articles demonstrate the competing discourses of the Asian American movement and "America's Japan" through
which Eiko & Koma's early works were received. The Asian American
movement gained momentum in the wake of the civil rights movement
in general and the "Third World Strike" demanding ethnic studies at
San Francisco State University in 1968 and the University of California, Berkeley, in 1969. *Bridge* was a national publication started by Basement Workshop, a New York Chinatown–based community arts center
formed in 1970 and active until the late 1980s. In addition to publishing *Bridge*, Basement Workshop published a collection of art and poetry
called *Yellow Pearl* and initiated projects like the Asian American Resource Center. As evidenced by the recent exhibition *Serve the People:
The Asian American Movement in New York*,[5] Basement Workshop was
just one part of a vibrant network of Asian American activist and cultural organizations active in New York in the 1970s. *Bridge* covered national politics from an Asian American perspective, including articles on
the Vietnam War, national elections, immigration policy, Asian American studies, the Asian American women's movement, and busing. The
magazine showcased culture and Asian American cultural production

side by side with political coverage.[6] In this context, the *Bridge* special section highlights dance as one of many approaches to defining and enacting Asian American identity and politics.

One of the founders of Basement Workshop, Eleanor Yung, also founded the Asian American Dance Theatre in 1974.[7] Under the direction of Yung, the Asian American Dance Theatre performed original dances based in modern dance vocabularies with titles like *Identification in Progress #1, #2, #3*; *Sheng Sheng Man*; and *Water Portrait*. Along with the choreographers featured in the *Bridge* roundtable — Alejandro, Ichinohe, and Lee — Yung also participated in a series of concerts in 1979 and 1980 under the name Asian New Dance Coalition.[8] In both cases, the company and coalition names claim membership in the American contemporary dance scene while asserting the presence of Asians and Asian Americans.

In contrast to *Bridge*'s focus on Asian American cultural politics, the Chin *New York Times* article is part of a long history of articles about Japanese performances in New York City. Barbara Thornbury argues that coverage like this had enormous influence, determining for American audiences not only how particular performances were to be understood, but also what it meant to be "Japanese" more broadly. Thornbury maintains that "Japan" was discursively constructed for Americans largely through its synecdoche, "Japanese culture," which was defined through exposure to Japanese performing arts and particularly kabuki in New York City beginning after World War II and continuing through the 1970s.[9] In particular, she argues that the way these New York–based performances were presented and interpreted for American audiences, particularly through reviews in the *New York Times* and other similar publications, had an impact far beyond the actual performance halls, producing a discourse of "America's kabuki-Japan" that not only determines how Japan is understood in America, but also at times supplements or even supplants official diplomacy. Key to America's kabuki-Japan is the idea of "a Japanese culture characterized by tradition and ahistorical continuity."[10] This supposed out-of-history quality allowed kabuki to stand in as a counternarrative to the reality of contemporary politics even as it was an important Cold War prize and an actual tool of diplomacy (e.g., a Grand Kabuki visit timed to mark the centennial of the 1860 US-Japanese trade agreement). In other words, the "timeless" and "refined" qualities ascribed to kabuki allowed American supporters of the art form to present a friendly Japan that both predated and transcended Japanese imperialism, thereby smoothing the way for mutually beneficial postwar military and business arrangements between the two countries.

Although these two discourses, Asian American and America's Japan, as represented by *Bridge* and the *New York Times*, were contemporary with one another, the reach of the former—700 subscribers at its height[11]—was no match for the latter, with a daily circulation of 879,000 in 1978.[12] How could the Asian American discourse even begin to make an impact in the face of such a dominant discourse of Japan? And yet as the changing representations of Eiko & Koma demonstrate, representations of them have remained under contestation for the past forty years.

"The Vanguard of Modern Dance"

Before Eiko & Koma first arrived in New York, there was already a long history of contemporary dance by Asians in America as well as a more recent history of Japanese avant-garde performances at La MaMa E.T.C., a well-known downtown Manhattan venue for experimental and radical performance. In fact, venues like La MaMa provided a frame for understanding avant-garde Japanese theater by artists such as Shuji Terayama[13] and Kōbō Abe[14] and provided an impetus for other venues to eventually expand their own programming to include new and avant-garde works that could challenge audiences to see something other than "America's Japan." Thornbury observes, "Although visits to the United States by figures such as Terayama, Abe, and Ono[15] decontextualized them and their output from the networks with which they were associated in Japan, their ties to La MaMa in New York gave them a new, substitute context and 'downtown' identity."[16] Like these artists, Eiko & Koma's performances at noted downtown venues contextualized them in the American avant-garde performance scene, even if the Japanese and European frames of reference for their work were not well understood.

Performances by Japanese avant-garde artists at places like La MaMa, Thornbury suggests, demanded a reevaluation of assumptions about Japanese performance that had cohered in the previous decades, and by association, a reevaluation of the country and culture they were understood to represent. Moreover, they demanded critical attention as art, rather than the more anthropological interest in performance as demonstration of culture that kabuki, gagaku, bunraku, and other classical art forms attracted. Eventually the success of these productions impacted the broader producing scene in New York, with organizations like Japan Society cosponsoring La MaMa productions and then eventually diversifying their own programming.[17] Other key "downtown" institutions like BAM and the Joyce Theater also began programming Japanese performance.

During Eiko & Koma's first tour in 1976 and in the following year when they moved to the United States, they were billed as "Japanese avant-garde dancers," and their work was called "avant-garde dance in the Japanese manner."[18] Rather than understanding this as meaning coming from the specificity of the avant-garde in Japan, however, it was generally interpreted in reviews as two separate, and conflicting, categories. Rather than a national identifier, "Japanese" was taken by many critics — in the language of the time — to mean "Oriental," which not only meant foreign but more importantly, "traditional," despite the fact that this specific work had no precedent in traditional dances like nihon buyo or bugaku. Reviews reflected this assumption, freely comparing Eiko & Koma's work to Zen, kabuki, noh, and other Japanese arts. For example, one critic described what she saw as "an unstudied absorption of the classical elements of their native culture."[19] Others saw parallels to what they called "Oriental stone gardens."[20] As dancers from Japan, Eiko & Koma were assumed to have a background in traditional dance (not unlike in the *Bridge* roundtable), despite their lack of any training in these forms.

Eiko & Koma's case was not unique. Despite solid downtown credentials, avant-garde works by Terayama and Abe were also filtered through the kabuki discourse with its attendant expectation that the performances represent Japan in some way. Steven Clark explains that artists like Terayama "faced a strange paradox: at home the troupe typically fit into universal categories like the avant-garde or underground theater, but when they performed in Europe or America they often found themselves representing geopolitical particularities like 'Japan' or even 'the East.'"[21] Even when the pieces themselves challenged the discourse, the discourse was nonetheless evident in reviews of those pieces. Not only were these performances understood as essentially "Japanese," the kabuki discourse went a step further to render them traditional and ahistorical.

Shoko Letton observes that "the art world's acceptance of and famil-

iarity with Japanese art movements readied American audiences to wel-
come and accept Eiko and Koma's dance — but also created a filter for how
their works were perceived."[22] Indeed, as Bert Winther has shown, there
is a long and complex history of what he calls Japaneseness in American
art, including a European-influenced *Japonisme* of the late nineteenth
century that was interested in the formal properties of Japanese art, and
a midcentury "Oriental thought" period that sought to digest and apply
perceived "Asian ideals" into "original," abstract art.[23] In dance, well-
known examples of this include Merce Cunningham's use of chance pro-
cedures involving the *I Ching* and the uncredited though widely recognized application of aikido techniques in the formation and practice of
contact improvisation.[24] Whereas white American dancers were credited
with originality for their avant-garde pieces, Eiko & Koma's own original works, in the eyes of presenters and critics of the time, slipped easily
from avant-garde into an essentialized Japaneseness. Deborah Wong's insightful observation — "Given the susceptibility of American audiences
to orientalist pleasure — their willingness to give themselves over to it — I
must ask what happens when performers think they are saying one thing
and audiences hear something else entirely, and whose responsibility it is
to redirect the reading"[25] — guides this chapter.

This unselfconscious Orientalism notwithstanding, critics and presenters firmly concluded that the pair fit into the postmodern or "New
Dance" scene, calling them part of the "vanguard of modern dance"[26]
and "a force in the avant-garde to be reckoned with."[27] Presenters, too,
agreed. Though the pair's first performance was at Japan Society, they
were quickly booked at spaces that specialized in postmodern and avant-
garde dance and performance. Moreover, Eiko & Koma appeared in festivals and seasons with luminaries of American modern and postmodern
dance alike, including Sophie Maslow, Hanya Holm, Rudy Perez, Bill T.
Jones and Arnie Zane, Molissa Fenley, Sarah Rudner, Margaret Jenkins,
Lynn Dally, ODC, Bella Lewitzky Dance Company, and Mangrove. They
were reviewed alongside Dana Reitz, Dance Theater of Harlem, Lucinda
Childs, and Susan Rethorst. This suggests that despite the persistence
of a discourse of ahistorical Japaneseness evident in reviews, in practice
Eiko & Koma were understood in the context of modern and postmodern dance.[28]

Butoh and the Bomb

By the early 1980s Eiko & Koma began to receive their first important commissions and grants from American agencies and organizations, including the American Dance Festival, the Walker Art Center, BAM First Wave, and the National Endowment for the Arts. Even as they were incorporated more and more into the American concert dance scene and its accompanying presenting and funding structures, the larger Japanese-American relationship began to shift, within and without the US borders. The relationship between Japan and the United States, which had been closely intertwined since the postwar occupation and subsequent structural investment, cooled in the face of the declining status of US industry and increasing economic competition from Japan. In the United States the movement for reparations for the internment of Japanese Americans gained strength even as the model minority discourse held up East Asians — and specifically Japanese Americans — as ideal, yet still separate, citizens. It was during this time that butoh began to be known internationally and the first butoh dancers, including Eiko & Koma's teacher Kazuo Ohno, performed in New York. I argue that the appearance of butoh provided the impetus for a new discourse about "America's Japan." Whereas the kabuki discourse persuaded Americans after World War II that the Japanese were a refined and highly cultured people with whom we could safely do business, a developing butoh discourse linked Japan with the cataclysm of the nuclear bomb, reassuring struggling Americans of their modernity in comparison to the postnuclear Japanese, who were, thanks to butoh, imagined as prehistoric.

In his book *Asian/American: Historical Crossings of a Racial Frontier*, David Palumbo-Liu argues that the borders between Asian/American are continually being redefined and renegotiated. In particular, Palumbo-Liu draws our attention to moments when distinctions between "Asian" and "American" are newly (re)constructed, suggesting that the need to distinguish them arises precisely when the possibility exists that they might merge.[29] The economic situation of the United States vis-à-vis Japan in the 1980s, for example, required a renewed distinction between Japanese and American. Palumbo-Liu links the advent of the model minority myth with the rise of Japan's economic power, noting that "appearances of the myth are haunted by a sense of America's weakened position at home and globally."[30] Lifting Japanese Americans up as a successful group that should be emulated domestically would seem to be an admission to full citizenship: If all Americans should strive to be more like Japanese Americans, does this not mean they are already fully so? And yet being singled out as a model minority perpetuated their always apart status and highlighted Japanese Americans' metonymic relationship to Japan.[31] Like their counterparts in Japan, Japanese Americans — suggested the myth — had overcome a difficult past through hard work and perseverance. Internationally, the model minority myth worked as a clear call to emulate Japanese approaches to work ethic and economics. Domestically, however, the myth served to divide and conquer communities of color previously aligned through movements like the "Third World Strike." In particular, Japanese American success was defined over and against apparent African American failure and, as Palumbo-Liu observes, "was deployed to contain and divert civil rights policymaking, to neutralize activism, and to promote a laissez-faire domestic urban policy."[32] If Japanese Americans could succeed, clearly the solution was not in policy or structures, but in an ethnic or racial group's own makeup, or so the logic went.

In addition to his legal, political, and economic analysis, Palumbo-Liu is interested in the ways that culture participates in constructing the Asian American body, psyche, and space. While his attention is largely focused on literature, we can consider the ways performance participates in this process. For example, Japan's economy was not the country's only notable performance in the 1980s. Kazuo Ohno's 1980 international debut at the Nancy International Theatre Festival produced a widespread buzz about the "new" modern dance from Japan, which was first seen in the United States the following year at La MaMa E.T.C. A central figure in the development and spread of butoh, Ohno himself had a deep history in Japanese modern dance. Reviews of Ohno's first US performance noted Eiko & Koma's relationship to him; as established figures in the city, it was Eiko & Koma who could provide a frame for Ohno for New York audiences. Even with Ohno, the pull of the kabuki discourse was strong, as is evident in Anna Kisselgoff's review of Ohno's *Dead Sea*, in which she attempted to explain his cross-dressing via her previous experience with kabuki.[33] Though Ohno's cross-dressed character is based directly on Divine from Jean Genet's *Our Lady of the Flowers*, Kisselgoff's reading of his dance places him on a continuum with *onnagata*, men who perform female characters in kabuki, which serves to take the performance out of a very specific artistic and political referent and fix it instead as traditional and timeless.[34]

I am not suggesting that this process of framing the avant-garde as traditional was intentional. As Thornbury has skillfully shown, visiting gagaku, kabuki, noh, kyōgen, and bunraku artists in the 1950s and 1960s had already cemented the association between Japanese performance and descriptors like "national treasure" and "intangible cultural property." In fact, those very concepts can be traced to the 1950 Japanese *Bunkazai Hogohō* (Cultural Properties Protection Law), which sought to develop a strong postwar Japanese cultural identity precisely through those performance forms. American audiences, then, came to understand Japanese performing artists as purveyors of cultural heritage, an understanding that was then unconsciously transferred to any artist who was seen as "authentically" Japanese, even if that artist's practices were not actually traditional. So rather than (or sometimes in addition to) contextualizing butoh as an avant-garde or modernist performance practice parallel to performance art or postmodern dance or theater, critics attempted to place it in what Thornbury calls "the discourse of cultural continuity."[35] Ruby Shang, for example, wrote that butoh "is as diverse and confusing to the Western eye as the rest of Japanese culture may seem. However, a sense of proportion, or *'ma no kankaku,'* steeped in years of tradition, pervades choreography, as well as the other art forms."[36] Shang was far from alone in such proclamations, which in effect told audiences that they were seeing something they could not understand because it was foreign (or that the way to understand it was through recourse to tradition). Such descriptions not only divorced performance practices like butoh from their own modern and radical histories, but also fixed them as essentially Japanese. This is particularly ironic for something like butoh, which had in its formation a strong critique of what it meant to be Japanese.[37]

Until mid-1984, the kabuki discourse dominated reviews of Ohno, Dairakudakan, and even Eiko & Koma. Even though critics called the artists avant-garde, they persisted in comparing the performers to kabuki. This changed with the 1984 North American premiere of Sankai Juku and the accompanying introduction of the term "butoh" in the *New*

York Times. Kisselgoff wrote, "This sense of the unreal, of hallucination and of pain in a visionary context is part of the imagery in a new, current dance trend that specializes in the grotesque. I am speaking here of the Butoh movement in Japan, an underground phenomenon that is nonetheless already the a [sic] favorite on the international festival circuit."[38]

Dairakudakan was founded in 1972 by Akaji Maro, an actor, dancer, and director who had participated in Hijikata's dance experiments alongside Ohno throughout the 1960s. Maro, still an active performer and dance maker today, has always encouraged his dancers to start their own companies, and Ushio Amagatsu was one of the first to take his advice, starting Sankai Juku in 1975. Sankai Juku is notable for being one of the first butoh companies to have significant international success; the company has split its time between France and Japan since 1980 and is often both celebrated and criticized for producing an aestheticized butoh for Western audiences. Even though Amagatsu was a third-generation butoh performer and choreographer, in the United States his work became a template for explicating the form as a whole.[39]

A frequently quoted passage from a 1984 *New York Times* feature article about Eiko & Koma and Sankai Juku by Kisselgoff, "Japanese Avant-Garde Dance is Darkly Erotic," proved key in establishing a popular understanding of butoh. The article proffers a definition of butoh as a "compound of the grotesque and the beautiful, the nightmarish and the poetic, the erotic and the austere, the streetwise and the spiritual."[40] This collection of surprising juxtapositions—also including creation and destruction, metamorphosis and transcendence—is still an apt description of many butoh dances because it puts into words the physical processes Hijikata and others developed for layering multiple, often impossibly contradictory, images into one body. But then Kisselgoff introduces the uncited assertion that the Japanese word butoh "derives from a word having to do with ancient ritualistic dance," which leads immediately to the incorrect conclusion that "certainly the prehistoric and the ritualistic are among the prime concerns of Butoh's choreographers."[41] As discussed in chapter 1, butoh's concerns were in fact specifically postmodern, developing new corporealities in response to rapid industrialization and fundamental changes in Japanese society in the late 1950s and 1960s.[42] The title of Sankai Juku's performance in Toronto, *Homage to Pre-History* (*Jōmon Shō*), was likely a major influence on Kisselgoff's assumptions about the connection between butoh and prehistory. In fact, "Jōmon" refers not to a generic prehistory but to the Jōmon period in Japan (approximately 12,000–300 BC). As discussed in chapter 1, Japanese avant-garde artists were interested in the Jōmon period as a mythological source of a Japanese culture untainted by outside influences (e.g., Buddhism and the Chinese writing system) and also as something predating and therefore outside of Japan's recent imperialist and violent history. The past of the Jōmon became for artists a source for actively imagining another present and future. The translation of the Sankai Juku title from "Jōmon" to "prehistory" erases this specificity.

If kabuki was seen to be timeless and therefore ahistorical, then butoh was seen as prehistoric, not because it had always been that way, but rather because something had caused the prehistoric state. Kisselgoff writes, "Moreover this emergence from the primordial begins with an image that suggests that an unnamed cataclysm has preceded it."[43] Though Kisselgoff does not herself refer to the atomic bombing of Hiroshima and Nagasaki in her article, audiences and other critics soon began to associate the cataclysm they read into the damaged bodies they saw on-stage with bodies damaged by the bomb. For example, Mindy Aloff, in a review of Eiko & Koma's *By the River* at Asia Society, writes, "The style is grounded in Butoh, a mutant species of dance theater that developed in the couple's native Japan a quarter-century ago. You can taste in it well-known performance traditions (Noh, Kabuki); Western modern dance (notably the Wigman school); the unconventional wit of its founders (including Eiko and Koma's teacher, the late Tatsumi Hijikata); and nuclear terror (evoked through film noir lighting, vaporous tableaux and dire, incandescent moods)."[44] Aloff's comments are particularly interesting for the way they explicitly link the avant-garde to both the traditional and the bomb at the same time. That same year, Debra Cash observed in a feature article on Boston's Dance Umbrella's Japan season: "Butoh's nuclear message both titillates American audiences and sends them on a guilt trip."[45] What her comment does not acknowledge, however, is that the nuclear message is one inserted by those very audiences.

Butoh's growing reputation in the United States fit nicely into the mode of holding up Japanese (economic) performance as a singular accomplishment. More important, however, is that it offered an opportunity to discursively renegotiate the Japanese-US relationship. While the kabuki discourse was useful for making Japan seem nonthreatening and aestheticized in the postwar period, the new context of economic competition required a new discourse, and Sankai Juku's version of butoh provided that through the specter of the atomic bomb.[46]

The reading of butoh as a response to the bomb is a uniquely American response to the form. "America's butoh," just like Thornbury's "America's kabuki," was a particular discursive construction that developed out of the reception of Japanese performance in a specific historical and political context. Whereas the kabuki discourse attempts to cover over evidence of the war and smooth away inconvenient images of the former enemy, now ally, with recourse to a timeless tradition, the developing butoh and the nuclear discourse acknowledged destruction, but in a way that erased modernity, not to mention postmodernity. In effect, the nuclear discourse moves Japan back in time before the economic miracle and freezes it in August 1945, a moment of absolute American supremacy over Japan. A discursive turn morphs the postnuclear into the prehistoric. Even the word "mutant" suggests a postnuclear creation, something like Godzilla: a prehistoric monster brought to life by a modern (Western) invention.[47] It is almost as if butoh provided the evidence that, as the saying goes, we "bombed them into the Stone Age."[48] "America's butoh" is an effective reminder of who has the power. The underlying message of the 1980s butoh nuclear discourse reminded American audiences that we bombed Japan and suggested that the Japanese people's response is to dance about it in a way that reveals their prehistoric state. If the Japanese are prehistoric, then clearly they are not serious competition. The discourse worked to reassure American audiences of their own modernity and thus their superiority vis-à-vis Japanese prehistory.

Through the kabuki discourse, Japanese performing arts, and by extension Japan, were considered high culture. In calling butoh primitive or primal, however, comparisons to "Africa" begin to crop up in reviews.[49] Whereas model minority discourse defines Japanese/success over and against African American/failure, with the prehistoric and primal qualities of the butoh discourse, "Japanese" could be associated with "African." Eiko responded specifically to the "prehistoric" association in an interview: "It is not a prehistoric thing, it is our fundamental existence. . . . I am as much a human being as I am a mammal, and animal, a part of nature. All of that is connected."[50] Eiko's attempt to universalize the themes of their work ("our fundamental existence") was a challenge to the nuclear discourse that sought to impose an evolutionary time line on geographic, political, and cultural difference.

Like the model minority discourse, the nuclear discourse led to Japanese performers being singled out by presenters in Japan seasons and festivals. Instead of reinforcing parallels of modernness as previous modern or postmodern dance bills or festivals had, these new Japan-oriented titles and seasons emphasized difference, a categorization that also conveniently supported ascendant multicultural programming practices of the time. Multiculturalism singles out on the one hand exceptional individuals and on the other hand practices that are seen to represent entire groups and offers their inclusion as proof of successful incorporation of difference into the nation.[51] Orientalist discourses such as America's kabuki-Japan and the nuclear discourse work hand in hand with multiculturalism to satisfy the needs of the nation by on the one hand incorporating artists of color through multicultural funding policies and on the other hand maintaining a division that affords only white artists the ability to be abstract, while requiring that artists of color be "ethnic" and remain other. Multicultural presenting practices certainly benefited from categorizing Eiko & Koma and other dancers as Japanese, a move that further reinforced the duo's foreignness, even as they were becoming more and more American.

In these circumstances, butoh provided a convenient label for Eiko & Koma's work, setting it in a Japanese performance context rather than an American postmodern dance context. As discussed in chapter 1, Eiko & Koma briefly studied with the two key figures of butoh, Tatsumi Hijikata and Kazuo Ohno, but left Japan soon after and never associated themselves with the form. Even though Eiko & Koma have never called their work butoh, critics and presenters began using the term more and more to describe them. Kisselgoff's comment, "perhaps we have been seeing Butoh in the United States without being aware of it,"[52] became a matter of fact for other critics. Increasingly, Eiko & Koma began to be compared to other Japanese dancers (even ones not associated with butoh), like Kei Takei and Min Tanaka, in reviews and articles.[53] On the one hand it makes a certain kind of sense that Eiko & Koma would be compared to other Japanese performers, if only because there was a growing number of artists to compare them to. But on the other hand, the implication of the comparisons changing from white American modern and postmodern dancers to Japanese avant-garde and postmodern dancers who were nonetheless made out to be "primal" is significant. Increasingly Eiko & Koma were programmed in "Japan" seasons and discussed in articles not about modern or postmodern dance, as they previously had been, but in articles such as "The Year of Dance from Japan"[54] or "Japanese Avant-Garde Dance Is Darkly Erotic,"[55] or simply "Dark Art."[56] At precisely the moment when Eiko & Koma were being incorporated into American modern and postmodern dance, they were separated out as Japanese and "prehistoric."

In the face of these dominant discourses, Eiko & Koma did attempt to intervene in how they were written about and presented. As early as 1985 the dancers released a statement asking presenters and reviewers not to call their work butoh. It is worth quoting a 1991 version of that statement at length to understand how Eiko & Koma did and did not want audiences and critics to approach their work. They wrote in part:

In English the term "Butoh" has no historical meaning to the general audience, it gives no explanation other than the fact that it is foreign. Since we started to work as Eiko & Koma in 1971, we have never billed ourselves as "Butoh," not in Japan, Europe nor in America. We have always given credit to two wonderful dancers we studied with, Tatsumi Hijikata and Kazuo Ohno, who started calling themselves Butoh dancers in the early '60s. . . . However, we feel just as indebted to our German teacher as well as other performers we have seen and other teachers we have studied with. . . . Many people may think the outcome of our work looks like Butoh, this we do not deny. By all means, we do not think of ourselves as new or original in what we do. We are, however, individualists belonging to no party, responsible only for what we do. We would like to present our work as such and not as a part or example of something like Butoh, which we feel may draw an audience of people curious about an exotic oddity. . . . In our work we question our own and the audience members' individual concerns. This questioning creates a direct relationship between individuals so that if they dislike us, they dislike us and not Butoh.[57]

Despite such a clear message released over a period of time by the artists themselves, the word "butoh" still frequently comes up in relation to Eiko & Koma, demonstrating just how enduring and influential the butoh discourse has been. Casual conversation among dancers and dance fans, and even official sources such as newspaper reviews and the New York Public Library for the Performing Arts topic headings, still persist in categorizing the duo as butoh. And as Bruce Baird is fond of reminding me, Eiko & Koma are second only to Sankai Juku in hits in a LexisNexis full-text search for butoh.[58]

In an interview with *Ballet Review*, Eiko discussed ideas similar to those expressed in their statement but without mentioning the word "butoh":

> I am very discouraging to those people who would like to mystify us as coming from Asia. (However I do not deny those differences.) I don't want to reinforce the possibility of your encountering us because of cultural difference: "Oh, we must go see that *because* she's Japanese or Asian." Then if you don't like what I'm doing, you can put it aside. Instead, I want you to ask, "Why don't I like what she's doing?" Or "Why do I like what she's doing?" You start to think and feel in return. I like this better than "Oh, she's Asian, she's Japanese."[59]

In both cases, the choreographers were asking presenters, audiences, and dance critics around the United States to engage with their work on its own terms, not through ideas of what it means to be Asian or Japanese, whether those ideas come from a specific word, like butoh, or from more generalized Orientalist concepts of what the work is or does. Eiko & Koma even raised these issues in a review of their official Japanese premiere in 1989 at Spiral Hall in Tokyo. Giving the reviewer their assessment of what it means to be Japanese performers in New York and what they face, Eiko said, "We're always fighting the mystification process in New York. . . . We don't want the audience to think that our work is beautiful just because it's from Japan and they can't understand it so we put in extra effort to make it fundamental." Koma added, "The cultural export business is something that we don't want to be mixed up in."[60]

Koma's comment about cultural export draws our attention to a fascinating contradiction: in the United States the dancers are frequently categorized as Japanese, whereas in Japan they are considered American. Other than their youthful performances in the early 1970s, they have only performed in Japan a handful of times, and when they do, their names are spelled out in *katakana*, the Japanese alphabet reserved for foreign words and names. Eiko & Koma are not alone in bearing the burden of this contradiction. Borrowing from Aiwah Ong, Thornbury calls artists like Eiko & Koma, Yoshiko Chuma, Yasuko Yokoshi, and others "flexible-citizen artists." Though these artists typically do not live in Japan, through preexisting professional ties or links established later they "reinstantiate their Japanese identity."[61] For example, invitations to perform at Japan Society, funding from the Japan Foundation, and participation in Japanese-themed festivals serve to forge or reforge cultural connections that then "metaphorically 'return' [them] to Japan."[62] Thornbury writes, "flexible-citizen artists enter the narrative of America's Japan because they *and* their artistic practices are linked with and, by extension, considered representative of Japan,"[63] even if those links are in fact tenuous or have been mythologized. To complicate matters further, these dancers are also are singled out for awards that recognize them as exemplary American artists, a move that reinforces both their status as model minorities and American myths and practices of multiculturalism.

More recently, a discursive tension has developed between a desire for an "authentically Japanese" artist and a "global" one. As Yutian Wong reminds us in her discussion of Michio Ito and the "international artist," this discourse dates from at least the first half of the twentieth century.[64] Exotic yet familiar, the exceptional "international artist" is granted the ability in the public eye to float over borders, with no concern paid to social or legal boundaries such as race or immigration. At the same time these artists are not allowed to be grounded as American, nor is their work deemed capable of engaging in American discourses on race or identity. At best, these artists are seen as producing work with transcendent themes capable of universal impact. Ultimately, however, Wong demonstrates that the trope of the international is a (failed) attempt to gloss very real material and political conditions with a romantic vision of the artist (usually an artist of color) as able to transcend race, bridge cultural gaps, and heal social wounds. To become international then is to be deracialized. As Ito's internment and subsequent repatriation to Japan demonstrate, however, the international artist remains in the end not a bridge, but an Other.

Terms like "flexible-citizen artist" and "international artist" describe the types of binds in which the kabuki and butoh discourses put Eiko & Koma. Moreover, they illustrate the functioning of the constant flux between "Asian" and "American" theorized by Palumbo-Liu. In each case, Eiko & Koma are honored for their contribution to the American dance scene, but are never quite allowed to be seen as American.

Japanese/American

Eiko & Koma's work became so overlaid with American ideas of Japaneseness in the 1980s and early 1990s — valid or not — that it became difficult to see their work as American. Moreover, their style does not explicitly tell Asian American immigration or discrimination stories and therefore was not always recognized by an Asian American audience. Yet in 1994 Eiko & Koma were invited to participate in a yearlong Festival of Asian/Asian American Dance at the University of Wisconsin–Madison. Sponsored by the Dance Program and cosponsored by the Asian American Studies Program, the festival featured concerts of Indian and Balinese dance and music ensembles by Mallika Sarabhai and Ngurah Supartha; three shows called "Making Waves," featuring University of Wisconsin faculty and students and guest artists; and a panel discussion, "Dancing Identity: What Does It Mean to Be Asian American?" In many ways the festival paralleled the *Bridge* special section sixteen years earlier with its combination of traditional dance forms, new works, and discussion of the field. In addition to Eiko & Koma, Sun Ock Lee also appeared in *Bridge* and at the University of Wisconsin.

Eiko & Koma were invited to perform their 1991 work, *Land*, which revisits the nuclear issues explored in *Fission* (1979), albeit from a different angle.[65] Elsewhere I have argued for *Land* as a dance that enacts Asian American cultural politics.[66] The dance stages a relationship among Native American musicians and Japanese American dancers in an American Southwest landscape, a site of containment for Native Americans and Japanese Americans alike and for testing of nuclear weapons, including those used on Japan. While creating the dance, Eiko & Koma spent time with musician Robert Mirabal in New Mexico, and he accompanied them to Japan, where they visited Hiroshima and gave a work-in-progress showing of *Land* at the Hiroshima Museum of Contemporary Art. In this dance, rather than appearing as survivors of nuclear devastation as they did in *Fission*, Eiko & Koma are seen to be coinhabitants of the desert landscape, sharing the space with the musicians. Clearly festival organizers saw something in this combination they wanted to feature.

That same combination puzzled dance critics when the dance first premiered; their view of Eiko & Koma as purely Japanese, even after they had spent fourteen years in the United States, seemed to prevent the critics from seeing the significance of Eiko & Koma's role in this particular *Land*. As discussed previously, the assumption of incomprehensibility often attends performances understood to be Japanese or Asian. A sort of Orientalist superficiality keeps the performance remote and exotic. Kishi and Bradshaw take a generous approach to this type of performance, suggesting that not being able to understand a theatrical performance linguistically allows a greater focus on nonverbal aspects of the performance.[67] Thornbury challenges this belief, arguing instead that when "productions are in Japanese, they are remote and exotic—and 'safe' to like. When they are in English, they become transgressive—and subject to critical disapprobation."[68] I would go even further to say that the English-language productions, or ones that draw attention to an American context, are no longer remote and exotic and therefore are simply no longer interesting. In other words, the pleasure of watching the "Japanese" performance is precisely in its remoteness and exoticism. Once something interrupts this distance, whether English in text-based performances or a recognizable context or situation in body-based performance, the source of the Orientalist pleasure is removed. This phenomenon was evident in critics' negative reception of Eiko & Koma's dances *Fluttering Black* and *Nurse's Song* (discussed in chapter 2), both pieces with strong associations with New York and American punk and hippie subcultures. I believe the same phenomenon was active in critics' reception of *Land*. Deborah Jowitt wrote of Eiko & Koma: "We attend their performance to be refreshed by simplicity, by essences, by the single burning gesture that sums up a moment, or an age, of living."[69] Although she was not writing about *Land* in particular, her statement reveals the kinds of expectations that had accrued around Eiko & Koma's work. According to Jowitt, one attends Eiko & Koma's dances to enjoy a timeless, Zen-like quality, not to be challenged by pressing current issues.

Though Eiko & Koma were not present for the Festival of Asian/Asian American Dance panel discussion, many of the issues they repeatedly raised in the 1980s and 1990s were echoed by panelists Kumiko Kimoto (now known as Koosil-ja), Mel Wong, and Sun Ock Lee.[70] Moderator Peggy Choy, a longtime University of Wisconsin–Madison assistant professor, indentified in her opening remarks a tendency in American twentieth-century dance to borrow or invent dances that seem "Oriental," with "no need to accurately represent Asian dance." This tension between the lived experiences of Asian American dancers and representations and appropriations of their dancing is at the heart of the questions she posed to the panelists. Though the panelists varied in the extent to which they identified as Asian American, they all spoke about ways their dance was impacted by larger discourses of what it meant to be Asian or Asian American. Lee spoke of how she always was labeled with "the Korean tag," not "the US tag," despite her US citizenship. Wong spoke with deep frustration about how critics and funders viewed his work. Unable to recognize the Chinese aspects of his choreography because it was not "traditional," Wong lamented, "they couldn't see how I was breaking ground." Kimoto, much like Eiko & Koma, made a plea for her work, not her identity, to be the focus. Grappling with her background as an ethnic Korean from Japan living in the United States, Kimoto said, "My art has my history, my contradictions, ambiguity, my complexity." She felt that complexity was erased, however, when funders and presenters asked her to identify as one thing or another.

Eiko & Koma encountered many of the same issues articulated by the festival panelists. They disappeared from the *Bridge* Asian American dance roundtable because they were not connected to tradition, yet according to many dance reviews in the *New York Times* and other publications, Eiko & Koma were traditional because they were Asian. On the one hand they were too postmodern to be ethnic; on the other they were too ethnic to be postmodern. The butoh discourse acknowledged their postmodernity, but tied it to a primitive, prehistoric (and even pretraditional) past. In none of these cases were Eiko & Koma presented as Japanese/Americans living and raising a family in New York, gathering American concert dance accolades. Acknowledgment of how their lives in the United States and their experiences as transnational Japanese/Americans might influence the work they were making was lacking from all sides.

Asian/American Dance Studies

In the twenty years since the University of Wisconsin panel, scholars such as Yutian Wong, Priya Srinivasan, and SanSan Kwan have led the way in developing a body of literature on Asian American dance including early twentieth-century modern dancers, diasporic South Asian dancers from the late nineteenth century to the present, circuits of popular dancers on the "Chop Suey" circuit, and contemporary companies.[71] The next generation of Asian and Pacific Islander American scholars is already contributing work on Filipino American hip-hop, contemporary hula, and other transnational dance practices.[72] But even as the idea that dance participates in the construction of Asian American identity is further developed, issues raised in *Bridge* in 1978 and at the University of Wisconsin in 1994 about the inclusion of Asian Americans in dance and dancing Asian American identity are far from resolved. Palumbo-Liu's assertion that the link between Asian and America is always up for (re)negotiation remains relevant. For example, in two 2014 blog posts *Dance Magazine* editor Wendy Perron muses about "Martha Graham and the Asian Connection" and "When Martha Got to Be Asian."[73] Much like Chin's article thirty-five years earlier, Perron's first post observes a notable number of Asian dancers in Graham's company and lists a number of singular performers, but without any sort of critical examination of Graham's Orientalism or what it means to be an Asian or Asian American dancer in the United States today. Her second post takes former Graham dancer and current Dance Kaleidoscope artistic director David Hochoy's drag appearances as Martha Graham to mean that Graham finally got her wish to be Asian, as if the fact of her appearance on his Asian American body made her so. Perron misses the opportunity to examine how Hochoy dressing as Graham might actually expose the deep history and continued workings of Orientalism in American modern dance.

While the larger discourse surrounding Japanese performance in the United States has moved on from butoh and the nuclear to the much-discussed "cool Japan" of anime and manga,[74] butoh has been unable to rid itself of the nuclear discourse, as evidenced in the almost mythic repetition of the butoh-bomb association by dancers and audience members alike. Eiko & Koma have likewise continued to struggle to separate themselves from butoh (not to mention all the mystification that still adheres to "Japan"). It is not lost on me that even as Eiko & Koma distance themselves from butoh, they do actually engage with the atomic bomb and its legacy. As I argue in chapter 6, however, Eiko & Koma's engagement with the atomic bomb constructs complex networks of complicity and shared experiences across time and continents, a level of complexity not admitted in the nuclear discourse surrounding butoh. Indeed, by taking the dances themselves as the starting point, the following four chapters attempt to demonstrate what Eiko & Koma's choreography does, in addition to or in spite of what discourses tell us it does.

CHAPTER 4

ᴅANCING-WITH SITE AND SCREEN

According to Eiko, she and Koma are attracted to nature (trees, rivers, land) in their work because it evidences "its own sense of time, and a grotesqueness that in our eyes can be beautiful."[1] Their first dance teachers, Tatsumi Hijikata and Kazuo Ohno, may have had some influence on this interest. When Eiko and Koma met Hijikata in the early 1970s, he was transitioning away from his experimental style of the 1960s, centered on an aggressive male body, toward a movement philosophy grounded in (but not limited to) his upbringing in Japan's northern rural farmlands. Beginning with a collaboration with photographer Eikoh Hosoe in the second half of the 1960s, Hijikata developed a method for generating dance vocabulary inspired by life in the remote and harsh Tohoku region: the stooped posture of farmers, animal behavior, and the unpredictable activities of local demons.[2] While rooted in a particular landscape and environment, this work was not, however, about nature or the relationship of humans to their environment in the way that Eiko & Koma's dances are. Instead, nature served as an inspiration for images that then formed the core of Hijikata's surrealist choreography.

Ohno, too, used nature images as inspiration for movement; for example, the process of standing up was imagined as the blooming of a flower. He also occasionally made site dances on farms, on the beach, in a harbor, and in a field of flowers. In fact, many of Ohno's later works took direct inspiration from his favorite subject, flowers, including *Water Lilies* (1987), *Flowers-Birds-Wind-Moon* (1990), *White Lotus Bloom* (1992), *Hana* (Flower, 2000), and *Hana-gurui* (Flower master, 2001).[3] Each of these was more about the idea of flowers, or flowers as mediated by art, however, than about a corporeal encounter with the natural world.

While Eiko & Koma were certainly aware of the ways that Hijikata and Ohno engaged choreographically with remembered landscapes and the idea of nature, their own nature-based projects developed along different lines. The duo touched on nature themes in their first two dances, *White Dance* (1976) and *Fur Seal* (1977), primarily by printing poems by noted twentieth-century Japanese poet Mitsuharu Kaneko in their programs.[4] The poems "Moth" and "Fur Seal," respectively, provide a nonhuman context for the movement onstage, but it is largely left for the audience to make the connection between what they see in the movement and the poetry. A more sustained choreographic engagement with themes of nature began in 1981, when after five years of being based in New York City, Eiko & Koma retreated to the Catskills to live in a farmhouse. Just as living in Manhattan had led Eiko & Koma to engage in sometimes unexpected collaborations with the people they met, their time in upstate New York led to new sorts of imagined and material collaborations with their environment. Even after they moved back to New York City, the duo continued to spend summers in the Catskills through a series of residencies at Art Awareness in Lexington, New York.

This period of immersion in nature in upstate New York would be decisive in their transition from a decade of experimentation to the distinct choreographic style for which they are known today, first evident in 1983's *Grain* and 1984's *Night Tide*. *Grain* bridges the strong characters and relationships seen in their early works with their developing signature style. Taking place largely on a rice-strewn futon, the dance is characterized by angular arms, spread legs, and stuttering, sudden movements. The piece is anchored by two striking images. Early on, Koma curls into a ball on his side on the futon as Eiko perches on him, a vulture on her prey. Near the end of the performance, Koma again supports Eiko's body, this time forming a wide base from a crouching position into which her splayed body easily fits. Oblivious to all else, she is consumed with the handfuls of rice that she shoves again and again into her mouth. Though some critics have described this piece as a fertility rite, the term seems to me too tame to describe the physical and sexual hunger Eiko & Koma openly display.[5]

In contrast to *Grain's* ingestion of nature in the form of rice into the bodies of the dancers, *Night Tide* saw the dancers using their bodies to enact an abstracted landscape.[6] On a bare stage, Eiko & Koma use their naked bodies to create a mountain range that migrates across space at its own pace, measuring time in millennia rather than hours or days. In this piece and others like it, Eiko & Koma offer their own bodies as land-scapes: buttocks could be seen as mountains, outstretched legs perhaps a long valley. Whereas nudity typically exposes specificities of a body no longer hidden by clothing, Eiko & Koma employ nakedness as a choreo-graphic tool in this performance and others to expand the possibilities of their moving bodies to be something nonhuman, or even for those bodies to be a point of connection to something larger than themselves.

These dances marked a turning point not only in Eiko & Koma's choreographic style, but also in their career. Eiko & Koma were awarded one of the first New York Dance and Performance Awards (commonly called the "Bessies") in 1984 for their presentation of *Grain* and *Night Tide* at Dance Theater Workshop. When American Dance Festival direc-tor Charles Reinhart saw *Grain* in a loft performance in New York City at the prodding of Lucas Hoving, Reinhart commissioned Eiko & Koma to make a dance for ADF, the first in a series of more than ten com-missions since 1983. Other commissions and grants soon followed, from the Brooklyn Academy of Music (BAM), the Walker Art Center, Dance Umbrella (Boston), Dance Theater Workshop, and the National Endow-ment for the Arts, to name a few.

In addition to nature coming to the fore of Eiko & Koma's choreo-graphic concerns, the period of creativity in the Catskills also includes their turn to media dance as a creative practice.[7] *Wallow* (1984), one of their first dances for camera, was choreographed on site at Point Reyes National Seashore in California as a media version of the 1977 prosce-nium dance *Fur Seal*.[8] The transition from the proscenium absurdity of *Fur Seal*—with a hanging tree trunk set, score of Shubert and The Beatles, and the dissonance of humans that act like seals and seals that dance like humans—to a seemingly straightforward presentation of Eiko & Koma *as* seals is enabled in *Wallow* by the conjunction of site and camera. The transformation of the dancers into seals is given credence by the setting, a rocky coastal scene that annually hosts scores of breed-ing elephant seals. The embodiment of seals is accomplished through an organization of the body that unifies the trunk and legs as a ponderous seal body and a movement vocabulary propelled by forearm flippers and stretching, expressive necks and chests.

Wallow is an early representation of the convergence, common across Eiko & Koma's repertoire, of site and screen, particularly in works that engage nature themes. These dances immerse the pair, if not also the audience, in an environment partially or wholly of their own construction. A key question, then, is how and to what end Eiko & Koma employ these choreographic practices to elaborate a relationship among humans and their environment. I approach this question through a close reading of *River* (1995). Designed to be site adaptive — that is, to be modified from one performance setting to the next as necessitated by the specificities of a new environment — *River* was presented in ten bodies of water in the United States and Japan. The performances generally took place at dusk and lasted forty-five to sixty minutes, depending on the particular location.

I suggest that *River* and dances like *Husk* (1987), *Breath* (living installation 1998, dance for camera 1999), and *The Caravan Project* (1999) evidence a choreographic method I call "dancing-with," in which links among human bodies, technology, and nature are initiated such that the elements work together to create a new entity. Unlike other pieces in Eiko & Koma's repertoire that engage in a practice of sustained mourning (chapters 5 and 6) or that form intercultural alliances (chapter 7), this body of work emphasizes the process and product of generating linkages with nature and technology through dance. Eiko & Koma's "adagio activism" gives all the elements involved time to form novel connections that they otherwise might not be able to generate. I conceptualize these connections as interfaces that unsettle the divisions among humans, nature, and technology and respond to Donna Haraway's call to "find another relationship to nature besides reification and possession."[9] This is not dance as representation or signification, but dance that does something in the world, generating another way of being resonant with calls within the environmental movement and environmental studies to shift how humans relate to nature. Interface, however, avoids an approach that suggests humans can either ruin or save nature in favor of a recognition that both necessarily must change when coming in contact with each other.

Dancing-with *River*

Audience members gather at the water's edge at twilight, making themselves comfortable on blankets or beach chairs they've brought from home.[10] As their eyes adjust to the dim light, they begin to take in the wide landscape before them, noticing how the dwindling light and the formality of the occasion have transformed a familiar recreational spot into a watery stage. In the current waits an unfamiliar monument: two statuesque human figures clinging to two thin vertical poles about five feet apart. Stretched between the two poles is a blank white canvas, which hangs well above the heads of the apparently motionless figures. The screen is not merely functional, however. Its presence is also sculptural, creating a strong angular image that stands in contrast to the flowing water below it and rustling leaves above. This structure quite literally provides a frame for the performance that draws the attention of the attendees, a focal point in the midst of a larger terrain.[11] The humans are submerged from the waist down; the bottoms of the poles similarly disappear beneath the surface of the water. The intense stillness and seeming silence of the scene signals to the assembled crowd the necessity for a different kind of focus than is demanded by their day-to-day activities. The open environmental setting likewise requires an attention different from a traditional proscenium, where all attention is directed forward and center by the very structure of the room. Conversations quickly fade and breathing slows as the audience tunes their awareness to the alternative time and immense geographical scale being enacted before their eyes.

A note plucked on a shamisen resonates through the air as light flickers on the suspended canvas, resolving into the projection of two naked bodies—the head and shoulders of one, the torso and arms of another—alternately splayed and hunched on an artificial rivulet.[12] For the next ten minutes all attention focuses on the screen, where the 1985 media dance *Lament* shows close-up video images of Eiko & Koma filling the display as they curl up in, reach out through, or arch over a thin film of water.[13] Although the pair shares the screen space, their physical separation in foreground and background suggests a more fundamental existential chasm. Viewed on its own, *Lament* is a corporeal cri de coeur in which unrelenting sorrow literally drips from the dancers' skin. As part of *River*, however, the shallow pool of tears is recontextualized in relationship to the water that flows around the makeshift screen. The media dance shows two people dancing on a glistening film of water, the same two dancers who stand suspending the images against the darkening background of water and sky. The confluence of live and mediated performance in the middle of a river moreover suggests that Eiko

& Koma are choreographically intervening in the enduring nature/technology dichotomy by creating a link between live and screenic action. The two are not posed as equals, however. Instead, the media dance is there to interact with the performers and create affect as a prelude to the subsequent live dance.

The couple imperceptibly loosen their grip on the poles, letting the screen drop forward into the river, gently pulling the focus away from the memories of the media dance and onto their partially submerged bodies. Koma, now distinguishable from his partner, drifts with the screen downstream, leaving the focus on Eiko. Accompanied only by ambient sounds of flowing water, chirping crickets, and any sounds of the audience shifting in their shoreline seats, she stirs, a lone figure in a darkening landscape. For ten minutes she reaches out of the stream from the waist, rotates in the current, and submerges to her armpits, arms still elevated. Despite the limitation of dancing almost entirely with arms and torso, the number of distinctive relationships Eiko develops with the water is astonishing. Time seems to slow as she and the water negotiate her presence there.

Soon Koma returns from downstream, pushing before him a collection of driftwood, twice as long as it is wide. With only his head visible, the long, curved branches undulating through the water give the impression of being Koma's limbs. For the first time since they let the screen fall out of their grasp, Eiko rejoins Koma. She approaches the driftwood and levers a branch above her head, moving it off the surface of the water such that the assemblage of wood juts diagonally out of the river, revealing that the seemingly random collection of branches is in fact a fan-shaped, floating driftwood sculpture, perhaps five feet tall and twelve feet wide.[14] A gently arching bough is joined to a long, straight one by smaller curving sticks, forming a vault interrupted by a slab of glass at its base. Responding to Eiko's invitation, Koma enters into the sculpture, which she then lowers around him. Much like the makeshift screen at the beginning of the performance, the driftwood frames the dance and the river itself. Alternately a home, a trap, or a lifeline, the structure serves to draw attention to the two small bodies caught up in the current of a body of water as it travels from the mountains to the sea.

The sculpture is more than a visual focal point, however. Eiko & Koma maneuver the collection of branches such that it becomes a key tool for creating a link between them and between the pair and their watery environment. While the performers are individually constantly in physical relationship to the water, they are only connected to each other when both are moving in relation to the screen or the sculpture. That is, the introduction of the driftwood impels a bonding process. The dancers reach to one other across the driftwood, becoming extensions of it as their limbs reach out along branches, complementing the arc of a wooden arm, the ligneous half-moon forming a whole with its reflection in the water.

Eiko & Koma together lift the sculpture up vertically so that most of it is out of the water, holding this position for almost three minutes, their bodies seeming not to move although they are continuously buffeted by the water flowing past them. Their still shouldering of the wood echoes the opening of the dance, when they held the screen aloft, only now the audience members are left to project their own vision onto the driftwood's negative space. More than that, however, when Eiko & Koma hold the wood aloft, they reveal how much of it has been hidden from view. In the near dark, they challenge the edge of visibility: What other unseen connections does the running river facilitate? What else is happening that we cannot see?

They lower the sculpture back into the current, which they allow to carry them away from the branches that previously connected them. As if changing their minds, they make a heavy-limbed effort to approach one another again. Meeting finally, their bodies are completely submerged so that all that can be seen is a tight cluster of four heads, blooming. Although they have not quite seemed human throughout the piece, at this moment the pair joins with the water to create a never-before-seen creature. Interconnected, the two rise out of the water as one, their choking embrace recalling the ambiguous space of the driftwood sculpture in which they could be caught, trapped, held, or protected. As Eiko & Koma slowly disentangle themselves and give themselves over at last to the downstream current, the lights begin to fade, creating the second twilight of the evening.

While the choreographers dubbed their work in *River* "dancing in water," I propose "dancing-with" as a more appropriate description. Dancing in water is hardly unprecedented, as evidenced by the popularity of Esther Williams's "aquamusicals" in the 1940s and early 1950s and the appearance of synchronized swimming in the Olympics begin-

ning in 1984. But what Eiko & Koma do is very different from water ballet. Neither do Eiko & Koma perform specifically human activities in the
water, such as swimming, fishing, or boating, even though each performance took place at a location where the audience would have regularly
engaged in such activities. Nor do their movements attempt to imitate
or resemble fish, waterfowl, or other specific riverine creatures. Instead,
they move with the water as a partner in a sort of contact improvisation in which the two or more entities meet at a point or points of contact. Normally, the pair moves with the ground as a sort of partner that
alternately cradles their weighted limbs and provides resistance against
which they may twist or propel. In *River*, Eiko & Koma dance with the
current in much the same way, with the added variation that their partner now flows with and around them. When they transpose their signature movement vocabulary into a fluid environment, the water becomes
both floor and mirror for the dance, allowing the pair to choreograph
quietude, stillness, and lingering alongside resistance and flow. They are
both moved by the water and moving in the water. In addition to the
solid surface of the riverbed, against which they may push, the dancers
must deal with a host of variables. They may choose to passively drift with
the current, be buoyed by a wave, or create drag by moving deliberately
upstream. Submerging to different depths permits the movers to play
with the different resistances experienced by body parts in and out of the
stream. For example, when Eiko lifts her hand from under the surface as
if pulling it from black sludge, the effect is markedly different from when
she allows her torso to be pulled along by the course of the waterway,
arms wafting lightly above her head.

By placing themselves in the body of water, Eiko & Koma stage themselves as belonging in this particular flow, but also more broadly in these
American landscapes. Entering into the river provides a means of entering into partnership with an already existing community site. Unlike
their audience members, however, Eiko & Koma are interlopers in these
particular community waters, strangers who nonetheless develop a sort
of intimacy with them through repeated rehearsals and performances.
Their presence in the river allows them to emphasize a metaphor of the
connectedness of a community, or rather the formation of a community through a common bond to the river. This link is evidenced spatially
through the choreographic connection of upstream to downstream, in

which the lives of unseen or hitherto unknown beings are connected. The choreography also frames the river as a temporal link; the audience does not see Eiko & Koma enter or exit the river, giving the dance a feeling of being an excerpt from an ongoing process.

To strengthen their relationship to each body of water and to share their concern for the rivers they danced with, Eiko & Koma connected with community ecologists and environmental groups at many performance locations, beginning with Judd and Pam Weisberg, codirectors of Art Awareness, the Lexington, New York–based co-commissioner of *River*. Eiko & Koma sought out Judd Weisberg's services not only as presenter and set builder, but more importantly as an environmentalist who monitored Catskill streams. Eiko & Koma were artists in residence at Art Awareness for nine summers, including the summer of 1995, when the site dance was developed in the shallow, slow-moving Schoharie Creek, which flows past a theater where the pair had often performed. *River* and the choreography of dancing-with so clearly evident in the work were both strongly influenced by these long-term relationships with the Catskills and with people who cared deeply about the local waterways. These types of linkages were also evident in their Pennsylvania and Minneapolis engagements with long-term Eiko & Koma presenters Lafayette College and the Walker Art Center. Lafayette College joined with the Environmental Performance Network, a project of Dancing in the Streets, to present workshops and panels on clean water, water resources, and river history. In Minneapolis, Water Ways: Celebrate the Arts and the Environment was a weekend-long festival that included a panel discussion with artists and environmentalists, an Eco Info Fair, and an outdoor Delicious Movement workshop.[15] While Eiko & Koma's collaboration with local environmentalists came at the moment of the presentation of the dance, rather than at the research or choreographic stage, it nonetheless added another layer of meaning to *River*. By including those who are concerned with the ecology of the waterways in the temporal and spatial links established by the dance, Eiko & Koma suggest that the community established by the river must do its part to take care of the water.

These multiple layers of partnership—with the water, the community site, and environmental organizations—are an important facet of dancing-with. But Eiko & Koma explore many of the same movement ideas in the studio and teach them in their Delicious Movement Workshops. Two-hour workshops are a common feature of their performance engagements, but the first Delicious Movement Workshop was a three-week event at their farmhouse in the Catskills. Although Eiko & Koma are careful to differentiate between the exercises they teach under the Delicious Movement designation and their performance style onstage, which they prefer to leave unnamed, from my experience as a frequent workshop participant and as a close observer of their rehearsals and performances, I discern a clear connection. For example, the most commonly taught exercise, "sleeping," generates the kind of languid, continuous movement that can be seen in a number of Eiko & Koma's works, including *River*. The following description from a common Delicious Movement exercise shows how the practice of dancing-with is not limited to material conditions, for example, submersion in a body of water, but may also be explored via movement prompts in the form of images: "Imagine that water is moving inside your bodies. If your body fills up with water, you can release water though your pores. Feel the difference between your body when it is full of water, and when it is parched. Next, imagine that you are in water. Feel the different ways your body is in the water: water running over your skin, water dripping from your fingers, etc."[16]

In exercises such as this one, students are prompted to explore how the image of internal and external water can stimulate movement. Imagining lapping waves in the torso, for example, may result in a rippling motion in the limbs, while working with the image of a body submerged in water provides opportunities to experiment with gentle floating or being carried off in the rush of a rapids. Similarly, picturing a body engorged with water may produce a weighted and laborious locomotion. In both of these examples, *River* and the Delicious Movement exercise, dancing-with is a choreographic and performance methodology that generates movement choices through a relationship with a nonhuman partner, whether materially present or imagined.

Dancing-with is also site adaptive (though site adaptivity does not always imply dancing-with). While *River* was Eiko & Koma's first explicit engagement with site-adaptive work, the fact is that all of their work is site adaptive, not only pieces that are explicitly designed for multiple outdoor locations. Sets, costumes, and even music may change according to performance conditions. This adaptability is ingrained both in the way

Eiko & Koma develop the concepts of their pieces and in their approach to each specific performance. Underlying *River*'s transposition to many different rivers is Eiko & Koma's belief that the themes deeply connected to their work are worth visiting many times. Moreover, it is precisely their method of performing a piece, such as *River*, at multiple sites that allows them to understand what the core of the piece is. For example, at twilight the specific histories, names, and experiences of each particular river are still visible; as darkness comes, however, those specificities vanish and the commonality of all rivers—bodies of water that have been flowing and will continue to flow—is revealed.

Each of the ten locations for *River* was chosen in conjunction with arts presenters and local environmental groups. After a preview in Schoharie Creek in September 1995, the dance premiered a week later at Eddyside Park's municipal beach in Easton, Pennsylvania, on a gentle stretch of the Delaware River. The following year Eiko & Koma danced in the lazy river that winds through the national recreation area at Chattahoochee River Park in Roswell, Georgia, famous for fishing and boating; the Teien-eiko Garden Pond in a Japanese-themed section of the Sarah P. Duke Garden, Durham, North Carolina, a site arranged by the American Dance Festival, and the only location where *River* was performed over a number of years; the Clifton E. French Regional Park on Medicine Lake, a popular recreation spot in the greater Twin Cities, Minnesota; and under the auspices of the Association to Preserve Tanzawa's Nature in the Nakatsugawa, near their second home in lush Kanagawa-ken, Japan. In subsequent years the choreographers danced in a stretch of the Huron River that flows through the University of Michigan's Nichols Arboretum, which has the mission of connecting people with nature; at the Winooski One Hydroelectric Project, Park and Fishway on the Winooski River in Burlington, Vermont; and on a stretch of the Monongahela River in Pittsburgh, Pennsylvania. Finally, Eiko & Koma revived the piece for a performance at the concrete-lined urban Confluence Park, at the point where Cherry Creek joins the Platte River in Denver, Colorado.

I list each of these sites along with some defining characteristics to emphasize how Eiko & Koma's performance of *River* in different bodies of water reinforces the idea of a continuously running river that connects its makers and audiences across time and space. Moreover, this bringing together of different times and spaces into the performance is another characteristic of dancing-with. That is, the piece poses a temporal link that connects the audience and the dancers with what came before on the river and what might come after, as well as a spatial one among those who witness the dance at different locations. For example, the choreographers explicitly draw on the metaphor of the "river of time" by projecting a screen dance of themselves recorded more than a decade before their live performances, suggesting that time is not only a chronological flow from past to future, but is a copresence in the now.

I also enumerate the various performance sites to emphasize how the practice of site adaptivity requires that each time Eiko & Koma move their dance to a different site, they form a new relationship in response to the particularities of that location. Is the riverbed rocky and slippery, or soft with plenty of give? Is the current swift and deep, or does it move more slowly than even the dancers? Is there anything in the water that could make the dancers sick? Attending to the particular conditions of a site not only demands a focused bodily attention to conditions, but will also have an impact on the dance itself. That is, the dance cannot stay the same. Nor can the river, for that matter; one cannot, as they say, step in the same river twice. At the same time, the river-ness of each site connected it to all the others.

Dancing-with acknowledges that not only will the dance change, but all partners in the dance will be altered by the process, forming something together that they could not possibly become on their own. For example, in *River* Eiko & Koma take advantage of the reflective qualities of their setting to choreograph a doubling of their bodies and the set on the water below. The dusky performance, illuminated by soft lights focused on the two movers, transforms the surface of the river into a mirror. Reflections of the exposed fragments of Eiko & Koma dance across the surface of the water, multiplying their images, disjointing and duplicating shoulders, arms, and faces. Eiko reaches her arms up, away from the surface of the water, and yet in reflection they also reach down below. Koma's Narcissian face sinks halfway under the surface, merging with its spectral self, water flowing in and out of his open mouth like breath. Floating on her back, the Janus-like Eiko simultaneously looks straight up into the sky and straight down into the murky depths. In this way, the gaze of the audience is (re)focused through the use of lights and time of day, shifting the possibilities of what is and can be seen.[17] The choreography draws the audience's attention to Eiko & Koma's upper torsos, arms, and heads, which remain above the water, while leaving everything under the surface up to the audience's imagination.

Throughout the live performance section of *River*, Eiko & Koma choreograph a fragmentation and doubling of their bodies, beginning with holding a screen on which their own images are projected. The way they subsequently work with the water in the live performance is resonant with yet distinct from *Lament*. In other words, much of what Eiko & Koma do with their watery site is also evident in their approach to dance for camera. Just as they use the properties of a site (e.g., water that hides the lower parts of their bodies and multiplies the upper body) in conjunction with lighting and framing to specifically focus the audience's gaze, so do they design their camera shots to disturb a unified human form, choosing instead to focus on fragments in relationship to their environment; this conjunction of fragments of human bodies and "natural" elements is shown to have its own coherence that is a thing apart from its component parts. In *Lament*, for example, the thin layer of water covering the black floor creates a double image of Eiko's body in the background, only to be interrupted by Koma's head and torso crashing into the water in the foreground from the right side of the frame. Slow cross-fades and layered images of different sizes also serve to magnify and multiply their bodies, so that they are no longer two distinct beings, Eiko and Koma, but manifold entities generated through a joint choreography of dancers, site, and camera. These three elements dance with one another, not only in the media dance, *Lament*, but also in the way video is used in the live performances of *River*. Dancing-with, after all, is premised on an active intermediality. Eiko & Koma dance with a projection of themselves dancing on camera. The screen dances with the water, and its simple construction is evoked by the introduction of the wooden sculpture that similarly frames the live action.

Even though Eiko & Koma may become something in *River* that is not entirely human, the piece can be read as a model for how humans may enter into relationship with nature. In the dance, the pair begin as more or less themselves, holding a screen on which their own images are projected. As the choreography transitions from the screen dance to the live performance in the river, who they are morphs until they are not quite human, yet neither do they become the river itself. Instead they choreograph a give-and-take partnership with the flowing water, a process through which all partners will be altered. This way of working evidences a careful attention that engages in a constant process of coming into relationship with the environment.

On Nature, Humans, and Technology:
Dancing-with as Interface

Dancing-with initiates linkages, particularly among entities that might not typically be seen in relationship to one another, such as human bodies, technology, and nature. It occurs in material or image-generated conditions, is site adaptive, and evokes connections across time and space. As we have seen, in *River* Eiko & Koma initiate bonds with the water, each other through the screen and sculpture, and the larger river community by working with ecologists and by choreographing metaphors that link upstream and downstream. These multiple concurrent points of connection can be described as interfaces. Like the flowing river in which the experimental links are formed, interfaces are never fixed points, but continue to shift and reform as necessary, actively intervening in nature/culture binaries as they do.

My use of interface is inspired by philosopher Elizabeth Grosz's work on the relationships between bodies and cities, which she argues are mutually constitutive, "not as megalithic total entities, but as assemblages or collections of parts, capable of crossing the thresholds between substances to form linkages, machines, provisional and often temporary sub- or micro-groupings."[18] In these interfaces exists the possibility, she suggests, for unexpected and temporary connections between bodies and their surroundings. I extend Grosz's concept beyond the city, multiplying the possible microgroupings to include all manner of links among nature, humans, and technology. For example, in *River* when Eiko & Koma come together around the driftwood sculpture, the arc of branches not only provides the audience a focal point in a broad expanse of water, but also physically demarcates a new space in the water. Previously, Eiko was one body alone in a flowing waterway, but now she and Koma are in relationship to one another in the interface created with the water and the set. The screen at the beginning of the piece functioned in much the same way. Eiko & Koma further foreground their in-process relationships with nature and technologies through the ongoing physical negotiations in their movement vocabulary. Their constant (if not always discernible) activity suggests that the labor of generating interfaces through dancing-with is an ongoing process. When the performance is over, the interfaces dissipate, although their effects may linger in the audience.

In order to understand the interfaces formed through the choreography of dancing-with—the points of connection and the qualities thereof—it is necessary to tease apart the constituent parts. Though I have been using the broad term "humans," I in fact am referring to the specific bodies of Eiko and Koma, who have their own particular histories and lived experiences that they bring to their performance. When I speak of technology, I refer broadly to both processes and products of mechanical arts or applied sciences. In Eiko & Koma's case, I apply it to the way they use built set pieces or props as well as video projection in their intermedia site and screen works. Technology here, whether it be a driftwood sculpture or a video camera and editing software, is not a tool for mastery or destruction, but for generative transformation.

The nature component of interface requires a more in-depth consideration because it is there that I see Eiko & Koma's most significant contribution. For the dancers, nature is not imagined as some untouched landscape with which they can have a direct encounter. After all, even places where we believe ourselves to be encountering "nature," such as national parks and nature reserves, are in fact human made. The ten sites for *River*, for example, were chosen very carefully for qualities such as a nonslippery riverbed; a specific distance from the land; water of a certain depth, temperature, and lack of contaminants; and so forth. While *River* takes place in outdoor settings ("nature"), many of Eiko & Koma's other works in fact participate quite literally in the construction of a "natural" environment in the form of sets for pieces such as the media dance *Husk* or the indoor "living installation" *Breath*, for which they built an environment complete with dirt, leaves, wind, and video. In both examples, the "natural" sites in Eiko & Koma's dances can be seen as constructed. In turn, these "nature" settings determine the parameters of the dance: how Eiko & Koma can move and the types of interfaces that may be generated are significantly impacted by the environment. Therefore, when I use the word "nature" in association with Eiko & Koma, I employ the word not only to mean specific outdoor environments, but also to reference a larger discourse around the term.

Raymond Williams calls nature "perhaps the most complex word in the language," reminding us of its long history as discourse.[19] He identifies three enduring and often interrelated senses of the term: the essential quality of a thing (e.g., "human nature"); forces in the world such as hurricanes and earthquakes; and material conditions that may or may not include humans, like wilderness or national parks. Indeed, "nature" carries with it a loaded history of essentialist assumptions in which it has typically been understood as the preexisting raw material from which civilization is built.[20] In this sense, "nature" has been defined by white, Western men as something that is primitive yet powerful and thus needs to be carefully managed. This dichotomy has been extended to the body, such that the mind is associated with reason and culture and technology, while the body is linked to emotion and nature.[21] In the latter, "human nature" comes to represent seemingly inherent or inborn qualities or behaviors that are considered inevitable. An alternate valuing of the nature/culture dichotomy calls for a "return to nature," accompanied by an understanding of nature as pure and uncorrupted and thus in need of preservation or emulation.[22] Likewise, ideas of a "natural" body romantically envision a human body unsullied by cultural norms or habits. Paul Wapner contrasts these two positions in contemporary times as a "dream of mastery" (science and business can solve environmental problems) versus a "dream of naturalism" (a retreat from technology into nature is both possible and urgently needed).[23] Other environmentalists, such as Bill McKibben, see the Enlightenment project of the management of nature as no longer possible because nature itself has been utterly vanquished by humans.[24] In fact this period of the earth — commonly linked to the beginning of the Industrial Revolution, but which some say began as early as the creation of agriculture — takes its very name from humans: the Anthropocene. First published in scientific discourse in 2000 by biologist Eugene Stoermer and Nobel Prize–winning chemist Paul Crutzen, the Anthropocene describes a period in which human activity has fundamentally changed the earth, resulting in significant geologic impact distinguishable from previous epochs.[25] The logic of the this new epoch would suggest that even as-yet-unidentified species living in the remotest areas of our world, such as the Marinara Trench, have been impacted by human actions that have, for example, warmed the oceans and changed sea levels. Of course these ideas of nature, even those significantly critiquing human impact on our environment, maintain a human-nature divide and discount the agency of nonhuman actors in the world.[26]

What I find so compelling about Eiko & Koma's dancing-with is the way it foregrounds how human activity has always engaged in changing and constructing nature, while simultaneously demonstrating that humans are themselves changed in the process. Interface conceptualizes how dancing-with generates new linkages through which each of the constituent parts is affected by the others, and none is left unaltered.[27] This approach is specifically nonanthropocentric, seeing humans as only one of many components. I am particularly inspired in this respect by Donna Haraway's thinking about cyborgs as entities that reject the boundaries or evolutionary hierarchies separating humans from technology and nature, focusing instead on the generative possibilities of unruly constructions and connections at areas in common.[28] Haraway's cyborgs offer a model for a different kind of being (both noun and verb) in the world very much in line with what I am arguing for the choreographic interface of bodies, nature, and technologies: the possibility of a relationship in which entrenched binaries are interrupted in and through Eiko & Koma's work.

What makes Eiko & Koma's "dancing-with" such an important intervention into the nature discourse is the way the choreography decenters anthropocentric logic. In an interface, one constituent does not dominate the others, but all come together in relationship — in contingent connections — to form something new, with previously unthought-of possibilities and unforeseen opportunities generated as a result. At the same time, this is not a naïve process, but one that is investigated, planned, rehearsed, performed, re-rehearsed, and re-performed, each time with different results. Rather than perpetuating a discourse that keeps humans dominant, Eiko & Koma engage in a corporeal practice that seeks not one-sided mastery or destruction but mutual transformation.[29] For Eiko & Koma, this choreography of interface results in new beings that could not have existed except through dancing-with. This choreography resonates with Jamie Lorimer's call to develop a "set of embodied and skillful processes of 'learning to be affected' by the environment."[30] Although he is advocating a new kind of conservation practice, his description of the needed approaches sounds intriguingly close to dancing-with. The implications of these new processes sought by Lorimer are profound:

nothing less than an "alternate ontology" that replaces "Nature" with a "hybrid and lively character of a world animated by a vast range of human and nonhuman difference adhering to multiple and discordant spatio-temporal rhythms."[31] I argue that this alternate ontology is already in practice in the world, formed through interfaces, and animated through the process of dancing-with.

Choreographing Interface

In *River*, the flow of the water suggests a somewhat easy interconnection among the various elements, which dance a sort of contact improvisation together in a model of community partnership. This is but one example of how the confluence of technology and nature through a choreography of dancing-with elaborates a relationship among humans and their environment in works from across Eiko & Koma's repertoire. Below I discuss works that posit a connection between humans and nature, paying particular attention to how different approaches to dancing-with impact the interfaces created.[32] For example, whereas *Husk* (1987) deconstructs a human body to form new connections with nature, *Breath* (1998), a live installation at the Whitney, conjoins bodies, technologies, and a constructed nature to form an interface in which the component parts are not only *not* diametrically opposed, they are mutually constitutive, each putting the other parts in motion. *The Caravan Project* (1999), on the other hand, creates a mobile interface that can travel from one location to another.

Husk, a nine-minute dance for camera, opens on an abstract scene accompanied by nature sounds. Leaves, dirt, and the outline of a mountain or a sharply angled branch are discernible in the dim light. A steady breeze blows a leaf through the shot, and everything in the frame softly undulates. After less than a minute, the camera begins a slow pull back, and it becomes evident that the opening landscape was in fact an arm tucked behind a back, elbow pointed up. Leaves are scattered across the ground, and all around the figure is a deep darkness, as if the moon were shining a light on this specific scene. The lone figure's face and neck are smeared with dirt, while the rest of the body is enveloped in a heavy cocoon of leaves, feet occasionally visible at the other end. The insistent crickets on the sound score and the constant breeze outpace the slow, constant shifting of the figure. Movement is simultaneously initiated from multiple points of the body and does not proceed sequentially, giving the impression of innumerable smaller organisms at work in this one figure.

Although the body is eventually identifiable as Eiko, this revelation does not change the viewing of the piece. The angle of the camera at ground level interrupts a unified viewing of her body and contributes to the perception that there are multiple organisms present and that they are merging in and out of one another. As in *River* and *Lament*, dancing-with fragments the human body in order to enable linkages that generate another entity. For example, from a supine position, feet planted on the floor, Eiko arches and twists her upper back and neck around so that her right cheek rests in a nest of leaves on the ground. A medium shot captures her face, her sternum, left shoulder, and left leg, but the leaf sheath that covers her skin from sternum to just above the knee blends in with the leaves on the floor, and her black hair bleeds into the black background, fragmenting her body and distorting any sense of a singular human body. The parts do not seem connected to the same individual, but rather form a whole with the surroundings. The entire media dance is a single shot, with the frame smoothly moving around Eiko so that sometimes her feet are closest to the camera, and at other times her head is. Often it is Eiko herself who moves in and out of the frame, as in one shot where a lone leg is dragged across the screen. About two-thirds of the way into the nine-minute film, Eiko begins to shed her mulch cocoon, her torso emerging leisurely from it. In the final scene, her torso disappears from view, leaving the cocoon, blowing leaves, and crickets behind.

By the time Eiko & Koma created *Husk*, they had developed their own approach to camera work. *Husk*, like the earlier *Tentacle* (1983), was created through studio experimentation with the camera and video playback as creative process. Eiko & Koma's interest in what they call "eye-angle" is evident in the placement of the camera on the floor at the same level as the body and in the way the camera seems to glide along the floor, dancing-with Eiko as a partner.[33] In fact, Koma operated the camera, mounting it on a tennis ball with the idea that he could smoothly maneuver the camera around the space while maintaining its contact with the floor. Eiko & Koma are so known as a duo that audiences familiar with their work may read the camera as Eiko's dancing partner; in this way, Koma is present in the media dance despite his apparent absence. The camera shifts to frame the body's movement while at the same time the body continues to move, with or against the camera, and in the process redefines the frame. There is both coordination and tension between the two intentions. This eye-angle of the camera — and particularly its close proximity — disrupts a view of Eiko's body as a single unit. Typically, a severing of the body, and particularly the female body, in visual media is linked to violence.[34] Here, however, the interruption of the unity of the human body works in the service of generating new microlandscapes; rather than a misogynistic violence, this technique rejects a hierarchical relationship of humans to nature in favor of establishing an interface among them. The focus of interface is not cutting down, but building something new out of points of engagement.

Husk effects a literal co-construction of nature, in which new environments and beings are manufactured on and through a mediated human body. Eiko is both body and landscape, enabled equally by movement, setting, and filmmaking techniques. This interface, taking up little more room than an adult skeleton, is furthermore portable and accessible to anyone with a computer. Eiko & Koma stream the dance for camera on their Web site and often distribute a DVD of the piece for free or for a nominal cost at their workshops and performances.[35]

Intrigued to see how Eiko & Koma's work would look in a museum, Mathew Yokobosky, curator of video art at the Whitney Museum of American Art, invited Eiko & Koma to create *Breath*, their first "living installation." As had been the pair's occasional practice, they were to include video in the installation. For almost four weeks, from May 28 to June 21, 1998, the duo performed *Breath* seven hours a day in an intermedial landscape they designed, including video projection; dappled lighting; and a set made of raw silk, dirt, and dry leaves. The two dancers performed alternately for one- or two-hour stretches, overlapping for only short amounts of time. As one replaced the other, their choreography created a continuous scene of a lone but not lonely creature nestled underneath a tree in crackling brown leaves and rich humus, propelled in the space by muscles and joints shifting with the subtlety of breath (see figure 4.1). A museum visitor who happened upon the installation might not notice the naked body at first, blending as it did with the pri-

FIGURE 4.1 *Still from* Breath, *1999.*
Courtesy of Eiko & Koma.

mal scene: an ur-being who has just been disemboweled from the earth, or perhaps an ancient creature decomposing along with the vegetation.

For the installation Eiko & Koma had to make choreographic decisions not only about their media dance, but also about how to integrate that dance into the live installation. To begin, they worked with ideas of body as landscape earlier explored in pieces such as *Night Tide* and *Husk*. Whereas in *Husk* Eiko was eventually identifiable as the dancer, the media dance used in the *Breath* installation concentrates on the type of abstract images that open *Husk* and that typify *Night Tide*. The camera here enlarges, blurs, and abstracts the dancers' body parts such that a shoulder becomes a rock, the curve of a hip a rolling hill, a sharp joint a mountain peak. When this co-construction of landscape is incorporated into the installation, it is not used as a mere backdrop for the live performance, nor as a representation of the bodies that are in the installation, but as an essential component that cogenerates the environment. Projected without a border and with darkened bulbs, the video image bleeds into the surroundings, dancing-with the stippled and subtly shifting light. In fact, Eiko & Koma choreographed the media dance as a co-performer, dancing-with the duo and the breathing set.[36]

What makes the interface generated by a work like *Breath* unique is that it may be visited in person and is further co-constructed with the audience. Museum visitors may come and go as they please: walking around it, sitting up close, observing from a distance, for a minute, an hour, or multiple times over the course of a month. They see, hear, and even smell the environment. This aspect of the audience creating the space along with the performers was again evident in *Naked* (2010).[37] In both installations, the audience members provide essential—and constantly changing—components of interface.

The Caravan Project offers an interesting twist on the method of dancing-with and the interfaces created by the museum installations. Rather than having their audience come to them, Eiko & Koma created a "mobile performance installation"—a black caravan, the size of a two-horse trailer—that they hauled behind their vehicle and set up in town squares, parking lots, city streets, museum plazas and lobbies, or open plots of land across the United States. The performance began when their assistant opened the specially designed double doors on all four sides of the trailer one at a time to reveal a cave-like interior, stalactites and stalagmites glowing cream, orange, and gold. As do many of Eiko & Koma's outdoor performances, this one takes place at dusk, a time when what was plainly visible even moments before begins to morph before one's eyes as shadows grow, and light fails to penetrate every nook and cranny. As darkness falls, the lights within the caravan seem to glow all the more brightly. The doors of the caravan stood open anywhere from fifty minutes to three hours, depending on the location. Ambient sounds of the site provided a sound track for the dance, along with occasional recorded or even live music.

Passersby need to be quite close to the trailer before they can perceive the two forms within. Even observed from up close and from all possible openings, the bodies of the dancers appear fragmentary: a torso and arm here, a head there. The bodies and the set seem interfaced at all possible points. The structure is pulsing with barely perceptible movement; even the stalactites seem to have a softness, a give. It is only by watching for an extended period of time that the movement of a head from side to side or the raising of an arm would be noticeable. It is as if these bodies are growing from and in symbiosis with this strange environment. Like a view under a 3-D microscope, *The Caravan Project* offers passersby a magnified chunk of a landscape teeming with life.

Similar to the gallery installations, much of the choreography of this piece is executed by the audience members, who decide when and how to approach, circle, stand, shift, whisper to a companion or a stranger, and exit. Yet the properties of the trailer — self-enclosed, mobile — distinguish this installation from the gallery performances. When the doors are closed on the cave still seething with life, the audience is left with the impression that what is displayed is happening all day everyday, wherever the caravan is, whether the doors are open or not, whether anyone stops to watch or not. *The Caravan Project* is as continuously operating and as mobile as an interface generated by live performance could be.[38]

Conclusion

Eiko & Koma choreograph a relationship among humans, their environment, and technologies, dancing-with sites and (on) screens. In the process they generate interfaces in which binaries of nature and technology are unsettled. The effect of the interfaces varies from piece to piece. In the *Breath* installation, for example, Eiko & Koma set their bodies in motion along with video and a constructed "nature" such that each component influences the other, and none can exist on its own. Just as the duo move in and are moved by the water in *River*, their breathing bodies both initiate and respond to the leaves and cinematic images around them at the Whitney. *Husk* employs camera work to deconstruct the human in favor of forming new human-nature connections.

Just as various dances demonstrate the different interfaces that may be generated, they also posit ways that audiences may interact with these nonpermanent creations. *River* and *The Caravan Project* show that a particular interface may be generated repeatedly at different locations, while the gallery installation proves that an interface can have duration. Those created solely through screen dances such as *Husk* are portable and accessible, traveling from DVD players to laptops to screening rooms.

This body of work is a recurring reminder of the potential for creating alternative ways of being in the world, in which the relationship between nature and technology has many complex possibilities beyond an either/or binary. In fact, as *Water* (2011) shows, dancing-with does not have to be in "nature"; it can be in the middle of a city. Created as part of Eiko & Koma's three-year Retrospective Project, *Water* calls up memories of *Lament* and *River* to create a new work that connects recent experiences of the destructive forces of water like the tsunami in Japan with questions of what about water links all of us, even if that water is a reflecting pool at the heart of the Lincoln Center. Eiko & Koma continue to choreograph these possibilities in rivers, museums, and city plazas, on screens and stages, even into the fifth decade of their partnership.

CHAPTER 5

*S*USTAINED *MOURNING*

When Eiko & Koma premiered *Mourning* in 2007, they announced that they created the piece by drawing movement directly from dances across their body of work, with the intention of furthering their choreographic investigation that had begun more than two decades earlier with *Elegy* (1984) and continued with other works over the years.[1] The revisited, repeated, and reimagined movements of *Mourning* are accompanied live by avant-garde pianist Margaret Leng Tan playing grand, prepared, and toy piano compositions by Somei Satoh, John Cage, and Bunita Marcus. Danced on a bed of dry leaves and dirt, *Mourning* reaches a crescendo when Koma attacks Eiko with a violent embrace, followed immediately by her collapse, his remorse, and efforts at caretaking that lead not to a resolution, but to renewed aggression that ends in a sort of stalemate. The pattern of attack and counterattack at the heart of the dance is bookended by a stretch of barely perceptible movements that are a hallmark of Eiko & Koma's work. A Japan Society commission, the evening-length dance premiered in New York City as part of a celebration of the Japan Society's centennial and the 101st birthday of the choreographers' mentor, Kazuo Ohno.

What happens when dance explicitly engages with mourning as a physical state in a way that mobilizes the emotion as a long-term, corporeal practice? What occurs when this process is taken out of the private spaces in which it is thought to normally occur and brought into the public sphere? How does such an artistic commitment to mourning impact public discourse? This chapter addresses these questions by examining several works in Eiko & Koma's repertoire, elucidating how the choreographers rework not only the process of mourning, but also fundamentally what it means to mourn. That is, in the choreographers' practice, mourning is no longer just an expression of sorrow in response to a loss;

it also may encompass the emotions tied up in the loss itself, like conflict, anger, or a desire for revenge.

I open this chapter with a close reading of *Mourning*. Although it may seem counterintuitive to begin my analysis with the most recent dance rather than to trace the evolution of mourning chronologically through Eiko & Koma's body of work, I use this approach precisely because I am interested in the way Eiko & Koma drew on previous works to choreograph sustained mourning in 2007. After the close reading, I then turn to Asian American studies, psychoanalysis, and art criticism to provide a theoretical context for the labor of Eiko & Koma's prolonged mourning and its effects. I argue that Eiko & Koma's body of work over more than three decades theorizes mourning as not merely a private, individual process, but a societal, public melancholia that highlights issues and events that can never be fully resolved but must nonetheless be grappled with. As David Eng insightfully observes, "The melancholic leaves history open for continual re-negotiation."[2] Eiko & Koma's choreography, I suggest, accomplishes this with performances of a prolonged mourning through which Eiko & Koma evidence the ability to dwell in a space of heightened emotion without necessarily effecting a transformation of those strong feelings. Grief in this case becomes a physical labor — sometimes even a battle — on endless repeat. Here their "adagio activism" effects an Asian American critique that extends beyond a specific dance to their body of work over decades. This corporeal theorization of mourning is a crucial reworking of the process that rejects the beginning-middle-end ideology of Freudian psychology in favor of a postwar temporality in which such a linear resolution is no longer possible. I conclude by discussing how dances from across Eiko & Koma's repertoire, including *Elegy* (1984), *Lament* (1985), *Wind* (1993), and *Duet* (2003), participate in choreographing melancholia. I also consider a project in which Eiko & Koma danced at a hospital (2005), courses the pair taught at UCLA, and courses Eiko continues to teach at Wesleyan University.

Mourning

As the audience enters, Eiko & Koma lie center stage, unmoving on an expanse of dirt, both wearing a version of the furry shifts they donned for *Fur Seal*. Each apparently in his or her own world, they acknowledge neither one another nor the audience. Behind them, a massive tree trunk constructed of raw silk rises up from a blanket of dry leaves. The odor of humus pervades the theater, establishing a paradoxical copresence of decay and fertility, death and renewal. Stage right, seemingly incongruous with the nature scene, is Margaret Leng Tan, coaxing the first notes of her mentor John Cage's "In the Name of the Holocaust" from a prepared piano as the house lights dim. This extended opening effects a detail-heightened expansion of time and invites the audience to adjust to and enter the performance's alternate temporal frame, simultaneously slowing down the pace and sharpening focus on subtleties that would otherwise go unnoticed. The first section of the dance is in a style closely associated with Eiko & Koma: small and subtle movements generated nonsequentially across the body and kept low to the ground in a slow-moving performance often discernible only in hindsight. In noticing that the dancers have shifted from here to there, the viewer understands that movement has happened even if he or she did not see it occur.

Whereas many works in Eiko & Koma's repertoire consist entirely of such glacial progress, *Mourning*'s still opening serves to prepare the audience for what follows. As Tan sounds the rumbling opening chords of Somei Satoh's "Litania," the dancers—having almost broached the distance that previously separated them—seem to sense the urgency and foreboding of the music as they themselves leave the slow and subtle behind for the sudden and forceful. Eiko comes to stillness facing the audience as Koma drags himself behind her with much effort, suddenly slapping a piece of leather to the ground downstage of her such that his arm covers her—whether to protect her or hold her down is as of yet unclear. He pulls her to him, onto her back, as if to see if she is dead. His head on her chest, he scoops his hand under her right thigh and begins to move her leg, perhaps in an attempt to reanimate her. He manipulates her right leg, bending her knee into her chest and then opening the leg to the ceiling, leaving Eiko splayed and vulnerable while she lies there, apparently without any means of controlling her own body. Wrapping her calf around his neck, Koma uses his shoulder and torso to pin her leg, the lever action of which lifts her chest toward the sky, head back, arms draped open to the sides. Although she makes no audible sound, her unexpected arch conveys a deep breath in, a gasp that fills her lungs, expanding her chest and reviving her body. At the height of her expansion, Koma's furrowed brow conveying concern and exhaustion suddenly shifts into a blank gape, lower jaw dropping open, eyes becoming vacant. His head does not even face her as he reaches over her to take hold of the cloth and calmly strangles her with it. She lets out a bloodcurdling scream, which freezes them both in place—she in her death pose and he in shock.

This scene lasts only two minutes but is nonetheless the crux of the entire dance. What I have just described could certainly be interpreted as domestic violence. Koma clearly attacks Eiko and seems to kill her, a reverse of the scene in *Before the Cock Crows* thirty years earlier, in which Eiko was the aggressor. Viewing the scene again reveals subtle indications that there may be more going on in the dance than at first appears. Koma's own weakened state before the violent act suggests that he, too, has been victim to whatever attack has left Eiko motionless. His desperation to reach her and the urgency with which he examines her lead the audience to believe that he is distraught to find her in such an unresponsive state. In such a context, Koma's actions could be seen as an attempted mercy killing.

What immediately follows Koma's attack on Eiko also colors how we view this crucial scene. The scream still resonating in the air, Koma slowly releases his hold on Eiko's leg, his head again turned toward her, his body arched protectively over her. As he releases her leg from around his neck, his hand rests protectively on her stomach, his forearm between her legs. The intimate gesture quickly turns to desperation as he frantically tries to lift her lifeless body. Unsuccessful, he departs the stage, returning soon with an armload of green branches, a symbol of regeneration after the death of winter that stands in stark contrast with the dry, brown leaves that cover the stage. Koma presses the branches to her body and finally succeeds in raising Eiko from the ground, both in a wide, deep squat, torsos leaning heavily into one another, arms hooked under shoulders. At first she is just a limp body in his arms, but the higher he lifts her off the ground, the more she seems to regain control of her own torso and limbs (see figure 5.1). Any impression that this is a happy revivification of the dead is fleeting, however. The pair may be on their feet, but this is no egalitarian sharing of weight. Every second is a struggle for balance as their feet shift in the dirt, knees wobble, arms push, and spines aim in vain for equilibrium.

When at last they seem to have found a moment of equipoise and stability, Eiko upsets it by pushing firmly and steadily against Koma, send-

FIGURE 5.1 Mourning, *Summer Stages Dance, Concord, Massachusetts, 2008.*
Photo: Jaye R. Phillips.

ing the upright pair careening toward stage right, where Tan is situated
with her grand and toy pianos, playing bright and staccato sixteenth
notes. Eiko now becomes more aggressive. Her back is to the audience,
her focus on Koma unwavering as she slams her body into his, pushing
him into the piano and even sending him to the ground, continuing the
cycle of violence with her retaliation. Here the pair removes any simple
binary of victim/aggressor, insisting that they are sometimes one and
the same. But soon the tables turn again, and Koma backs Eiko roughly
toward the tree, pressing a handful of dry leaves against her mouth as her
body is pressed into the tree. Eiko's left hand joins Koma's two hands as
they begin to gently release, sending leaves floating to the ground and
collecting in Eiko's lap.

Mourning asks its viewers to act as witnesses to unresolved violence,
and by naming these actions "mourning," the choreographers demand
that the audience question the nature of the emotion itself. He strangles
her; she charges him. These are not incidental gestures, but actions central to the rhetoric of the piece. The physical labor of mourning is shown
here as bodies that rub up against one another with friction and push
each other away. The charged energy between them prevents them from

connecting yet compels them together again and again, even if an erup-
tion of violence is the result.

It is furthermore significant that the violence of the piece is intimate—hands that strangle, a chest that shoves. This is not massive, in-
discriminate violence from above, not a bomb or a plane. Here the violence is delivered from up close, hidden in a caress. Not only does this
scene suggest that massive acts of violence are only comprehensible at
the individual level, but also that these events are repeated across generations in small and personal ways.[3] Moreover, the remorse demonstrated
immediately after the violent attack does not necessarily foreclose future
assaults, as seen in Koma's advance that sends Eiko into the tree. Indeed,
the kind of violence I describe here has appeared in previous dances. In
some, such as *Before the Cock Crows*, in which Eiko's character pursues
and shoots Koma's, the violence may be followed by remorse, but it is not
linked to mourning. *Wind*, which I discuss later in this chapter, does link
violence, culpability, and mourning, although these acts receive a more
literal treatment in that piece than in *Mourning*.

Audiences viewing *Mourning* likely expect to see sorrow, but instead
see violence and an intensity of emotion that is sustained across the
piece. How may this gap be reconciled? I believe what Eiko & Koma
are proposing with this dance is that it is impossible to mourn without
remembering *why*. The cause and the effect must be viewed as part of a
whole. While publicly staging an act of violence does not necessarily lead
to mourning, it may provoke remembering; in Eiko & Koma's dances,
these steps are crucial precursors that make mourning possible. Thus we
witness a grieving process that is not divorced from the specific violence
that produced a loss in the first place. Accordingly, it is imperative that
we witness not only Koma's desperate attempts to revive Eiko's lifeless
body, but also his actions that left her lifeless in the first place. For Eiko
& Koma, then, mourning is closely connected to human violence and
cannot be separated from an acknowledgment of its repeating cycles. As
they dance it, mourning is also inextricably linked to remorse and a sense
of responsibility. These qualities are expressed choreographically as the
act of giving over to emotion and remaining in its intensity. Accordingly,
the dance lacks a linear trajectory, offering no resolution, only a brief respite. In Eiko & Koma's body of work, it is less important what is being

mourned and why, than how mourning is defined, activated, and then publicly repeated.

While some critics have interpreted these movements as representative of a sort of primal consumption or mating ritual, they do not acknowledge the brutality or viciousness of the encounters.[4] The connection these critics see in the work between nature and sex is certainly present in the dance's wooded setting and references to previous pieces (*Fur Seal*, *Tree*). In this context the image of male aggression and gender-based violence might stand in symbolically for larger domains of meaning. For example, Koma's attack could signal "man's" treatment of nature, or a similar argument that associates men with aggression and war and women with peace. Eiko & Koma themselves write in "Choreographer's Statement" that "to mourn is to grieve not only for man's cruelty to man, but to feel remorse for the pain that humans have inflicted upon the earth and all of its living beings."[5] The essentialist man/nature reading is interrupted, however, when Eiko returns the aggression, a move that complicates the dance's violence as a back-and-forth cycle rather than a one-way street.

As the dance comes to an end, the amplified tension of the dancers' bodies begins to subside, although one has a sense that instead of relenting, the cycle of violence and remorse may have begun anew. Koma recedes away from Eiko, pulled from the small of his back deep into a hollow in the tree. She, too, sinks into the tree, becoming camouflaged in its leaves as Tan leans in to play the keyboard with her forearms, creating a cacophony of low rolling tones and higher insistent chaos. As she transitions into the hushed, spare notes of Satoh's "A Gate into the Stars," the dance shifts back to the alternate timescape of the opening. Eiko & Koma's white-painted legs begin to emerge from the base of the tree, new shoots slowly reaching upward into the light and toward one another. An echo of the opening scene, this time oriented to the tree rather than the dirt, the closing is no resolution to what has come before. Rather, it marks a resting period, a stalemate, or perhaps a period of forgetting, before the inextricable violence/mourning complex is reactivated.

Bookending their dance with sections of slow movement aimed to intervene in an everyday temporality, Eiko & Koma choreograph mourning as a particular understanding of time. Eiko has written of their work that "space and time, in which we move, is not a white canvas that stands alone and empty. Here and now are continuous parts of a larger geography (space) and history (time) and as such are dense with memories, shadows, and possibilities."[6] I argue that this density to which Eiko refers — a sort of copresence of other times and places — is a quality common to Eiko & Koma's works that sustain mourning. They are continually attempting to assert with their bodies an alternate temporal realm. In this, Eiko & Koma do not seek to stop time, nor do they attempt to revert to the past. Rather they slow time and expand it, lingering in moments of particular significance such that they are brought into the present of performance. Central to the understanding of the kind of time I am arguing for here, and specifically a prolonged mourning, is Walter Benjamin's "Theses on the Philosophy of History," in which he argues for a historical materialism capable of disrupting the additive and progressive march of time characteristic of dominant historiography. Instead Benjamin espouses a view of history in which the past is radically present. Rejecting a before/after, past/future dualism, Eiko & Koma are always present in a now that embraces the past and the future.

Moreover, Eiko & Koma insist that a viewing of their performances takes time. The act of viewing requires that the audience participate in the dancers' stillness. Through this experience, the spectators begin to feel in their own bodies what it is like to slow down, expand time, or be faced with a moment in time that holds greater weight than the others that surround it. Thus, the choreographic manipulation of time for Eiko & Koma becomes both an expression of major ruptures in history, as well as a space for taking time to grapple with, or mourn, those ruptures.

Consonant with the link Eiko & Koma make between mourning and time, they choreograph the emotion less as a noun and more as a verb. That is, they treat it not as a state but as an action, an emotion that requires repeated practice and that needs time to be experienced. While *Mourning* is dated 2007, it in fact draws heavily on their earlier repertoire, including costumes from *Fur Seal* (1977), sets from *Tree* (1988), and movement sections from the touring version of *Offering* (2002) and *Tree Song* (2004).[7] For audiences familiar with their work, memories of these previous pieces resonate in the midst of the current choreography. The latter two dances are especially evident in the section in which Koma revives Eiko by pressing her with fresh, green boughs, and the final scene in which the pair seem to merge with the tree. The imported elements bring with them a human connection to animals and plants and the sense of renewal or rejuvenation, but interestingly not elements directly related to a common understanding of mourning. The choreographers' choice of these elements to stage mourning suggests that their conception of the emotion goes beyond a straightforward display of loss or grief. Indeed, I am arguing that this habitual return to the choreography of mourning is constitutive of the choreographers' conception of mourning itself as something that is ongoing and therefore must be constantly worked at. I return to this idea later in this chapter.

The emotion choreographed in *Mourning* is not just sadness or grief, but a complex of affect that Eiko & Koma stage as the side-by-side performance of three middle-aged artists, each drawing from across his or her substantial body of work. These bodies do not always meet easily, and friction is often in the air between Tan's avant-garde virtuosity and Eiko & Koma's humanist deliberations. Yet the meeting of these two performances of mourning, the overpowering and the subtle, the aural and the corporeal, in forms that for the artists are deeply familiar, rehearsed, and repeated, is an attempt to describe—to both detail and to mark out— the energy and qualities and effects of mourning. The point of the relationship between Tan and Eiko & Koma is precisely not how they meld together but how they sustain the conflicts, contradictions, frictions, and tensions that their concurrent performances generate.

Eiko & Koma have collaborated with a number of noted composers and musicians over the course of their career, often sharing the stage live with these artists. The first instance of this practice was *Fluttering Black* (1979) with noted avant-garde guitarist and composer Glenn Branca.[8] Here music and dance, perhaps in the spirit of a Cage/Cunningham collaboration, are staged as separate but equal endeavors: neither influences the other (and in fact all the performers wore earplugs and blindfolds so that they could not), but their performance alongside one another creates a whole that neither could generate without the other. This approach differs from most of Eiko & Koma's musical collaborations, in which performances by artists such as Chanticleer (*Wind* 1993), Kronos Quartet (*River* proscenium version 1997, *Fragile* 2012), and Joan Jeanrenaud (*Be With* 2001) establish an atmosphere for the dance but never emerge from the background; even when the musicians themselves share the stage with the dancers, Eiko & Koma remain the main focus. The choreographers' relationship with Margaret Leng Tan's performance comes somewhere in between these two extremes. Her intense music is not a spare background, nor does it proceed in synchronization with the dance. But neither does the pianist function entirely separately from the dancers. Instead, she is a strong partner and coperformer, much like Robert Mirabal in *Land* (1991) and *Raven* (2010), who participates in the generation of space with his presence downstage and ceremonial drumming.[9] The mood and energy of the movement and music sometimes run parallel with one another even as they refuse to synchronize. For example, Tan's rumbling sixteenth notes in "Litania" are constantly shifting tone and tenor, careening full speed ahead, such that they provide neither solid ground on which the moving bodies may depend nor a clear path that the dance may follow. If anything, the dance and music charge around one another, occasionally falling into step. They are allies in mourning, each progressing in its own way through a common process. This relationship between the movement and music of *Mourning* is reinforced by the physical relationship between Tan and Eiko & Koma onstage. The three performers exist in their own worlds — Eiko & Koma a pair of creatures in their wooded set, Tan a solitary figure at her pianos — yet their worlds are situated alongside one another, equally visually accessible to the audience. Moreover, these seemingly disparate partners share constituent parts, the wood of the piano gesturing to its ancestor in the tree.

As I discussed previously, the fact that Tan would be playing well-known pieces of music from her repertoire prompted Eiko & Koma to also draw from their own repertoire. In particular, they wanted to have movement that could stand up to the powerful and indeed emotional piano compositions, such as John Cage's 1942 "In the Name of the Holocaust." While it is unclear if Cage was actually addressing, or was even aware of, the mass murder of Jews taking place in Germany at the time of his composition, the piece has certainly come to embody, with its haunting and discordant sounds, a powerful lament. The piece of music is interestingly resignified by Eiko & Koma in *Mourning* such that the "holocaust" of World War II is not only the Jewish Holocaust, but also the atomic bombing of Japan.

Eiko & Koma tell the audience that what they have witnessed is *Mourning*, and yet they show us tension, violence, and desperation. Koma displays seeming regret; Eiko seeks revenge. But there is no expression of grief, as is expected of mourning. This is a signal that Eiko & Koma believe that to mourn entails more than feeling sadness or lethargy. Mourning is a response to actions that result in great loss. Part of Eiko & Koma's intervention is to demonstrate that staging and witnessing the destructive events that warrant mourning—sometimes over and over again—is an essential component of an extended mourning process. Even when the specific trigger events are not in evidence, the pair asserts the absolute necessity of staying in the intensity of the situation. They expand and reformulate our notion of what mourning feels like and how it is accomplished, even as they pull the audience into their drawn-out intensity of emotion.

Moreover, Eiko & Koma's remembrances effect a mourning that is constantly present in what Grace Cho describes as "a temporality in which the past is in the present, returning over and over to a traumatic moment."[10] Since the movement does not portray a simple victimhood, but enacts a complex relationship of complicity and remorse that appears to cycle through human and nonhuman lifetimes, *Mourning* suggests that addressing past wrongs is not a one-time action or event, but an ongoing and intergenerational process that cannot be settled in any final way. In fact, trying to resolve it might itself be a further injury, an idea I return to below. Contra Freud, mourning is not a process whose linear path leads directly from loss of a beloved object to acceptance of the loss. Acknowledging the recurring cycle, looking at it head on and not shying away from it, experiencing it visually, aurally, kinesthetically, viscerally—this seems to be the main import of *Mourning*. By allowing the violence of a past event to be present onstage alongside the remorse and grief that result, by repeating and revisiting these experiences and dwelling in their conflicts, Eiko & Koma rework what it means to mourn and how and why it is of vital importance to do so. By sitting in the theater for the duration of the piece, the audience sits with the dancers, and with the dance and music, as they chafe at one another for almost an hour, sometimes anxious to connect and at other times insisting on widening the gap. The experience of lingering in these conflicts in the theater could potentially continue to resonate with viewers for hours or days, drawing them in as participants in prolonging mourning.

Some have seen the performance of a recurring cycle of violence and remorse as a reactionary message that does not offer the possibility of ending the violence. At a talk back after a 2008 performance of *Mourning* at Summer Stages Dance in Concord, Massachusetts, Tan observed that the piece is a microcosm of the real world. "We are so horrible to each other but there is also a tenderness there," she remarked. "We love the earth, we hate it; we have remorse about what we do, but we continue to do it." It is this sort of acknowledgment that Eiko & Koma seek by performing mourning—an honest, hard look at what it feels like to commit and suffer acts of cruelty, and how easily those acts are repeated even in the face of remorse. Attempting to rectify a wrong as if it were an event in the past that could be finally left there is to do further violence by effacing the very real effects that remain in the present. What is needed instead is restaging and remembering it as often as necessary to keep the event productively present. It is precisely the practice of staying in such a contradictory and contingent place—a present that activates the past, a public mourning that encompasses the violence being mourned—that ironically offers the only real possibility for the violence to ever end.

Mourning and Melancholia

The mourning choreographed by Eiko & Koma represents a fundamental reworking of the concept of mourning, in which the point is to stay in the visceral and kinesthetic experience of violence and loss rather than attempting to progress through it. Here the focus is not on a Freudian letting go of a loss or moving beyond it, but on an insistence upon staying in the original event and all its potential contradictions. Eiko & Koma stage mourning as a kinesthetic intensity, a push and pull between the dancers reinforced by a failure of the music and dance to resolve into agreement. All this adds up to the absolute necessity of the public performance of mourning, in which mourning is understood not as an individual process, but a collective one that points to issues and events with which society must grapple. For Eiko & Koma, it is the performance of mourning that is key; the object of mourning may shift, but the emotions inclusive of the actions and emotions that caused the lament process must be prolonged. It is precisely the repeated practice of the emotion and its potential efficacy that are at stake here in staging this non-Freudian theorization of mourning.

Examining prolonged mourning means grappling with questions of pathology and melancholia head on in order to more finely articulate what is happening in Eiko & Koma's choreography. That is, the significance of their reworking of mourning—and the stakes of it—must be considered in relation to the dominant twentieth-century understanding of mourning and its pathological twin, melancholia, as first articulated by Freud. Equally essential is an understanding of how those concepts have been employed in relation to major societal traumas, including World War II and the AIDS pandemic.

In his 1917 essay "Mourning and Melancholia," Freud attempts to delineate what differentiates mourning, which he considers a "normal" process of dealing with loss (of a loved one, an ideal, an object), from melancholia, a pathological response to loss. Common understanding of the difference between the two is that mourning is a process that is worked through and ends, while melancholia is pathological precisely because it is turned inward and does not end. But even Freud admits that mourning takes "a great expense of time and cathectic energy" that cannot be predetermined.[11] If I am arguing that Eiko & Koma's choreography is a sustained and necessary mourning for major societal traumas, who is to say how long is too long, or that its sustained nature is pathological? Mourning occurs precisely because of the significance of a lost object, which Freud describes as "a significance reinforced by a thousand links."[12] While he presumably is referring to links established before the loss of the object, I submit that in the case of a massive societal, human loss with ongoing repercussions, those links are continually reestablished. For example, in the case of the atomic bombing of Hiroshima and Nagasaki, the cancers and other physical ailments experienced by *hibakusha* and their descendants continually bring the bombings into the present in new ways. Alan Tansman writes of the annual events in Hiroshima and Nagasaki that mark the atomic bombings: "It is a commemoration that seems to guarantee that it will always continue to repeat its process and expression of mourning," but "when is enough enough, and is enough ever enough?"[13] In this case, it seems completely reasonable that mourning should, and indeed must, continue for decades. Indeed, the German word for mourning is *Trauerarbeit*, which can be translated as "the work of grief." At the same time, Freud believes that melancholia does in fact end. So if both processes can take place over an extended period of time, and both eventually end, what then distinguishes them?[14]

Dominick LaCapra utilizes mourning and melancholy, which he examines via Freud's allied terms "working through" and "acting out," to consider problems of memory and history after the Holocaust.[15] For Freud, the latter concept is a compulsive return to a trauma, in opposition to the former, which like mourning to melancholia is healthy cousin to "acting out." LaCapra attempts to mitigate the binary between these paired concepts with intermediary solutions, by acknowledging that acting out is necessarily bound up in the process of working through, a process that itself may never be complete. In fact the idea that working through could ever be entirely successful is cast into doubt; some traumatic events or deplorable actions may never be "made good." LaCapra helpfully expands the purview of these concepts beyond the individual to historical, political, and ethical concerns. The drawback for those of us invested in corporeality is that even though he rejects a normalcy/pathology binary in favor of a spectrum of necessary actions, it remains clear that he favors a "reasoned" approach in which memory is the desired medium.[16] LaCapra thus maintains a body/mind hierarchy by subsuming acting out as a component of working through, which is considered the appropriate primary process. Working through, accomplished via memory and critical perspective, belongs to the domain of the mind, while the less desirable but sometimes necessary acting out—defined as compulsive repetitive behaviors—is clearly a bodily practice. LaCapra's investment in working through moreover presumes that historical events are all accessible to memory in the first place, ignoring the possibility that some traumas may be unspeakable or even forgotten due to the marginal status of the victims and survivors.[17] Scholars grappling with the AIDS epidemic, Asian American racialization, and Asia-Pacific wars have addressed this crucial oversight. These scholars have attempted to understand why melancholia and acting out are prevalent in those cases and, perhaps more important, how these can in fact be constructive responses to destructive circumstances.

Beginning in the late 1980s, Douglas Crimp notably engaged Freudian theory to address assumptions about publicly performed mourning and activism that swirled as creative direct action escalated to meet skyrocketing HIV transmission rates and AIDS-related deaths. Within the activist community, mourning and protest were considered to be mutually exclusive activities done by two separate groups: a somber candlelight vigil attended by individuals, for example, versus a raucous demonstration organized collectively by the AIDS Coalition to Unleash Power (ACT UP). Articulating common opinion at the time, Crimp wrote: "Public mourning rituals may of course have their own political force, but they nevertheless often seem, from an activist perspective, indulgent, sentimental, defeatist."[18] This is attributable to the fact that mourning is seen as an all-encompassing and solitary process, in which an individual slowly detaches from a libidinous connection to the deceased and thereby returns to reality, that is, society.

One of Crimp's contributions to the understanding of mourning was to demonstrate that normalcy did not exist for gay men in the time of AIDS, and mourning therefore could offer no possibility of returning to reality or normalcy. Instead, there was a wholesale rejection of mourning and a funneling of grief into public anger. The danger was that "by making all violence external, pushing it to the outside and objectifying it in 'enemy' institutions and individuals, we deny its psychic articulation, deny that we are effected, as well as affected, by it,"[19] leading Crimp to famously call for "militancy, of course, then, but mourning too; mourning *and* militancy."[20]

Crimp points to multiple modes of responding to large-scale violence and strongly argues the need to couple inward and outward, individual and public expressions of anger and grief. Chungmoo Choi similarly outlines possible ways to deal with the wartime experiences of Korean comfort women, who were forced into sex work by the Japanese military during World War II, experiences that were not publicly acknowledged until fifty years later.[21] The most prominent response, she claims, has been on the level of the nation-state, in which an anticolonial nationalist discourse metaphorically links the comfort women's bodily pain with that of the Korean nation. The women as agentive subjects are replaced wholesale by the nation, and the women are safely (re)inscribed into the dominant patriarchal structure. In another scenario, the women are able to speak their personal experiences, expressing their physical and emotional pain—what Choi, via Adrienne Rich, calls "speaking silence"—through public or private testimony and various media that document their stories. One danger of testimony in the official public sphere is that in cases in which such testimony may deem the women deserving of government reparations, the women's status as passive victims is reinforced when their honor is seen as restored from an outside (official, male) source.[22]

Choi highlights one intriguing, nonofficial public mode of embodied "speaking silence," further elaborated by Hyunjung Kim, in which comfort women have taken on the role of shaman.[23] Shamanic ritual is available in Korean culture as a setting in which otherwise inexpressible issues, especially those of marginal peoples, may be brought to the fore. Hyunjung Kim's examination of Young-hee Kim's 1997 dance *Here Myself Alone* explores the possibilities of not only speaking silence, but bringing the body to bear as a site and agent capable of grappling with histories of violence and the attendant complex of emotions. Young-hee Kim reworks the traditional Korean dance, *salp'uri*, to reject the traditional femininity the performance typically represents and instead call on the dance's purported shamanic roots to publicly stage an alternative mode of confronting the ever-present but rarely spoken past.[24] Confront is an appropriate word here, because rather than passively accepting the evil sprit, Young-hee Kim actively engages it. She invites the demon into her body, keeps it present, and attempts to cohabit with it. She doesn't allow it to take her over, nor does she allow it to disappear, and by so doing she asserts herself as an agentive, corporeal subject capable of grappling with legacies of enormous violence and pain. Similarly, in Japanese noh drama, plays are structured to allow a ghost that suffered a traumatic death to recount its story to witnesses and thus gain some measure of comfort and rest. While Eiko & Koma do not propose to give expression to particular stories or to embody specific individuals, their choreography does give space to the bodies of the lost as well as those left behind. The audience is provided with an opportunity to powerfully witness the evidence of a great loss and to participate in the mourning of that loss.

Inspired by Crimp, David Gere asks critical questions about the nature of mourning:

What if the subject—the gay male subject—is unable to recover from the loss of a loved one? Or what if he grieves not just a single person but the very "ideal" of an entire culture, with its own social and sexual practices? Or what if, by reason of his fear for his own life and his anger at political and cultural forces that failed to prevent the death of the loved object, he actually *chooses* not to complete his mourning? Or what if he cannot, will not, return to "normal"?[25]

Like Choi, Gere is focused on a loss affecting a marginal population whose pain and suffering is invisible to the larger society because they themselves are not seen. How their mourning might be expressed and what form it may take cannot conform to established paths. Gere points to the complex interworkings of self and society tied up in mourning and begins to suggest the resistive potential that lies with the choice to mourn. It is precisely this kind of intentional, purposeful, willing, and willful expression that I am theorizing here. It is a mourning that is fraught with violence, culpability, righteous anger, and a determination that there is something worth holding onto.

In the past, what I am describing would have been pathologized as melancholia. However, scholars working on gender and minoritarian group identities have embraced melancholia as a powerful concept with which to articulate and analyze individual and group experiences and subject formation. Anne Anlin Cheng, for example, developed the idea of racial melancholia to elucidate the contradictions and ruptures produced when nation formation is played out at the level of subject formation. That is, as the ego processes the abjection of Asians that was mobilized on behalf of the nascent American nation in the form of immigration exclusions and Japanese American internment, followed by a period of model minoritarianism, the same irresolvable contradictions of exclusion and absorption arise at the level of the individual psyche, particularly around issues of (the impossibility of) assimilation and whiteness.[26] Cheng proposes that racialization is itself a melancholic activity, in which an "identity built on loss is symptomatic of both the dominant and the marginalized."[27] In other words, what the white subject and the minority subject have in common is that both identities are formed through an exclusion of the minority. White melancholia takes the form of "a history of legalized exclusions . . . . [I]t is, however, also a history of misremembering those denials."[28] For minority Americans, to use Cheng's term, the result of racial melancholia is a desire for whiteness, for the ideal of the dominant other, which nonetheless is thwarted by the persistent contradiction of "simultaneously becom[ing] the illegal alien and the model minority."[29] This same process plays out on the societal level as multiculturalism concomitantly celebrates assimilation while marking difference.

It is worth asking at this point what happens when Cheng's ideas are played out on another national level, or on a diasporic or transnational level. Can one, for example, speak of a racial melancholia of Japan? This is also part of nation building, but in an external sense. Japan's leaders felt the need to define their nascent nation-state above and against the rest of Asia in order to align itself with (and thus avoid intrusion and invasion from) the Western powers that were literally waiting on Japan's shores. Can abjection be applied to what Japan did to Asia?[30] Can it be applied on the international and transnational levels? Japan's melancholia would have to deal with being both the abject and the deject, the aggressor during World War II and the victim. Zooming in on the student movements of the late 1960s and the early 1970s in which Eiko & Koma participated, was the violence and dogmatism of the movement a reminder of imperialist aggression? Was this the reason to pull out? That those who stood for revolution and an overthrowing of old ways had become exactly that which they stood against? So then the mourning/melancholia of Japan is not only linked to the atomic bombs, but also to imperialism. It is a mourning of the violence suffered, accompanied by a knowing of one's own capacity to inflict violence.

Central as melancholia is to Cheng's theory of racialization, she resists the easy dichotomy between healthy mourning and pathological melancholia, suggesting that Freud's version of mourning "goes beyond mere forgetting to complete eradication." Thus, "'health' here means killing a loss already lost"[31] and becomes itself a suspect concept, based as it is on pathology. For her, mourning *is* melancholy. What Cheng's statement allows us to consider is that it is precisely the process of "getting over" a loss that might itself be harmful. It is almost as if the call to return to health at the end of mourning becomes the ultimate denial of a history of violence and exclusion. This insight points to the possibility of another way of approaching issues of memory and mourning, in which the goal of mourning is not to "get over" loss, especially when dealing with catastrophic events.

To reiterate: to the extent that any productive grappling with a crisis event is possible, it must happen through a repeated or prolonged public performance of insistent mourning, which we can also term melancholia. Eiko & Koma's performances are focused on an unnamed loss, and while the violence of that loss and its consequences reverberates through their bodies and is forcefully repeated through their movements, the focus ultimately remains on the loss as the audience witnesses what it means to grapple with inconceivable catastrophe. Yet Eiko & Koma also complicate the easy tying up of the process of mourning that Freud offers by intentionally repeating their mourning over and over again, by in essence declaring that their melancholia will persist.[32] Freud asserts that "mourning impels the ego to give up the object by declaring the object to be dead and offering the ego the inducement of continuing to live,"[33] as if holding onto the object and continuing to live were two separate endeavors. According to Freud, the ego needs assurance of the finality of loss in order to find a way to move on. His teleological approach reflects a linear beginning-middle-end ideology that does not hold after the mid-twentieth century. The mass destruction of World War II, the Holocaust, and the nuclear age ruptured time, shocking and changing the human psyche such that the experience of time has been irrevocably altered.[34] An inevitable progression forward toward truth and resolution has been replaced by apparent inaction, which in fact becomes a sort of productivity in its own right. As I discussed in the introduction, Slavoj Žižek invests in waiting as a valuable tool of understanding.[35] Robert Diaz similarly identifies "delay, rather than immediate articulation, [as] an important counter-narrative around a traumatic event,"[36] while David L. Eng argues for valuing silence.[37] Similarly, Miryam Sas employs Gayatri Spivak's theory of strategic withholding in her analysis of Minoru Betsuyaku's plays dealing with post–World War II trauma, calling the characters' nonaction "a refusal to signify as a last but powerful refuge against the inscription of meaning within the framework of a dominant paradigm."[38] Waiting, delay, silence, or in this case a staying in the intensity of loss—these (in)actions in fact provide a way of dealing with catastrophe. Eng goes so far as to suggest that melancholia be viewed as "nascent political protest"[39] in its refusal to allow invisible or overlooked parts of the past to disappear fully.

Choreographing Melancholia

Much as Eiko & Koma returned to their repertoire for source movement for *Mourning*, the choreographers have repeatedly returned to the theme of mourning and a choreography of sustained intensity over the course of their careers, with the effect that the process does not end but is intentionally prolonged. The trauma is repeated, must be repeated, with each performance, each retelling letting more memory surface. Throughout the pair's body of work, they have responded to many crises — usually indirectly — including AIDS, friends dealing with abortion, the death of a loved one from cancer, and most recently September 11, 2001. They elect to prolong mourning in an intentional melancholia, saying, "We like to mourn, we don't want to not mourn." [40] The choreographers believe that knowledge of one trauma makes one aware of others.

Accordingly, while the practice of choreographing melancholia has been a constant across Eiko & Koma's body of work, *how* they accomplish it has varied. In what follows, I demonstrate how selected pieces in their repertoire stage melancholia. Some dances, like *Mourning*, reveal or elicit memories of a loss, exposing the violence inherent therein. Other dances physicalize the sadness, immersing the audience in a kinesthetic experience of grief. Still other projects pose melancholia as a mode and object of research. By deliberately discussing these works out of chronological order, I seek to interrupt the idea that there was some sort of evolution in Eiko & Koma's choreography of mourning. Rather, I want to draw attention to how all of their mourning dances across their repertoire have in common an insistent and persistent energy that does not abate. There is no attempt to abandon or transform the melancholic state; at best there is only a brief respite before the intensity returns once again. Eiko & Koma's melancholic dances drop the audience directly into the depths of emotion and leave them there.

Eiko & Koma's first significant engagement with mourning was the dance *Elegy*, which debuted at the American Dance Festival in 1984. Eiko & Koma perform the twenty-minute dance naked in two oblong, shallow pools of water separated from one another by a few feet of marley stage, accompanied by a score created by Eiko that evokes wailing. The black space between the two watery patches acts as a void that ensures the dancers' isolation, sealing them off one from another in grief. Though

Eiko and Koma move in tandem with one another—first collapsing into their respective pools, then creeping slowly downstage toward the audience—they exist in their own worlds, their reflection in the water as their only companion. Their physical separation powerfully manifests a greater existential separation that they cannot remedy, even though they maintain a connection through their parallel paths.

The water through which they move is too shallow to drown, yet both dancers struggle in their fluid environments; Koma in particular thrashes around, displacing pooled liquid with a heavy torso and sending spray into the air. Their nakedness suggests that they have lost everything they have; all that is left is the ability to keen with their muscles and bones, their sadness covering their skin with tears that emerge from their very pores as joints struggle to support the weight of sorrow. This is an incredibly vulnerable state: their bodies have become pure emotion, everything externalized, nothing left to hide. This is especially evident when Eiko & Koma both rise up into a crab-walk, supported on hands and feet, head thrown back upstage, genitalia splayed downstage. The audience is simultaneously confronted by and enveloped in a raw state of sadness rarely permitted outside of funerals.

Unlike *Mourning*, *Elegy* offers no evidence of what is being grieved.[41] The audience does not witness the violence of loss, only its aftermath as it sinks along with the performers into the experience of mourning. The dance does not present a reassuring arc—beginning, middle, end—but instead stays in the intensity of feeling throughout the entire dance; even as the lights fade, the dance continues. The piece asserts the value of letting the mourning be experienced fully, of giving one's whole self over to sorrow. In fact, what is most striking about *Elegy* is that emotions are presented as not only visceral but also muscular and skeletal. Normally we depend on faces to provide a window into emotion; keeping their faces largely hidden, Eiko & Koma do not allow us this privileged view. Instead, the pair mobilizes mourning through muscles, skin, and bones. Their skeletons often fail to support the weight of grief, sending them crashing again and again into their private pools, where their skin is coterminal with the liquid, appearing to both generate and soak in the expanse of tears. Although their trembling muscles keep them moving forward toward the audience, their movements, and therefore their mourning, do not change significantly over time.

One year after *Elegy*'s premiere, Eiko & Koma adapted the stage piece into an eight-minute screen dance, *Lament*. The video opens on Eiko, back to the distant camera. She is curled in on herself, solitary but for her reflection in faintly rippling, shallow water. Koma lowers himself down from off camera quite close to the viewer. His hair is already wet; this lament is ongoing. He drags his head through the water as she, out of focus, arcs her arm up and toward the viewer, reaching out unseeing from a distance, but the only soul nearby has already retreated off camera. She is splayed open, head flung back, torso arching, not knowing or caring that she is being watched. He returns, hunched over, hand attempting to skim the surface of the water, instead stuttering across the hard floor underneath. He stumbles again in the water, collapsing and then picking himself back up. Gravity pulls strongly on these requiem bodies, scarcely allowing them to break contact with the ground. The soundscape, created by the choreographers, resounds with a chorus of cries, creating a somber and mournful atmosphere that is underscored by the dancers' nakedness in their solitary pools of shallow water.

As in *Elegy*, the two dancers remain unaware of one another, but rather than the extreme dark isolation of the proscenium-based piece, the filmic *Lament* multiplies their figures — already duplicated by the water's mirror surface — with cross-fades and layered images, and in doing so creates a wash of light as manifold bodies swollen with grief unfold on the screen (see figure 5.2). Perhaps the most significant difference between the stage and screen versions of this melancholic choreography is the way the camera works with distance, proximity, and perspective to magnify and approximate the physical experience of mourning. The camera first establishes the space between Eiko and the viewer, then that between Eiko and Koma, emphasizing the feelings of isolation and separation that grief can exacerbate. But the camera remains neither stationary nor remote. Perspective shifts such that she is in front and he in back and later shifts back again. Focus zooms in from a wide shot to a close-up of a hand, water glistening, a myriad of tears dripping from every finger. These techniques unsettle the solid ground from which the viewer watches, simulating the disorientation of extreme emotion.

The intimacy and vulnerability of the staged *Elegy* is augmented in *Lament*, which as a screen dance offers the viewer the possibility of watching the DVD on a personal computer or television, alone with his

FIGURE 5.2 *Still from* Lament, *1985.*
Courtesy of Eiko & Koma.

or her own thoughts or memories of loss. Even a 2010 exhibition of the video at the Walker Art Center required that viewers — no more than a few at a time — move their bodies close in to the small screen displayed on the wall at eye level.[42] As the movement abates and the music softens to signal the end of the screen dance, the dancing bodies remain fixed in the water, and the viewing bodies remain near the screen. For both dancer and viewer, the mourning is not over; only the privileged view into it comes to an end.

The evening-length work *Wind* (1993) formulates mourning altogether differently than *Elegy* or *Lament*. The dance opens with the image of a lone archer kneeling downstage left and facing diagonally upstage. Tension builds as he draws back the arrow, which, when finally shot, arcs over a stage covered with large blue clouds and disappears in the far wing. Lights dim on the brief prelude, which taken on its own evokes *kyudo*, the art of Japanese archery. When the stage is again illuminated, however, the target of the arrow is revealed to be not the traditional *mato*, but a small boy (performed alternately by Eiko and Koma's two young sons, Yuta and Shin). The heavy grief of the parents pervades the dance. After the labor of carrying the dead child, Koma struggles to stand, wrists crossed low in front of him, exerting every effort to simply walk, to put one foot in front of the other. Eiko wanders the stage as if lost. Later, the piece is intercut with a ten-minute section echoing *Elegy* and *Lament*, in which the parents appear naked and writhing on the floor. A score of keening voices composed by Robert Mirabal, arranged by Joseph Jennings, and performed by Chanticleer, the famed men's a cappella chorus, vocalizes the parents' bodily grief as white feathers drift in the air and accumulate on the ground like snow, blanketing the stage in another layer of sorrow.

The image of the arrow in *Wind* recalls the intimate violence of *Mourning*. The bow and arrow is an incredibly tactile weapon that requires both close contact with the archer's body and intense concentration on the target. The very muscles of the body are responsible for the arrow's success, tensing in preparation and then releasing into flight. *Wind* also shares with *Mourning* the blurring of culpability and mourning. We do not know why the arrow was shot, or why the boy dies, simply that he does. Each performer carries an arrow at some point, touching the source of violence in order to own it, mitigate it, or simply maintain contact with it as a fetish that keeps the memory of the violence and the resultant loss present. The boy himself reappears throughout the dance as both a corpse and a living presence, and in fact the final image of the piece is of the small, solitary figure stirring, energy bursting beyond his bound movements. Whether a ghost or a memory, the boy's recurrent presence is a strong reminder of the source and purpose of mourning, one that does not disappear but is always present. *Wind* is at the same time more personal—and more literal—than other pieces in Eiko & Koma's repertory, in that it is clearly about parents mourning a child, who is in fact Eiko and Koma's own son. Perhaps the choreographers are grappling with their own responsibility for having brought children into a world full of violence and mourning, or their own fear that they might come to harm.

A decade later, *Wind* took on further contexts of mourning as Eiko & Koma performed a version of the piece in private for a dying friend, and then, under the title *Duet* (2004), performed it in her memory. The narrative of *Wind*—the death of a child—is abandoned in *Duet* in favor of a looser idea of affliction, collapse, and caretaking. The arrow remains a powerful motif of an unexpected and personal attack, but rather than invoking a past catastrophe or foreseeing a possible future, Eiko & Koma herewith create a dance contemporaneous with their own grief. It is around this time that Eiko & Koma began to link the choreography of melancholy with the idea of dance as an offering. Beginning with their large-scale *Offering* to New York City in 2002, they then quickly scaled back to focus on intimate offerings to and for a friend.[43] In 2005 they expanded their offerings to include dances for strangers as they performed for terminally ill patients at Duke University Medical Center, documented in the video *Dance at Hospital* (2005). Like the personal performance for their dying friend, these private performances were given at bedsides and in doorways. Here there are no violent attacks, just the suffering and caretaking; the arrow stands in for whatever illness has pierced the body. The audience members are themselves the loss in progress.

Influenced by more than three decades of choreographing melancholy, and proceeding from experiments in making dance as an offering, Eiko & Koma began an important new part of their practice in 2006 when they began approaching mourning and melancholy as not just something to be performed, but also researched and practiced. Although the pair had long coupled their performances with teaching Delicious Movement Workshops, Eiko began regularly teaching university courses, first at the University of California, Los Angeles, in 2006, and subsequently launching an annual course at Wesleyan University in 2007.[44] By coupling their movement practices with archival materials, literature, and films about atomic bombs, Eiko asserts melancholy as a valuable mode of knowledge production.

At the same time that Eiko & Koma began teaching university classes, Eiko herself was completing an interdisciplinary MA on atomic bomb literature. As part of her thesis, Eiko translated and later published Kyoko Hayashi's *Torinitei kara Torinitei e* トリニティからトリニティへ (*From Trinity to Trinity*).[45] Hayashi, herself a survivor of the atomic bombing of Nagasaki, writes a story of an aging hibakusha who visits the Trinity nuclear testing site in New Mexico, now open to the public only once a year. Surveying the bombed, barren landscape fifty years after the first detonation, Hayashi's protagonist recognizes in the land a fellow survivor of a nuclear attack. She stands at the original ground zero in the

New Mexico desert and imagines the blast that preceded the attacks on Japan by less than a month: "The flash of light boiled the downpour and, with that white froth, ruined the fields, burned the helpless mountains, and shot up to the sky. And then silence. Without time to defend and fight back, the wilderness was forced into silence."[46] In addition to the silence of the stone, Hayashi marks the space once held by the nuclear dead. "I wonder with what I can possibly fill the fifty-two spaces that were once lived by fifty-two schoolmates in my grade. I want to embrace the emptied spaces but my hand reaches towards nothing."[47] Eiko was working on the translation of Hayashi's story, not published until 2010, even as she and Koma were choreographing *Mourning*. Her writing and translation function as a supplemental creative practice and an insight into their artistic process. What *Mourning*, and by extension the performance of mourning, seem designed to do is enter corporeally into that sustained silence, those empty spaces, nudge them open, and give the landscapes and people frozen there an opportunity to "defend and fight back" across space and time through a corporeal testimony.

Conclusion

Whether Eiko & Koma set their melancholic dances in a fecund forest, a snowy expanse, or an isolated pool; whether they animate these settings with delicate feathers, sharp arrows, or sparkling drops of water; and whether they move with a feverish purpose, an exhausted urgency, or a heavy compulsion, they choreograph their prolonged mourning as unrelenting intensity. Tensions and contradictions may abate but are never resolved. As this structure repeats in one dance and across Eiko & Koma's body of work, the choreographers assert their commitment to mourning.

Governments around the world repeatedly demonstrate how grief is mobilized politically to justify state and vigilante acts of discrimination, war, and terrorism. Thus an understanding of the productive potential of a prolonged public mourning and the political implications of an intentional melancholia can be a crucial intervention. Melancholy, I have argued, has the ability to reopen the past in the present. Eiko & Koma's choreography of melancholy draws inspiration from catastrophes that have impacted their own lives, but leaves plenty of room for audience members to bring their own histories and experiences to bear. In this way, Eiko & Koma invite all manner of ghosts and demons onstage, into their bodies, where they may not only repeat the past in the present, but perhaps negotiate new terms of copresence.

While in this chapter I have focused on how the choreography of mourning prolongs past traumas and keeps them productively present in the now, in the following chapter I consider Eiko & Koma's performance in response to the creation of Manhattan's Ground Zero through the collapse of the Twin Towers on September 11, 2001. I suggest that Eiko & Koma's *Offering* (2002) to New York invites a transnational connection to previous ground zeroes in Trinity, New Mexico, Hiroshima, and Nagasaki — as indeed the experience of living through 9/11 as a New Yorker prompted Eiko to pursue the study of atomic bomb literature. These performances stage the possibility to choreographically shift out of the realm of mourning and melancholia into the performance of reparation.

$\mathcal{G}$ROUND ZEROES

In summer 2002 Eiko & Koma premiered *Offering* in six community parks across Manhattan under the auspices of Dancing in the Streets' "Reclaiming the City through Dance" series.[1] Although the hour-long site dance was proposed before 9/11, the duo reconceived their dance after the fall of the Twin Towers as an offering to the dead and an act of public mourning, even adapting their usual duet format to include South Asian American dancer Lakshmi Aysola.[2] Centered on a large coffin-like set—filled with dirt and extruding branches that resemble bones—the dance enacts what Eiko & Koma call a "ritual of mourning and regeneration."[3] Over the course of the performances, the dancers gradually submerge in and then emerge from dirt, evoking images of burial and rebirth, planting and new growth. Sited in verdant spaces across Manhattan at the height of summer, the dancers embody not only the missing dead of 9/11, but also the efforts of those left behind to go on with their lives. *Offering* does more than just offer a ritual space for New Yorkers to grapple with 9/11, however; I contend that it effects an Asian American critique of the attacks and their aftermath. In direct contrast to the impact and destruction conveyed by "ground zero," *Offering* engages in a contingent joining of Asian American bodies with public sites to create a critical transnational space that mourns—and proposes the possibility of emerging from—multiple horrors of American imperialism.

Offering differs from the choreography of the previous chapter in that it transforms rather than prolongs mourning; instead of being melancholic, I suggest, it is reparative. Asian American studies scholars including Robert G. Diaz and Joshua Takano Chambers-Letson adapted the psychoanalytic concept of reparation to open up the possibility that creative action may productively address crisis and loss. An important distinction must be made at the outset between reparative acts and paying reparations. The latter, for example, was what the US government did through the Civil Liberties Act of 1988, in which monetary redress was given to Japanese Americans subjected to internment during World War II through Executive Order 9066. In other words, reparations were paid as a state remedy for a wrong perpetrated by the state. Reparations may also be juridical, as in the voiding of conviction for avoiding internment, or symbolic, such as an official apology from the government.[4] Reparations seem to function on a sort of balance sheet — one thing makes up for another — whereas what Diaz calls "acts of reparation" are process-based, creative responses by the wronged people themselves that engage with loss and deal with it, rather than try to make up for it.

Centering my argument on a choreographic analysis of *Offering*, I work through the ways that the dance foregrounds the specificity of the dancers' Asian American bodies and the public parks, even as it is repeated at and adapted to different sites. I argue that this choreographic strategy brings multiple histories together, producing a critical simultaneity of the ground zeroes of New York City; Trinity, New Mexico; and Hiroshima, Nagasaki, and most recently Fukushima, Japan. This fundamentally historical and transnational relationship expands the idea of reparative acts both spatially and across time. To further explicate the intracity, transnational, and temporal relationality I ascribe to *Offering*, I examine the World Trade Center as a site and symbol that concentrates ideas of local and global even as it opens up a discussion of spatialization as the interactions of people and places. Finally, these ideas are explored further through other dances in Eiko & Koma's repertoire, including *Event Fission* (1980), *Land* (1991), *Raven* (2010), *Fragile* (2012), and a series of recent solo projects by Eiko.

Offering

Immediately after September 11, New Yorkers shared a literal intimacy with the dead: as Diana Taylor so evocatively wrote, "We inhaled the Towers, smelled them, tasted them in our mouths, rubbed them from our teary eyes, crunched them with our feet as we walked through the streets."[5] With the physical evidence of both the towers and public mourning — pictures, candles, flowers, teddy bears — quickly removed, however, what remained was precisely that which was missing: people and buildings. With multiple iterations of *Offering* taking place in parks across the city, Eiko & Koma sought to bring into focus this empty evidence of loss by creating a public mourning ritual in which people could take part in their own neighborhoods.

A fourteen-minute video document, *"Offering" in Manhattan Parks*, travels back and forth among five of the six 2002 performance sites, visually positing the temporal and spatial coexistence of each iteration of the dance.[6] The video of *Offering* opens on a sunny, summer day in a space identified with subtitles on the screen as Madison Square Park. As businesspeople pass by on the way to a meeting or perhaps lunch, we find in the middle of the square a strange, large, black structure, the size of a dumpster, filled with dirt and marked by branches stripped bare of bark and resembling long bones protruding horizontally from the top of the structure. We then come upon Koma busily drilling at the base of the structure, while Eiko and a few others look on. They chat in Japanese ("Do you understand? That's better.") as they continue setting up and practice rotating the set, which turns slowly counterclockwise. They make no attempt to hide their activities from the passersby who turn their heads out of curiosity, or the families who linger to watch. Like their dance, which will begin later in the day, their labor, too, is public. There is no hidden magic of performance to be revealed, no curtain to draw back.

In the video the setup process continues in the Clinton Community Garden in Hell's Kitchen, where a costumed Eiko walks matter-of-factly through the garden past mothers and nannies caring for small children. The camera peeks through flowers and leaf-laden branches as the choreographers set up lights and speakers. In this intimate, secret garden, the set is placed up against a fence; here there is no room for a theater in the round. In contrast, Dag Hammerskjöld Plaza, with its long, broad walkways and monumental art, affords more sweeping views. Although the plaza is sometimes the site of raucous protests, given its proximity to the United Nations, today the atmosphere is more contemplative, lacking the bustle of Madison Square. Here, people relax on benches in the shade, calmly taking in Koma's last-minute adjustments to the set.[7] In Bryant Park, the performance site is nestled against the foot of steps, with wide-open green space surrounding the dance on three sides, while at Tudor City Park, an imposing wrought-iron gate encloses the performance. In each of these sites, the audience begins to gather, with people sitting on chairs, benches, and the ground while others stand or stroll by.

Again, Koma's activities in front of the audience are casual, not ritual-istic. As Koma finishes his preparations, a helicopter is heard overhead, disturbing the serenity of the park and reminding those present of the bustling city that surrounds them, and perhaps of new post-9/11 security measures.

The performances pointedly did not take place at the site of the 9/11 attacks. Ground Zero was actually visible from some of the performance sites such as Battery Park City, but already within months of the attacks, as Taylor so succinctly observed, "There was nothing to see."[8] Instead the dance took as its location other sites, still green, still living, where people regularly gathered to publicly mourn, celebrate, or just pass the time.[9]

I begin my discussion of *Offering* with this enumeration of its different settings precisely because the meaning of this dance is so closely linked to its multiple sites and multiple bodies. The specificity of the sites and bodies is one notable difference — although not the only one — between *Offering* and *Mourning*, and therefore between performing reparation and mourning. At each of the parks a performance site was formed through the dumpster-sized set piece, lights, speakers, sound, and casual seating, all oriented to establish a focal point for the dance. Depending on the topography of each park, the resulting performance site was an informal theater in the round or a sort of thrust stage.[10] Yet this performance was choreographed to form a relationship with the parks, not to perpetuate the no-place of a proscenium stage. Rather than asking a self-selecting audience to come to them, for example, Eiko & Koma go to the audience as visitors and fellow users of the park. Indeed, each performance was cosponsored and introduced by the respective park's local committee or organization.

Although passersby and intentional audience members have been able to watch the transparent preparations for the performance, *Offering* officially begins with the entrance of Lakshmi Aysola, a West Coast dancer whom the choreographers met while working with Anna Halprin on the 2001 piece *Be With*.[11] Dressed in a full-length, goldenrod sarong, Aysola slowly and purposefully processes through the audience, approaching the black structure as if on her way to perform a ritualistic task known only to her. Minutes pass as she ascends past the branches, climbing steadily and surely, arriving finally on top. Once there, she stands upright and surveys her surroundings before slowly sinking into a supine position across the rich loam contained in the structure. The materiality of her actions — a literal going to the earth — powerfully signifies death.

As Aysola's movements in the dirt slacken to an imperceptible pace, an identically clad Eiko walks in from the audience — from the city, from the people. While Aysola is clearly younger than Eiko, their relationship is not that of parent and child. Instead they appear to be beings on a shared path, individuals undergoing similar circumstances. As Koma enters the scene in a simple gray short kimono and loose pants, Eiko circumnavigates and then turns the structure, in effect turning the dance itself counterclockwise, changing the perspective of the audience in the process. Accompanied by clarinetist David Krakauer's deep, haunting notes, Koma joins Eiko in laboriously leaning into and rotating the set piece topped by Aysola's now motionless body. The structure now begins to evoke a bier moved along by steadfast mourners. Eiko separates from Koma, however, to join Aysola atop the structure, her movements slowing as she comes to rest lying down in the dirt, a second corpse (see figure 6.1). Seeing these particular images in Manhattan public parks invites the audience to question who has access to the claim of victim and who has a right to mourn, and indeed poses a link between those two roles.

Eiko & Koma choreographed Aysola's presence in the piece in order to draw attention to the post-9/11 context in which Arab and South Asian bodies were targets of increased surveillance, particularly — but not only — in New York. Under those circumstances, bearded, brown-skinned men were spotlighted as terrorists, while women wearing headscarves or the hijab were seen as victims of antidemocratic (i.e., anti-American) regimes. While these bodies were hypervisible in the call to war in Afghanistan in 2001 and in Iraq in 2002 and 2003, other Arab and South Asian Americans — those who died in the Twin Towers, were detained and deported, were violently attacked, or were left behind to cope with all of these situations — became for all intents and purposes invisible.[12] While Aysola's dancing body cannot begin to encompass all of the complexity and diversity of those erased from public view, her presence nonetheless argues for an integration of South Asian bodies with urban American sites. At the very least, Aysola's corpse-like presence suggests that South Asians and people of Middle Eastern descent must be acknowledged and mourned as part of the dead, not just the living victims of post-9/11 racial profiling.

FIGURE 6.1 Offering, *Bryant Park, New York City, 2002.*
Photo: © *Tom Brazil.*

By publicly choreographing a South Asian American body alongside their own Japanese American bodies, in the political context of the time, Eiko & Koma ask the audience to view not only the dance but also their bodies as site-specific. That is, they call attention to the ways that Japanese and South Asians have been racialized in the United States historically and how that racialization was being modified and mobilized after September 11. We can read into this move a strategic essentialism that calls attention to their racialized bodies in order to stage the corporeal stakes of moving and mourning in public in the age of the "war on terror." The context of the dance draws attention to the extended history of US immigration and military policies, calling to mind a time when Japanese and Japanese American bodies were themselves the focus of US governmental and vigilante racial profiling, "a particular historical moment when being Japanese is synonymous, on all accounts, with being a terrorist."[13] The collocation of these particular three bodies in *Offering* thus serves to expand the space of mourning beyond the immediate context of the fall of the Twin Towers to the history of Japanese American internment during World War II and the American bombing of Japan.

Furthermore, by signaling similarities between Eiko and Aysola — in costume, movement vocabulary, and trajectory — the choreographers point to parallel histories and contemporary connections, for example the way Japanese Americans living with the legacy of internment lent support to Middle Eastern and South Asian Americans subjected to racial profiling and worse after 9/11.

When Aysola and Eiko lie dead alongside one another in the soil, they bring the histories of violence against South Asian, Arab, and Japanese Americans and the Japanese in Hiroshima and Nagasaki into one shared space and time. According to Nicholas Birns, this act of bringing recent and more distant histories into the present is not typical. He writes, "America is a society without any palpable relation to history, a society particularly ahistorical when it assumes it is ultra-historical. The ultra-historicism of official memorials makes us think the past is finished, when we still have the power to construct it. Even more so, race continues to be the arena where the American response to history is most resistant."[14] Birns goes on to suggest that the work of some artists — he is writing about Ralph Lemon's work in particular — "opens up a field of countermemory in which what was supposed to be 'historical experience' is in fact still taking place."[15] I argue that this is precisely what is happening in *Offering*: history being repeated in the present, made local and intimate.

All of these connections among bodies and sites are established in the first third of *Offering*. A major transition happens when Koma assumes the solo labor of rotating the structure. Up until this point, all dancers followed a common choreography of a slow, steady walk to enter the performance space, followed by a repeated, ritualistic circling of the black structure. Now, however, Koma's role diverges from that of Eiko and Aysola. Standing on the ground, he reaches his hands into the soil in the top of the structure and begins to scoop the dirt over the unmoving women. Using his hands he buries a leg, an arm, a torso with reverence and care. As he works, dirt audibly falls over the women to the ground. Their bodies are never deeply buried in the soil; they do not disappear into it. Elevated as they are — not lowered into a grave nor shut away behind the doors of a mausoleum — the women remain visible and identifiable under an uneven layer of dirt that here is more symbolic of burial than functional. This section enacts a gendered division of labor that is repeated more than once in Eiko & Koma's choreography: a dying or dead woman cared for by a still-living man. That Eiko and Aysola here are literally lying in dirt, contained by the structure, becoming one with the dirt, reinforces the trope of woman as land: cycles of harvest and barrenness, motherland, and so forth. Koma, meanwhile, remains erect and active, in charge of the structure and its contents, tasked as celebrant of this death ritual.

As sunlight fades, stage lights (and in some parks, lamplights) come up, and the bodies of the performers seem to glow.[16] With the lowering light, the *Offering* becomes more intimate, more hushed. The focus of the audience is drawn even more tightly in toward this central section of the dance. Koma lights candles pressed firmly into the dirt. The bier is now a pyre, one not edited from television cameras nor hidden from view behind construction fences, but out in the open for New Yorkers to see. In fact, this is one of the functions of ritual: to bring inner life or a private experience into a shared, sacred space.

In this way, *Offering* could be seen as a funeral ritual. But what kind of funeral is it? In his book *How to Make Dances in an Epidemic*, David Gere writes movingly about an activist funeral for Jon Greenberg, who died of complications from AIDS in 1993. Jon's brother, choreographer Neil Greenberg, and other family members and friends conducted a public funeral for Jon in New York's Tompkins Square Park before parading his casket down the streets of the East Village, in what Gere calls an insurgent act that serves a number of functions: "For the participants, it constitutes a demand for their grief and loss to be taken seriously and to be respected. . . . The procession also represents the (re)affirmation of emboldened activism: This grief will not be borne alone or in secret. It will be paraded down the street. For random onlookers the procession serves notice of the power of this grief and of the activist anger that attends it. Let this not be taken for granted. Mourning makes for powerful militancy."[17]

Greenberg's funeral aimed to make public a loss that at that time was still very much kept behind closed doors. The militant funeral procession was a powerful intervention into a society that denied not only the depth of the AIDS crisis, but perhaps more fundamentally the queer and otherwise marginal lives lost to the epidemic. After 9/11, however, there was no shortage of public mourning. Particularly prominent was a nationalist sentiment that beat the drum for war. As Eiko wrote in the program notes for *Offering*, she and Koma "saw how quickly people were orchestrated to forget the true meaning of violence and sorrow. In the process, victims were turned into heroes. And compassion was replaced by hate and swallowed with a song of freedom."[18] In opposition to this linking of national grief and patriotism, the choreographers sought to create local and intimate spaces for mourning. This is effected not only literally, through performing in various parks at a time of day when their dance might seem to blend in with its surroundings, but also in an act of synecdoche in which the soil they dance in comes to stand for the city, and their dancing enacts the burial of the bodies that were not to be found, as well as life growing from the detritus of the ruins. Through the connection with the soil, the dancers join, too, with the dead, who as Taylor pointed out, covered the bodies of the living in the days after 9/11. In this context I suggest that *Offering* was not, to use Dancing in the Streets' title, a "reclaiming" of the city in the sense of recovering something that was lost, but rather an attempt to bring specific bodies and sites together to create a new space of communal mourning.

Bringing his burial activities to a close, Koma rotates the structure once again. The women then begin to stir, their limbs alternately sinking into and reaching out of the soil, as if growing from some secret seeds planted there. Having been buried, Eiko and Aysola now emerge. As their torsos rise from horizontal to vertical, the two women twist slightly toward one another, acknowledging each other's presence with their bodies if not their eyes. Their earlier straight-spine stance and pedestrian actions — walking, standing, lying down — are left behind in favor of curving shoulders, spines that slowly coil and uncoil, and knees that bend to contract the body. Koma continues to tend and rotate the structure as Eiko and Aysola begin to exceed the borders of their grave, their arms and heads budding and stretching over the edge into the increasingly dark night. What was for a time a funeral rite is transformed as the two women emerge once and for all from the soil and begin their controlled descent. The dirt still clinging to their skin is the only visible evidence of the grave from which they came. One by one, the three dancers retreat slowly into the darkness, leaving the audience to consider the now empty coffin before them in the dim light of a New York City summer night.

This ultimate rebirth and departure occupies the shortest section of the dance, but instead of suggesting its unimportance in relation to the processes of burial, the effect is open-ended, pointing to possibilities of moving beyond mourning. Anne Anlin Cheng declares that "there will never be enough justice, enough reparation, enough guilt, pain, or anger to make up for the racial wounds cleaved into the American psyche."[19] She is right that some wounds cannot and should not be excised. In the previous chapter, I argued that dances like *Mourning* and *Lament* effect melancholy by actively prolonging an intense emotional engagement with loss. The mourning of *Offering*, however, is transformed at the end in a way not seen in those other pieces. Ending with reemergence, the dance suggests that it is indeed possible to do something other than prolong mourning, even if the loss cannot be gotten over. I propose that what Eiko & Koma choreograph here is akin to the notion of performing reparation.

Making Space for Reparative Acts

Some Asian American scholars have turned to reparation as a way to make room for that which is foreclosed by a focus on melancholia. While acknowledging the utility of melancholia for understanding racial formation and the Asian American experience, Robert Diaz, for example, is particularly concerned that the pathology has been reified, thereby, as he says, "limit[ing] the conditions of possibility for Asian American persons."[20] As a way out of that situation, Diaz turns to psychoanalyst Melanie Klein's concept of reparation, which, he claims, "unlike melancholia, does not just involve pining for the lost object but requires constructive creative action around emotions of loss, mourning, depression, and abjection."[21] This focus on creativity and process in reparation provides an opening for performance to intervene in what had previously been treated only within the realm of psychoanalysis. Reparative acts are not necessarily about mending a rupture, nor about "getting over" something, but about acknowledging that much of life is lived in fragments, and figuring out a way to do so.

Diaz sees reparative acts as "performances that seek to not necessarily contest, but strategically deal with, racial oppression."[22] His focus on performance is key. That reparative acts are performed and not built (nor paid) is central to their ability to deal with pressing issues of loss. Reparative acts are precisely not official monuments or memorials, but performances that can change as necessary. Monuments are fixed spaces, but what is needed are contingent spaces that can address issues immediately, come and go as needed, and shift over time. Eiko & Koma's *Offering*, for example, continued to have resonances with New York and 9/11 even outside the city. Trading the soil and lush greenery of Manhattan parks for a public fountain, the pair performed their reparative dance in Portland, Oregon, on the second anniversary of the collapse of the Twin Towers.

These creative engagements with loss that set aside needed space seem to be able to be mobilized much sooner than official reparations are paid or monuments are built.[23] For many years after 9/11, the plans for an official memorial were plagued by controversy. The initial inability to agree on a monument for 9/11 is not unusual; the Atomic Dome in Hiroshima was not dedicated as such until more than twenty years after the bomb was dropped, and the Holocaust Memorial (Memorial to the Murdered Jews of Europe) in Berlin was not dedicated until sixty years after the end of World War II. Reparations were not paid to Japanese Americans interned during World War II until 1990. Eiko & Koma, on the other hand, were able to publicly dance their mourning only ten months later and to sustain those performances amid shifting needs over the following ten years.

The National September 11 Memorial was dedicated September 11, 2011, and opened to the public the following day. The Memorial Museum opened in 2014. The memorial is a tree-ringed pool marking the footprint of the destroyed buildings that provides space for contemplation away from the everyday bustle of the city, not unlike the parks where Eiko & Koma performed *Offering*. Moreover, the memorial links the Twin Towers' collapse with the plane crashes the same day in Pennsylvania and at the Pentagon, as well as with the earlier 1993 bombing of the World Trade Center. Even in its absence the WTC continues to serve as a transtemporal nexus of multiple sites. The description of the memorial as a "powerful reminder of the Twin Towers and of the unprecedented loss of life from an attack on our soil"[24] continues the synechdochic logic that construes the attack on the towers as an attack on the nation, even collectivizing the almost three thousand individuals who died into a singular "life." Eiko & Koma's performance, on the other hand, brings together three individuals who undergo burial and emergence together, and through the interaction of the specificities of their bodies and the sites of their performances, mobilize histories erased by the official memorial narrative.

Another characteristic of reparative acts is that they are not necessarily contestatory. Eiko & Koma's reparative dances are not necessarily a call for "never again," in contrast with art like Käthe Kollwitz's famous *Nie Wieder Krieg* lithograph. In this strident image, created a decade after the end of World War I, Kollwitz writes the words "never again war" urgently across a page, underlining each for effect. The upraised arm of a determined, shouting protestor erupts from the bottom of the page, bisecting the space and partially obscuring the word "war." What Eiko & Koma offer instead is a recognition that in many ways it has happened again, and will happen again, a fact evident in the repetition of performances across many sites and in the repetition of choreography across many pieces. The dances do, however, offer a possible way forward—a sort of choreography for survival and beyond[25]—by corporeally working through a recurrent crisis and its aftermath. Saidiya Hartman, a writer whose work has influenced scholarship on reparation, offers the important insight that "redress is itself an articulation of loss and a longing for remedy and reparation."[26] Even amid Cheng's recognition that remedy (as in Freud's "health" or the balance sheet of reparations) is an impossible if not dubious goal, reparation as articulation and longing is a performative practice that continuously connects the past and the future through a constant reworking in the now. For Chambers-Letson, these acts focus on a "political *doing*" that is reparative, "providing options and alternatives for rethinking our conditions of existence through reparative practice."[27] So by dancing a loss, Eiko & Koma suggest a way of moving through it.

I do not mean to present this process as idyllic, for while reparation may not be directly oppositional, it does not shy away from dealing with difficult issues. Chambers-Letson clarifies, "The reparative act is not a sublimation of this violence so much as a coming to terms with it."[28] In *Offering* the audience only witnesses the aftermath of catastrophe: death and burial. But less than a year after 9/11, images of planes crashing, people jumping to their deaths, and massive buildings crumpling in on themselves were still fresh in people's minds; there was no need to provide a visual mnemonic for the violence.

In reflecting on their body of work and on the recurring treatment of death and crisis, Eiko writes, "Throughout the overwhelming part of our common history, to live has been to see others die and to anticipate our own death close by. This still remains so in many regions of the world. While people should of course work to lessen the suffering of others, we should not mask every pain as though it were a blemish to be disguised or swept away quickly."[29] The reparation that Eiko & Koma choreograph in *Offering* places death center stage, where it cannot be ignored. More specifically, it places the deaths of two specific people side by side and treats their loss with reverence and respect. *Offering* asks over and over at each performance site, "How can we live with this?" The answer comes with the emergence of the two women at the end: if we acknowledge our common histories and understand the similarities and differences, we can try to work through this together, through a patient, corporeal practice. This proposition stands in stark contrast to the state rhetoric of resilience that existed in the months after 9/11, which Inderpal Grewal has described as "consumer citizenship."[30] President George W. Bush himself linked the nation's survival of the 9/11 attacks with consumption, exhorting Americans to spend money and travel as a way to show the terrorists they had not won.[31]

Offering accomplishes all of this without ever explicitly referencing 9/11. There are no portrayals of the Twin Towers, no planes, no sudden collapses, no falling bodies, no flags, no images of heroes. Instead, Eiko & Koma present a simple process of being buried and surviving it, over and over again. In the case of *Offering*, the time and place of its performances—public parks in Manhattan less than a year after 9/11—give it a more detailed meaning. Moreover, the collocation of these particular three bodies in *Offering* serves to expand the space of mourning beyond the immediate context to the histories of Japanese Americans and the American bombing of Japan. While the movement vocabulary is not racially marked, the performers are, a fact especially significant in an age of explicitly legal racial profiling.

But it is precisely the nonspecificity of the narrative that makes the dance capable of connecting this crisis to other histories of disaster and perseverance. Each time *Offering* was repeated in different parks across Manhattan, meaning accrued. As the sites multiplied in number, each remained local and contingent—as evidenced by changes made in the choreography to adapt to each particular park—while also encompassing all the previous sites. This approach to site dance is resonant with geographer Doreen Massey's thinking on world cities. She "poses the question of whether, in certain realms, we could imagine (aspects of) other places as in a sense part of our own place, and vice versa . . . a kind of multi-locational place."[32] This is precisely the work that *Offering* does: Eiko & Koma create a ritual space that holds together individual sites in tension alongside each other. This same bound tension is evident in Eiko, Koma, and Aysola's physicality: their bodies are always contained, and while their movement is continuous, they do not exhibit an easy fluidity. When the performers are engaged in pedestrian activities such as walking, rotating the structure, or lying down, their energy is committed yet contained; it does not spill beyond their bodies. Near the end, as Eiko and Aysola emerge from having been buried, they extend and grow from multiple points simultaneously, for example from the top of the skull and the kneecap, so that the gestures cannot possibly flow in only one direction. In this way, Eiko & Koma reject the creation of a universal space of New York in favor of holding the specific sites in tension alongside each other in a way that underscores theories of the multiplicity and relationality of place.

This multiplicity of time and place in Eiko & Koma's choreography can be productively understood through Diana Taylor's notion of acts of transfer, which work through "doubling, replication, and proliferation"[33] and account for cultural continuities, even those that may not be immediately evident. Within Taylor's model, then, we can see the name "Ground Zero" given to the site of the fallen Twin Towers as an act of transfer of sorts. "Ground zero" is significantly the term coined to describe the location on the surface of the earth above or below the explosion of a nuclear bomb, with the experiments of the Manhattan Project and the bombing of Hiroshima being the first instances of the use of the phrase. The term suggests at once a presence—a ground, something solid—and simultaneously a nothing, a zero. Although it was a misuse of the term, the collapsed Twin Towers site was already being called a ground zero within hours of the attacks. Certainly, as Joseph Roach[34] suggests, this double naming evidences a replication of structures of power not necessarily apparent amid the post-9/11 patriotic fervor; in the earlier case, the aggression and destruction of ground zero was justified as an ostensible act of liberation from war, while the more recent attack was decried as an "attack on our freedoms" and therefore as justification to initiate a global war on terror. But while we might see in the name "ground zero" the repetition of erased structures of power, *Offering* could be seen as an example of challenging this doubling. In the midst of the frenzied buildup to the launch of the war on Iraq, *Offering* created a space in which multiple instances of American imperialism could be joined, mourned, and dealt with.

The World Trade Center

The gigantic mass is immobilized before the eyes. It is transformed into a texturology in which extremes coincide — extremes of ambition and degradation, brutal opposition of races and styles, contrasts between yesterday's buildings, already transformed into trash cans, and today's urban irruptions that block out its space. Unlike Rome, New York has never learned the art of growing old by playing on all its pasts. Its present invents itself, from hour to hour, in the act of throwing away its previous accomplishments and challenging the future. A city composed of paroxysmal places in monumental reliefs. The spectator can read in it a universe that is constantly exploding. . . . On this stage of concrete, steel and glass, cut out between two oceans (the Atlantic and the American) by a frigid body of water, the tallest letters in the world compose a gigantic rhetoric of excess in both expenditure and production.[35]

This is what Michel de Certeau saw when he gazed northward over Manhattan from the top of the World Trade Center. One of the countless "urban irruptions" captured in his vision of New York is Eiko and Koma's high-rise apartment building near Times Square, where they have lived since 1984. From their living room window on the twenty-ninth floor one can return Certeau's gaze straight down 9th Avenue, past the WTC site to the tip of Manhattan island and beyond to the Statue of Liberty. It is from this vantage point that Eiko watched the Twin Towers fall. This sort of sweeping perspective epitomized Certeau's understanding of place: power's totalizing — perhaps global — view that affords surveillance and control. Yet perched on one of the Twin Towers, he also recognized that the constant and unpredictable activity of people through the city's local buildings and streets escaped the towers' panopticon-like gaze, creating the space of the city through movement.

These oppositions between place and space and visualization and corporeality were crystallized for Certeau in the World Trade Center. What I am interested in here is the way the WTC complex—its construction, destruction, and reconstruction—concentrates those issues while also serving as a nexus of the local and global.[36] I employ it here as a tool to further open up my earlier discussion of Eiko & Koma's choreographic practices that seek to create space for reparation by posing particular relationships among multiple bodies and sites. Below I trace the various meanings of the World Trade Center, from its construction in the late 1960s and early 1970s to its destruction in 2001, to tease out its implications for the generation of local and transnational spaces. This in turn forms a foundation for my discussion of spaces of reparation in the following section.

My move to bring the WTC, spatializing practices, and Eiko & Koma into productive tension with one another is not without precedent. In fact, Eiko & Koma's choreographic engagement with New York City is in many ways tied up with the construction, presence, destruction, and absence of the World Trade Center. Even their identity as a singular construction (Eiko & Koma) made up of two distinct entities (Eiko, Koma) provides an interesting parallel to the Twin Towers themselves, which Eric Darton describes thus: "Standing side by side—not quite separate yet never merging into one—the WTC buildings divide their singular name in two. Each tower might be the clone of the other,"[37] or perhaps a cell that has undergone fission. In 2000 the dancers had a residency on the ninety-first floor of the North Tower, even though their choreographic project seems diametrically opposed to what the towers stood for.[38] As choreographers who frequently offer free performances in the parks and cemeteries and open spaces of New York, they relate to the city through movement practices that seek to create local and intimate relationships between bodies and specific sites. Their work as artists has sought to change the time signature in which a city is experienced, re-purpose urban sites, and question the relationship of humans to their surroundings.

When the Twin Towers of the World Trade Center were dedicated in 1973, they were briefly the tallest buildings in the world, only to be supplanted months later by the completion of the Sears Tower in Chicago. Upon Eiko & Koma's arrival in the city in 1976, controversies surrounding the WTC were still fresh in the minds of New Yorkers; issues of aesthetics, the displacement and destruction of Radio Row, local versus regional governance, private versus state funding, and looming late capitalism continued to roil long after the towers topped out.[39] Indeed, construction of the rest of the WTC complex continued until 1985, and the building of Battery Park City on the Hudson River from landfill from the WTC excavation extended well into the 1990s. Only in the wake of their destruction in 2001 have the towers coalesced into an emotion-laden symbol of New York, and by extension, America. Until that time, their meaning remained up for grabs, and Eiko & Koma as new citizens of the city readily participated in that contestation.

At stake was the identity of New York as local versus global; as city, (nation-)state, or the world.[40] The WTC site—whose purposes represented a conjunction of urban renewal for Lower Manhattan and a transition of the New York local and regional economy from industry to world finance—concentrated this debate. Although New York's position as a key trading port and point of entry to the colonies and then the United States long ago gave the city a unique role as conduit between the nation and the world, the Twin Towers were a bold, postmodern statement that materially and symbolically tied New York City's prosperity to that of the world. The success of this link was evident in the immediate aftermath of 9/11, when the whole world briefly seemed to be in mourning for the symbolic loss of its center.

What interests me about the WTC here is not the ways that it was celebrated or mourned, but how it complicates issues of global and local and articulates relationships among the two. Scholars like Massey and Saskia Sassen, who grapple with the construction and identity of "world cities" or "global cities," are helpful in this endeavor.[41] For Massey, a place is not just defined by its geographical borders and what is contained therein (e.g., the arrangement of built structures and geographic features) or by what comes into a city (people and capital, for example), but also by what goes out from it. For her, the local is certainly constructed by the global, as many scholars of globalization have argued, but her unique contribution is that she credits the local with also constructing the global. We cannot think of a place only as what exists or transpires within its boundaries; we must also take into account the relationships of that place with other places, whether across a river or around the world. In this way the sense of place of a city like New York is *both* local and global in complex ways that are not always immediately evident. Sassen's approach, although more narrowly focused on economic conditions than Massey's, also conceives the global and the local as intertwined places and processes. In other words, a focus on the local in the context of globalization is not just a romantic reaction to the perceived loss of the same, but is a real acknowledgment of the ways that the two are linked.[42]

In the case of New York, for example, the city is not just a conglomeration of the "poor, tired, huddled masses" immigrating to and living there; it is also a center of world finance and policy that is in large part responsible for creating the global conditions (at other local places) that make migration an economic necessity. That is, what is commonly simplified as global versus local is in actuality coexistence, or as Massey puts it, "Places are meeting-places of multiple trajectories whose material co-presence has to be negotiated."[43] The view from Eiko and Koma's window before 9/11 made this connection among the globalization of capital, the migration of people, and the local perfectly clear, even if the Statue of Liberty did stand on its own island in New York harbor, separated from the World Trade Center and the island of Manhattan by a confluence of flowing waterways.

If, as Massey says, place must be negotiated, then Eiko & Koma's choreography provides one possible model for doing so. The dancers treat the sites of their performances as key partners alongside the sets and other technologies they introduce to the parks (lighting, sound, etc.). This choreographic move suggests that it is not merely the dancing bodies that are significant. Nor is it simply, as some theories of globalization would suggest, movement of capital or goods that expands or contracts space. It is more the process of bodies forming relationships with sites, cities, and nation-states that forges the meaning of a place. Massey identifies this as a "reciprocity of multiplicity between the identity of place and the identities of multiply placed people."[44] In Eiko & Koma's case, for example, the dancers have deep roots in New York City. They have raised a family in the city and consider themselves New Yorkers. Yet at the same time they maintain their Japanese citizenship, returning to Japan two or three times each year. Following Massey's logic, Eiko & Koma bring their worlds/spaces with them. In a sort of translocal move, they can be said to have brought Hiroshima and Nagasaki, and later Trinity, New Mexico, and Fukushima, with them to New York, a fact they make tangible through their dances.

Choreographing Acts of Reparation

I argue that Eiko & Koma's contribution to reparation is the unique way their reparative acts are predicated on the convergence of multiple sites, bodies, and histories. In other words, the pairing of nonspecific narratives with specific sites and bodies in their dances allows various histories from different times and places to be brought into corporeal relationship with one another. The work of these dances opens up spaces that are transnational yet local and intimate, where performers and audience members alike may work through these histories.

Across their body of work, Eiko & Koma have provided a variety of techniques for performing reparation. In *Offering* they propose the possibility of emerging from crisis as a parallel and cooperative process that can bring together different histories. In what follows, I examine other dances from their body of work: *Event Fission*, *Land*, *Raven*, *Fragile*, and a pair of solo projects by Eiko. This collection of work proposes different ways of shifting from prolonged mourning into possibilities for reparation, including moving from attack to surrender, addressing past wrongs by finding ways to relate to others who have gone through similar experiences, and issuing a joint warning.

Eiko & Koma nearly forgot their 1980 performance, *Event Fission*, until 9/11 reminded them of their own modest attack on the Twin Towers. The *Event* was a site-specific version of their 1979 dance, *Fission*, on the Battery Park City landfill on the Hudson River at the southwestern edge of Manhattan.[45] In fact, the landfill at the site came from the excavation of land for the construction of the World Trade Center. More than two decades before 9/11, this part of Lower Manhattan was already "urban wasteland,"[46] a ground zero from the explosion of urban renewal. At one point in financial wrangling over the future Battery Park City site, the state actually agreed to condemn the landfill in a move that would allow it to take over the costs for the city.[47] The cycles of death and growth in Eiko & Koma's choreographic imaginary of New York could not be more resonant with the wtc: the detritus from the construction of the WTC site had to be condemned in order to be developed. Even the title, *Event Fission*, contains the sense of creating new life, as in biological fission when one cell becomes two, alongside the destructive potential of nuclear fission. Significantly, it is at this (much transformed) location that Eiko & Koma premiered *Offering* twenty-two years later.

Under the aegis of Creative Time's "Art on the Beach" program, *Event Fission* was performed on top of a sand dune and at its base, surrounded by four bonfires in the early evening. Covered in flour paste and fabric that cracks, flakes, and peels off them as if their skin were destroyed, Eiko & Koma here reject the aesthetic beauty of the smooth, white makeup that they typically wear in favor of a more frightening display of decay. Perched on high in profile, Eiko holds in her hands a long pole more than twice her own height. She sustains this still but alert pose until, with some effort, she raises the pole vertically overhead. Changing her facing, she brings the pole down with control, knees deeply bending until the pole and her thighbones are parallel to the ground. Eyes following the pole's angle, the gaze of both the audience and the performers is directed to the recent Lower Manhattan building boom, including the WTC Twin Towers, which at that time were less than a decade old and still stood as a contested symbol of capitalism rather than of the nationalist sentiment they now evoke in their absence.[48] As Eiko places the point of the pole on the sand, she quickly unwraps a white fabric from around her torso and adjusts her grip on the implement so that it now looks like a jousting lance or a vaulter's pole. Her body held at rigid attention like a pole vaulter gathering energy for her sprint, muscles taught yet ready, Eiko lifts her leg from the thigh, foot flexed, and sends it firmly into the ground in a bent-kneed stamp that, although unheard in this outdoor setting, seems to reverberate through the ground. Stomping her foot again, in a manner reminiscent of a sumo wrestler's *shiko* stamp, Eiko picks up speed and begins a flat-footed, bent-knee run away from the audience in the direction of the skyscrapers, white fabric billowing around and behind her torso. Will she attempt to sail over the Twin Towers in a world-record-setting vault? Or will she charge with her lance at the windmills of global capital? After running about fifty yards, our postmodern Quixote abruptly stops, awkwardly changes her grip on the pole, and charges back toward whence she came.

Waiting in her starting position is Koma, who marks time with a more restrained, nontraveling version of Eiko's runs. Eiko drives the pole in slow motion directly into Koma's torso and pushes him firmly yet gradually into a crouching position as she engages in a sort of reverse flag raising; the fabric that had previously been wrapped around her body has been revealed as a large white flag that now is driven into the ground. Koma extricates himself from the pole, and together the two flip the pole around and plant their white flag of surrender in the sands of lower Manhattan, counterbalancing their bodies against each other and the flag. In perhaps the most overtly political gesture of their entire repertoire, Eiko turns and raises her fist in the direction of the skyscrapers (see figure 6.2). Flag planted, the dancers begin to move in concert, stiffly, seemingly able to tilt only at the hips. A repeated rocking-horse movement slowly builds momentum and takes them to the edge of the dune, where they tumble down, kicking up sand as they roll downward toward the bonfires. Having reached the bottom of the dune, they descend even further into a predug pit, disappearing from the firelight and the view of the audience.

Certainly *Event Fission* is easily read as two naïve Japanese dancers, former student protestors at that, tilting at the windmills of American capitalism and global finance. In fact, this performance would seem to contradict the noncontestatory nature of reparative acts. But closer examination of the use of the white flag of surrender suggests that Eiko's solo head-on charge of the Twin Towers was not meant to succeed. Indeed, turning around, meeting Koma, struggling to negotiate a partnership, and then together planting their joint statement of surrender, they offer an alternative for how to strategically deal with an ongoing crisis. They choreograph a plan to attack by yielding. The image of them tumbling down the dunes and disappearing into a hole, then, is not a "fall" in the sense of a fall from grace, nor a collapse of ideals, but a joining with the audience that already stands watch below. The fires are watch fires, but also a symbol of renewal, of the creativity of destruction. What new thing will grow on this spot, this ground zero in reverse, this land(fill) created from nothing? After 9/11 the documentation of this site-specific performance took on a new significance: Eiko & Koma with their white flag are the ones who survived, not the seemingly unassailable towers.[49]

Midway between *Event Fission* and 9/11, Eiko & Koma choreographed *Land* (1991), a collaboration with Native American musician Robert

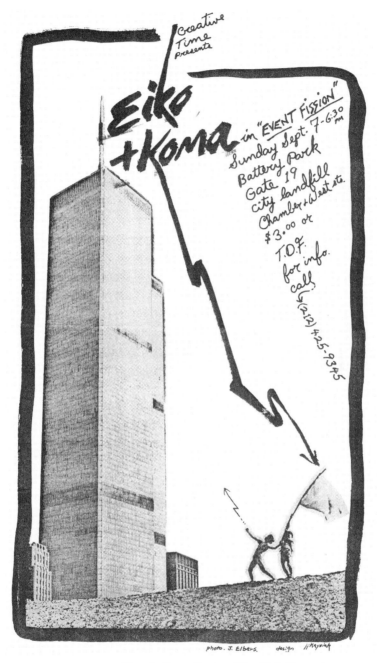

FIGURE 6.2 *Flyer for* Event Fission, *New York City, 1980.*
Courtesy of Eiko & Koma.

Mirabal, a lifelong resident of the Taos Pueblo. As part of the process of creating the piece, Eiko & Koma visited Mirabal in New Mexico, and the three artists then traveled together to Hiroshima, both places mutually implicated in a nuclear age.[50] *Land* thus connects the United States and Japan through the physical sites of Hiroshima, Nagasaki, and Trinity — the location in southern New Mexico where nuclear weapons technology was tested prior to being deployed on Japan. In the evening-length dance, Mirabal and a second Native American musician (alternately Reynaldo Lujan or Ben Sandoval) join Eiko & Koma on a stage covered with a canvas created by artist Sandra Lerner that echoes the colors and shapes of the desert: sand, rock, and minerals are evoked in the colors and textures of the massive painting. A buffalo head imposingly stands watch. Beginning lying curled on their sides, facing away from one another, Eiko & Koma slowly draw closer by minutely opening and lengthening their bodies until they meet, back to back. One lying atop the other, the pair then crawls downstage at the pace of a desert tortoise, only to later retreat back upstage side by side. Eiko & Koma's minimal movements keep them connected to the ground, and to each other, for the duration of the piece. They seem to not be able to move except in cooperation with one another. Unlike in modern or postmodern dance, in which exploitation of the entire space is imperative, Eiko & Koma use only a small part of the deep set, as if to imply that their bodies, while materially linked to the land, cannot and perhaps should not occupy it all. Meanwhile Mirabal, accompanied by Sandoval or Lujan, establishes a ritual space by playing music derived from ceremonial traditions of the Taos Pueblo. He and his fellow musician walk the depth of the stage playing the flute and drum. This choreography of dancers and musicians suggests a relationship between the two pairs, despite the fact that they seem to function in different realms.

Land, then, constructs a transnational space that asks how Japanese, Japanese Americans, and Native Americans can act in solidarity with one another, calling attention to the fact — surely no coincidence — that New Mexico and other southwestern lands celebrated in this dance were considered by the American government to be useless, and therefore to be equally useful for containing Native Americans on reservations, interning Japanese Americans, and testing nuclear devices with the intent of using them on Japan. Persistent inequities, however, mean that interned Japanese Americans received reparations from the American government as part of the Civil Liberties Act of 1988, but reparations for Native Americans have not been forthcoming. *Land* presents these multiple meanings and inequities together on one stage, holding them together without attempting to resolve them. Yet as we saw in *Offering*, even bringing these histories together on one stage is a reparative act, acknowledging past wrongs and suggesting possible ways of moving forward in parallel.

Eiko & Koma revisited *Land* through *Raven* (2010). Unlike the vast, still, but life-filled setting of *Land*, the twenty-five-minute-long *Raven* is centered in a postapocalyptic set of scorched canvases lined with straw and dotted with piles of black feathers. Mirabal's ceremonial-style drumming and singing initiate a ritual space, although in this burnt-out landscape—a nameless "ground zero"—images of physical struggle abound. When the lights come up on a prone Eiko, there is a strong impression that this is a dance that has been going on for a long time. Her efforts find her repeatedly splayed, joints jutting at awkward angles. When Koma joins her onstage, his stuttering walk evokes an injured animal. The performers seem to have survived, just barely, sure destruction. Their interactions are halting and sometimes brutal attempts at connection that result in sudden collapses or awkward embraces. Roles of aggressor and victim constantly shift, and Eiko & Koma flail about the space as if disoriented or uprooted. And yet the dancers determinedly mobilize exhausted limbs through familiar patterns as if compelled by some unspoken responsibility. Even when they tumble to the ground they cannot—perhaps will not—permit themselves to rest. Buoyed by the urgency of Mirabal's sound track, they press on. Even images drawn directly from *Land*—including *Raven*'s final pose of the two dancers lying head to head, bodies curled toward the audience—twitch with a nervous energy not evident in the original. If the 1991 dance was a rehearsal of Native American and Japanese solidarity, the 2010 version is a desperate joint cry of warning, characterized by Mirabal's drumming, which crescendos to a decisive boom. A raven, after all, is a symbol of a portent, a messenger. Can anyone hear them? Sometimes the frustration and longing for reparation take on an urgent note.

On March 11, 2011, less than a year after the premiere of *Raven*, a massive earthquake struck off the eastern coast of Japan's Tohoku province, triggering a devastating tsunami. In addition to killing tens of thousands of people and destroying hundreds of thousands of buildings, the tsunami caused major damage to reactors at the Fukushima Daiichi Nuclear Power Plant, including a meltdown in three of the six reactors. Fukushima was the most significant nuclear incident since Chernobyl in 1986, raising nuclear fears in Japan and around the world. Though Eiko & Koma have typically eschewed direct references to world events in their work, the Fukushima Daiichi disaster has resonated through their work in the years since 2011.

Fragile (2012) adapts *Raven*'s burnt-out desert landscape as an intimate environment for a four-hour durational collaboration with Kronos Quartet. The string players sit in startling proximity to Eiko & Koma, whose micromovements keep them grounded in a small nest of feathers.[51] Over and over again Eiko & Koma reach toward each other with heads, hands, limbs, as if seeking comfort and connection at the end of the world. The musicians both share the stage with the dancers and complete a circle with the audience. In addition to the live accompaniment, David Harrington of Kronos created a sound score of recorded audio about the atomic bomb, Hiroshima and Nagasaki, and Fukushima Daiichi. In *Fragile*, *Raven*'s earlier warning takes on a specificity previously absent from Eiko & Koma's repertoire. Though Eiko insisted to me that the recorded audio was entirely Harrington's contribution and expressed her opinion that it was "too obvious,"[52] I cannot help but observe that his linkage between the atomic bombing of Japan and the nuclear power plant disaster makes explicit the temporal and spatial connections already implicit in Eiko & Koma's work.

Explicit connections across time and space continue in Eiko's 2014 photographic collaboration with William Johnston, *A Body in Fukushima*, and her solo performance project that same year, *A Body in a Station*, both of which premiered in Philadelphia.[53] Eiko and Johnston, a photographer and Wesleyan University professor of Japanese history with whom Eiko has cotaught classes about the nuclear bomb, traveled to Tohoku on two separate occasions to visit abandoned train stations in the swath of lands evacuated due to radioactive contamination. Johnston's large-scale digital prints show Eiko dancing amid the jumbled contents of a still-standing house, on train tracks almost obscured by lush ivy (see figure 6.3), and on empty roads with the now-calm ocean and inoperative Daiichi plant in the background. In many of the photos,

FIGURE 6.3 *Eiko in Fukushima, Japan, July 2014.*
Photo: © William Johnston and Eiko Otake.

Eiko carries with her a Japanese futon and an expanse of red fabric, items which, along with Eiko's body, provide points of connection between the abandoned Fukushima stations and her performances in the bustling Philadelphia Amtrak station. In the program notes Eiko writes, "I want my body to be a conduit that connects the grandeur of 30th Street Station to the desolation of the abandoned stations in Fukushima, as well as the station and the museum gallery. Through a body, memory, and imagination, distance is malleable."[54] By corporeally working through the crisis of nuclear meltdown and bringing evidence of that process in the form of her body, the cloth and futon, and the photographs, into a place ostensibly untouched by the crisis, Eiko suggests that reparative acts must be performed well beyond the time and place of loss.

Conclusion

Across the span of Eiko & Koma's body of work, the choreographers have created dances that combine a specificity of sites with nonspecific narratives in a way that is capable of connecting a unique event like 9/11 to other cycles of death and new life. In these dances there are no towers and no bombs, only bodies—bodies that struggle, stab, push away, pull closer, awkwardly caress, collapse, and recover. These are bodies that take tender care of one another, bodies that persist. While their choreography leaves room for audience members to bring their own experiences to bear, Eiko & Koma's strategic collaborations with a Native American musician and a South Asian American dancer — at times and places where such identities and allegiances hold increased significance — serve to create a transnational Asian American space in which the ground zeroes of the Trinity and other American Southwest test sites, Hiroshima and Naga-saki, and New York City may be critically linked. Eiko's most recent work expands the space to include sites of nuclear accidents. Through dances like *Offering, Event Fission, Land, Raven, Fragile,* and *A Body in a Station,* Eiko & Koma offer this critical transnational space to their audiences, in-viting others to participate in their reparative acts.

CHAPTER 7

"*T*AKE ME TO YOUR HEART"

INTERCULTURAL ALLIANCES

———————————————

Cambodian Stories (2006) features Eiko & Koma alongside teenage and young adult painters from the Art School at the Reyum Institute of Arts and Culture in Phnom Penh.[1] Subtitled *An Offering of Painting and Dance*, the piece was performed on dirt-covered proscenium stages bordered with paintings created by Reyum students that served as both backdrop and wings.[2] Developed over a two-year period through a series of residencies and workshops in Phnom Penh, the hour-long dance stands out in Eiko & Koma's repertoire for the sheer number of bodies onstage; most of their pieces are choreographed for the duo alone. The piece opens with a series of spoken introductions followed by the first of two action paintings created live onstage and an initial unison dance by the entire cast. Peace and Charian, two featured Cambodian performers, then dance a duet that will later be echoed by Eiko & Koma.[3] From this point, Charian becomes the main focus of the piece as she collapses, is mourned, and then is revived as the other Reyum members create a second live painting on the backdrop. The piece ends with the entire cast once again moving in unison.

Though Eiko & Koma have often collaborated with other artists and musicians, *Cambodian Stories* evidences a particular understanding of interculturalism as a process of exchange centered in interdisciplinarity and intergenerational labor. This might not have developed as a choreographic concern for the pair had Reyum's cofounder, Daravuth Ly, not invited Eiko & Koma to do a residency in Phnom Penh after seeing *Offering* in New York. The subsequent month-long residency in 2004 led to Eiko & Koma's decision to pursue a longer-term project with the students.

The type of interculturalism staged in *Cambodian Stories* was not just a result of Eiko & Koma's choreographic decisions, but rather was inherent in Reyum itself. Ly was born in Cambodia, spent time in a refugee camp in Thailand in the post-Khmer Rouge era, and immigrated to France at age fourteen in 1983. He returned to Cambodia as an adult and started Reyum with Ingrid Muan in Phnom Penh in 1998 as a storefront gallery space to feature rotating exhibitions by contemporary Cambodian artists. Three years later they added a free art school for young people ages ten to twenty-five to supplement the half-day of schooling then provided by the government. Located across from the Royal University of Fine Arts and the National Museum of Cambodia in downtown Phnom Penh, Reyum places itself quite literally at the nexus of knowledge formation and preservation. In the wake of the devastating Khmer Rouge regime, during which many traditional artists were either forced into exile or killed, much of the recent focus in Cambodia has been on reviving and preserving traditional art forms.[4] By contrast, Reyum teaches students traditional art while also emphasizing contemporary practices. The school moreover provides the students with tools and opportunities to become working artists, including providing studio space to work on commissioned pieces and scholarships for further education.

While Reyum is explicitly dedicated to Cambodian arts and cultures, the "Cambodia" Reyum references necessarily exceeds national borders, formed as it is through emigration and return and postwar diasporic networks. Ly, like many Cambodian artists, returned to the country as an adult, while maintaining contacts and relationships in Europe and the United States. Accordingly, the founders — including the US national Muan — conceptualized Reyum as "a space of encounter for [Cambodian] students, professors, townspeople and foreign visitors."[5] In fact, many of the funders underwriting the Institute and School are European and American.

These physical and conceptual spaces of Reyum provide rich material for considering ideas of culture and exchange. The strong focus on the education of young people emphasizes the importance of intergenerational mentorship in the development of culture through the passing on of skills and knowledge and the availability of career opportunities. Moreover, Cambodian culture is understood as constructed through transnational circuits of exile and return, the influx of resources, and increasingly, the circulation of Reyum members and art out of Cambodia across Asia and beyond. In this way Reyum, and indeed even Cambodia, are already intercultural. In that context, *Cambodian Stories* is not so much an intercultural experiment as it is an engagement with issues already at stake for the painters.[6]

Cambodian Stories propounds an interculturalism less concerned with a spectacular final product than with showing the process of forging relationships, specifically relationships among Asians of different cultural backgrounds living at home and in diaspora. After all, Homi Bhabha has persuasively argued that "it is the 'inter' — the cutting edge of translation and negotiation, the inbetween space — that carries the burden of the meaning of culture."[7] Moreover, the dance suggests intercultural alliances may be forged onstage based on cultural commonalities even as personal histories retain their specificity. I specifically employ the word alliance here to convey a strategic, self-reflexive approach that is sometimes absent from projects described as intercultural exchange or interculturalism. I begin this chapter with a close reading of *Cambodian Stories* that unpacks this particular intercultural alliance grounded in interdisciplinarity and intergenerational links. I then compare Eiko & Koma's choreography of intercultural alliance with selected examples from the history of intercultural performance in order to tease out what intercultural alliances make possible. This discussion involves consideration of how we may further complicate the already complex debate on intercultural performance to move beyond dichotomies of East/West and traditional/modern to view agency in nonhegemonic practices and to engage in collaborations (e.g., south-south, north-south, regional, etc.) that challenge existing binaries. I then consider Eiko & Koma's collaboration with Anna Halprin, *Be With* (2000), before turning to a suite of post–*Cambodian Stories* performances created with Charian and Peace, including *Cambodian Stories Revisited* (2007), *Quartet* (2007), the revival of *Grain* (1983/2007), and *Hunger* (2008), to demonstrate how Eiko & Koma continued choreographing these issues. The chapter concludes with a consideration of the impact of intercultural alliances on Eiko & Koma's subsequent work, including their three-year Retrospective Project (2009–2012).

Cambodian Stories: An Offering of Painting and Dance

The first thing the audience notices when entering the theater is a massive canvas painted red at the front of the stage, flanked by floor-to-ceiling paintings of stylized Cambodian women, with bare breasts stage left and a cloth draped over their shoulders stage right.[8] The paintings, created by the students at Reyum, double as wings. The women depicted there reference the hand gestures of Cambodian dance, but do not take the form of traditional depictions of Cambodian dancers, eschewing the formal grandeur of headdresses and accessories in favor of simple bracelets and colorful clothing. This first impression draws attention to the piece's subtitle — *An Offering of Painting and Dance* — and signals that painting will play a key role in the performance alongside live dancing bodies.

As *Cambodian Stories* begins, seven young men dressed in bright yellow sarongs enter the stage one by one and stand facing away from the audience in front of the red canvas.[9] An eighth young man, Setpeap "Peace" Sorn, enters, distinguished from the others by his salmon-colored sarong, and proceeds to paint the backs of the others, brushing glistening water onto their backs with two deliberate strokes that lend a ceremonial air to his actions. Painting, then, is established as primary in these *Stories*, a fact underscored by the young men's self-introductions; each young man faces the audience in turn and in strongly accented English sketches his story: "My name is, I am this old, I have this many siblings, my parents are living or dead, in my free time I like to . . . ." The stories end in the common refrain: "In my future, I want to be an artist."

Following their spoken introductions, the young men pull down the red canvas with a dramatic flourish, revealing a stage covered in sandy soil and a blank canvas lying center stage like an island in a sea of dirt. The young men exit briefly, soon returning with portable scaffolding they place over the white canvas. Draping themselves over the scaffolding, they busy themselves painting. No sooner has the stage been transformed into a painting studio than Chakrya "Charian" So, the only female member of the Reyum collective, dances onto the stage with a striking and stately walk, arms outstretched, wrists flexed up, head in profile. When she reaches center stage, she turns her head to face the audience, states her name, and says, "When I dance I imagine I am walking in water. Sometimes I am a flower or a fish. In my future, I want to be an artist."[10] As she completes her cross-stage journey, the young men, seemingly oblivious to her presence, lift their painting until it is suspended midair from wires, revealing a woman in a pose that echoes Charian's. Immediately after the first action painting is revealed, the entire cast enters with Charian's slow walk, perambulating the painting, singing along to Preap Sovath's "Take

Me to Your Heart," which was popular throughout East and Southeast Asia.[11] The transposition of Charian's movement first onto the painting and then onto the bodies of the entire cast establishes a shared stance — across generations and genres — that becomes the basis on which the rest of *Cambodian Stories* is built. These first twelve minutes of the piece are rich with implications about the interdisciplinary relationships between painting and live dancing bodies and between the roles of painter and dancer, roles in which gender is also implicated.

Until Charian's entrance, gender has been divided between the live presence of the young Cambodian men and the two-dimensional, larger-than-life paintings of women that frame the stage. Males are presented as producers of art, while women are seen only as objects of a masculine artistic practice.[12] Furthermore, the young men have been established as individual subjects, whereas the paintings stand as essentialized symbols of femininity: exotic, traditional Cambodian women who at the same time symbolize the universal mother/goddess/eternal beauty/nurturer.[13] This division in gender roles would seem to confirm theories of a dominant male gaze, of which females are the object.[14]

The active male/passive female divide is complicated, though not resolved, with the arrival of Charian onstage. Charian's role is distinguished from that of her male colleagues in a number of ways. Interestingly, gender in *Cambodian Stories* does not seem to be constructed through the dance vocabulary itself; all of the performers use the same movement vocabulary throughout the piece. Members of Reyum paint; Eiko & Koma do not. Instead, gender is constructed in this dance through specific choreographic decisions. For example, Charian does not enter with the other members of the Reyum Painting Collective at the beginning of *Cambodian Stories*, but instead enters alone while her colleagues paint. During her separate introduction, Charian maintains her dancerly stance, unlike her male colleagues, who stand and face the audience in a pedestrian manner. Furthermore, she defines herself not through the facts and figures listed by her fellow Reyum painters and also later by Eiko & Koma, but by her dancing state. This discrepancy in the content of introductions, while perhaps intended to underline Charian's central role in the dance, only serves to emphasize separate gender roles.[15] This is reinforced by other choreographic structures that spotlight female bodies, such as the way the (male) Painting Collective functions as a sort of recurring balletic corps, framing the soloist Charian; later in the piece, they fulfill the same role for Eiko. Charian is further set apart from the male painters by sartorial standards of chastity that clad her in a modest and formal floor-length, pink-sand-colored silk *sampot* topped with a long-sleeve blouse, while the shirtless young men wear brightly colored, casual sarongs. Her dress is also in sharp contrast to the bare-breasted women depicted in the painted wings.

When the male performers reveal the completed painting to the audience, one could read the painting as a representation that objectifies — quite literally — the female dancer, who, as we have seen, is multiply distinguished from her fellow painters.[16] In dance studies, however — and this is a key departure from a gaze theory centered on film — the corporeality of gendered performing bodies is the focus. Not only do we need to pay attention to what Charian's body is doing in relationship to the painting, but also to the bodies of the young men producing it. Have the painters conjured up Charian with their act of painting, or has her presence triggered them to paint, much like a muse? Or is there a dialogue at work between Charian's dancing and the action of painting? Eiko & Koma choreograph painting as a physical act, rather than merely a means to an end of producing an object. Eiko clarifies that this choreographic decision was both a practical and artistic one, saying, "We had to find a way to show [the] audience . . . that they are painters. Their bodies in the action of painting are beautiful as they move [purposefully] and collectively."[17] In fact, their movement while painting exhibits an awareness and exactitude that is distinct from their movement while dancing. With an emphasis on the process of making art, versus art as object, Charian could be seen as an agent rather than an object, her slow walk not merely a journey from point A to point B, but a knowledge-producing passage that participates in a cocreation of the art. The simultaneity of the two actions precludes a simple causal relationship; rather, the actions of painting and dancing are mutually generative. Assuming that choreography "elaborates a theory, not only of gendered corporeal identity but also of relations among gendered bodies,"[18] we cannot look only at isolated images of gendered bodies — whether two- or three-dimensional — without placing them in the context of their relationships within the piece. If we choose to see Charian as a member of the painting collective — and she does finally paint later in the piece — we can shift our view of her from being an object of the young men's painting to being in alliance with the other bodies (who are admittedly predominantly male) onstage.

Following the unison circling, the young performers exit with the painting, and Eiko & Koma come to stand side by side center stage. Eiko projects: "My name is Eiko Otake. I was 19 years old when I first started dancing. Now I am 57 years old. I am an artist." Koma begins his own introduction in Japanese before switching to English: "*Watashi no namae wa Koma desu.* My name is Koma. I am 60 years old. I left my country Japan when I was 22 years old. I am an artist, and I want to continue to be an artist." At that moment, Eiko & Koma are both older versions of the young painters occupying the same space in time, as well as mentors showing the Reyum Painting Collective that their hopes for their lives are possible. These facts are reinforced through the middle section of *Cambodian Stories*, in which all eleven performers once again dance together in a flowing stream. Solos, duets, and groups form and dissolve as dancers enter and leave the stage. The young painters are no longer specific entities with particular dreams and goals, but rather indeterminate bodies searching and yearning with outstretched arms and open chests. Eiko & Koma appear sometimes as parents or teachers to the painters' children, gently leading them or appearing to guide their movement, only to send them on their way. At other times the choreographers appear as older versions of the same people, as when they speak as artists who have achieved the young painters' uttered dreams. Though they encounter each other in pairs or groups, the elder dancers evidence a responsibility for the younger ones, gently leading them by the hand, supporting their body weight, or setting them on a path before letting them go (see figure 7.1).

The section ends with a duet by Charian and Peace to the recurrent Cambodian pop song. Their tension-filled bodies suffuse the stage as they separate on the diagonal, reaching in unison toward some distant goal. Arms outstretched finally toward one another, Peace and Charian briefly, chastely connect—palms, cheeks, shoulders—only to separate once again. Peace exits the stage; Charian falls to the floor, and the side wings follow suit, slowly crumpling to the ground. The earlier doubling of stance between dancers and painting has now further developed into a kinesthetic relationship between the two. I argue that more than a case

FIGURE 7.1 *Eiko and Sok Than in* Cambodian Stories *(rehearsal),*
Novel Hall, Taipei, Taiwan, 2009. One of the side wings painted by
students of the Reyum Art School is partially visible behind them.
Photo by the author.

of mimicry, Eiko & Koma have choreographed an interdisciplinary alliance in which the movement of paintings in coordinated action with
Charian both reinforces and amplifies her collapse. On her own, her fall
might read as an individual breakdown or death. Performed synchro-
nously with eight large paintings, however, this individual collapse resonates on a larger societal scale: the destruction of Cambodia under Pol
Pot, the threatened loss of Khmer culture, the crumbling walls of Angkor Wat, and the pressures of conforming to traditional expectations of
womanhood in contemporary society are all brought to mind.

After the joint collapse of Charian and the wing paintings, two young
men lay out her lifeless body center stage. Eiko and Koma approach one
by one and struggle to make sense of Charian's state. Eiko hovers over

her like a protective and grief-stricken mother, while Koma lurches forward in desperation. It is a familiar trope in the pair's work: one dancer suffers injury or death — often at the hands of the other — while the other alternates among caretaking, remorse, and mourning. In a body of work that tackles broad, elemental concepts, large-scale violence seems to be embodied in the most personal and intimate of ways. In the case of *Cambodian Stories*, Eiko & Koma both take on the roles of the caretaker and mourner. At the same time that they stage themselves as mentors to the Reyum members, they also embody the parents whom the Cambodian performers have lost, ancestors, or the war dead. One loss particularly fresh on the minds of all the performers was of Reyum cofounder Muan, who was a mother figure to many of the students. Muan passed away suddenly at the age of forty while Koma was in Phnom Penh working with the Reyum students, rocking the tight-knit school and prompting Eiko & Koma and the Reyum Painting Collective to dedicate the piece to her memory.

Yet even as the mourning occurs — for Muan and for the symbolic death in the dance — the remaining Cambodians engage in an act of creation: they paint a massive portrait of Charian in her death pose on the backdrop of the stage. Charian's location at the center of the stage places her at the nexus of dancing and painting, mourning and creation. This powerful channel awakens her; whether she is now a ghost herself or is actually reborn does not seem to be the point. Instead, the dancing and painting appear to offer a way to make the unspoken past visible and perhaps even make living possible. The tools of representation become the means of imagining, remembering, and narrating the past in the present, and through the past, the future.[19] In fact, many of the painters told me that the process of developing and performing *Cambodian Stories* allowed them to speak to their families for the first time about the Khmer Rouge and the post–Khmer Rouge war that ended in 1993. They told me that when they perform, they are not alone onstage, but are joined by family members both living and dead.[20] Invoked in the young people's introductions at the beginning of the dance, these family members seem to rise with Charian and then materialize in the larger-than-life painting.[21]

As Eiko & Koma dance together for the first time in the piece, echoing the earlier duet by Charian and Peace, Charian herself steps up to the canvas for the first time, furiously painting a luminescent full moon over the woman in repose. Charian's rebirth in the dance, catalyzed by the collective, becomes a determined decision to continue to create in the face of inexplicable loss — whether personal, as in Reyum's loss of Muan, or national, as in Cambodia's devastation in the wake of decades of war. Charian's multivalent body takes on the trope of woman as nation and nation as motherland at the same time that she comes to stand for the particular mothers and mother figures missing from the young painters' lives.[22]

Near the end of the piece, Charian and Peace join Eiko and Koma in a quartet center stage while the rest of the young men put the finishing touches on the large backdrop before joining the dance. The white makeup covering Eiko & Koma's faces and arms stands in counterpoint to the paint splatters on the bare hands, arms, and torsos of the Reyum dancers. Each wears a marker of their art, their culture: painters' bodies, covered in paint; dancers wearing white makeup.[23] But the elder dancers are no longer helpers and mentors to the younger ones. Roles are now reversed, blurred, shared. While the piece began with the assertion of individual identities and a separation of painting and dance, it ends in simple unison: surrounded by revived though askew wing canvases and the massive freshly painted backdrop, the eleven dancers form three columns, sink to their knees in the dirt, and bow. At the beginning of *Cambodian Stories*, the young painters' introductions ask if becoming an artist is even possible in this situation, while Eiko & Koma's introductions answer a resounding "yes!" The arc of the entire performance suggests that the future is now, and that with Eiko & Koma's mentorship the young people have already become artists.

Interdisciplinarity and Intergenerational Relationships

The intercultural work of *Cambodian Stories* is concentrated in a staged interdisciplinarity of painting and dance that is reinforced by intergenerational roles of mentor and student. Whereas interdisciplinarity is often shorthand for "pulling a bit from here, here, and here," Eiko & Koma choreograph the encounter between painting and dance — and on a larger scale among Cambodia, Japan, and the United States — as a presentation and exchange of painting and dancing skills. This shifting interdisciplinarity is often linked onstage to the various corporeal modalities exhibited by the performers, who alternate among pedestrian gestures (walking, standing, speaking), functional activities (carrying, lifting, sweeping, brushing, bending), and a dance vocabulary that develops seemingly simple movements (reaching, twisting, arching) over time. All of the performers engage in pedestrian movements and sections of unison and collective dancing, while it is predominantly the young men who engage in functional activities that in the piece are associated with painting. Eiko & Koma do not paint, while the one young woman, Charian, bridges the two groups with her featured dance role throughout the piece and an act of painting that completes the second action painting at the climax of the dance. Whereas at the beginning of the piece each of these different movement vocabularies—and associated groups of people—is featured independently, they gradually begin to overlap and then blend so that by the end of the piece the actions and performers segue and coalesce with one another.

For example, at first the large painted wings seem to serve as decorative backdrops for the choreography, inviting a comparison of the live, dancing bodies with the stylized bodies in the paintings and suggesting that the stories being told hold in tension the traditional and the contemporary, the corporeal and the inanimate. As the piece progresses, however, the relationship between the two becomes more complex than one of action and its setting or a straightforward juxtaposition of static and live art forms. This is seen in the way the performers touch and interact with the paintings as if they were a corporeal presence; lower and raise the paintings to initiate a kinesthetic connection among the canvases and human bodies; and create two action paintings that demonstrate that the painting is not a mere representation of the dance, nor is the dance a simple enactment of the painting. Instead, *Cambodian Stories* posits a mutually generative relationship across these two disciplines that has profound implications for the stories told by the piece, in which the performers share experiences of violence, loss, and remembrance in order to strengthen their relationship with one another.

The interdisciplinarity of arts parallels the intergenerational bodies onstage: Eiko & Koma are middle-aged, established artists; members of Reyum are teenaged and young adult art students. When Eiko & Koma introduce themselves, the mentorship of the young Cambodian painters by the older Japanese American dancers is underscored. In fact, the young performers' status as students to the elder dancers' mentors is further emphasized through their various levels of proficiency with Eiko & Koma's movement style. Eiko & Koma's way of conceiving movement from familiar concepts and with no series of codified steps to learn means that it is possible for the choreographers to introduce untrained dancers to their style and within a relatively short period of time have them perform onstage with them. But that does not mean that the difference in training is not noticeable, or that it is insignificant. Various levels of dance proficiency in the piece draw attention to the generational difference among the performing bodies. At the same time, however, with multiple movement modalities sharing the stage in *Cambodian Stories*, the bodies less experienced in one form are also shown to be skilled in another.

Because the Reyum painters were not experienced dancers, painting was the point of departure for their rehearsals with Koma. Dance training for most of the Reyum students consisted solely of the Delicious Movement Workshops Eiko & Koma conducted when they were in residence at the Reyum Art School for a month in 2004. When Eiko & Koma decided to initiate a long-term project that led to *Cambodian Stories*, training the nine volunteers had to be a significant aspect of the development of the piece, a process documented in the short video *The Making of Cambodian Stories* (2005). Certainly the act of painting itself became a way of generating movement. Eiko believes that the art students' extensive experience in painting traditional Cambodian figures, many of which depict dancers, offered them a unique approach to visualizing bodies.[24] Koma asked the young people to investigate movement by literally dancing with their paintings. In rehearsal he had them lay their canvases on the ground and dance on top of them in both a standing and a reclined position. The painters also practiced dancing next to and up against canvases that were hung on the wall, a process that is visible in the middle section of the dance as the young men stand in front of the canvas wings and run their hands over them, as if feeling the texture of a temple wall. The opening scene from *The Making of Cambodian Stories* shows the painter/dancer Peace at Angkor Wat looking at, touching, and dancing with the bas-relief that covers the temple's surfaces. The image of Peace engaging with the three-dimensionality of the sculpture suggests that the collective was asked to approach both the painting of bodies and dancing as haptic experiences. In contrast, Eiko & Koma themselves have often used large-scale canvases as backdrops or as a dancing surface, the difference being that the canvases were not a source of movement for them, but a way of establishing the site of the performance.

The staged interdisciplinarity also marks out the parallels in the lives of Eiko & Koma and the Reyum Collective. The similarities among the young painters and elder dancers are gestured to in the introductions, although it is largely left to the audience to fill in the connections and historical parallels between Japan and Cambodia and their own connections to those two histories. Eiko & Koma were born just a few years after World War II ended with the atomic bombing of Japan, while the members of the Reyum Painting Collective, aged sixteen to twenty-two at the time of the premiere of *Cambodian Stories*, were born within a decade of the fall of the Khmer Rouge at a time when civil war was still raging in their country. The shared experience of growing up in the shadow of devastation and war while imagining a new role for art and artists in the rebuilding of the society created a strong bond between Eiko & Koma and the war refugee Ly, and among the elder choreographers and the younger painters. A significant influence on the decision to initiate a long-term relationship with the students of Reyum beyond the initial month-long residency was how strongly the students reminded Eiko & Koma of themselves when they were younger.[25] And while Koma claims that they worked with the Reyum Painting Collective not because they are Cambodian, but because they are art students, he does admit that they share "a lot of common things: Asian-ness. Being Asian. That is a big asset."[26] Koma claims that shared day-to-day experiences, such as eating rice and sleeping on the floor, provided a common ground from which to relate to each other, especially when language barriers were an impediment to understanding. Of course, it is important to note that the histories of the Japanese-American dancers and the Cambodian painters are also linked by the Japanese occupation of Cambodia from 1941 to 1945, a fact noted neither by Koma nor by any critics who reviewed the piece.[27]

The performers in *Cambodian Stories* form an interdisciplinary relationship among dancing bodies and painting. This relationship is choreographed as a process of exchange, in which each participant offers up his or her strengths and skills as if to say, "Here's what we do. What do you do?" Each group contributes to the final product: the dancers bring what they have; the painters do the same. What is on view in the final product is the collection of all these conversations and exchanges, presented alongside one another, each retaining its own distinctiveness while revealing similarities. By choosing to work with painters, Eiko & Koma utilized the distinctiveness of the two mediums to underscore the differences between their own Japanese American culture and the Painting Collective's Cambodian culture. At the same time, the intergenerational aspect of their performance, rather than highlighting gaps, actually posits a bond between the two groups.

The combination of interdisciplinarity and intergenerational relationships in *Cambodian Stories* produces a new kind of interculturalism for the global stage, one that is not based solely on collaboration across difference, but that seeks to find a mutually generative relationship from within that difference. It is undeniable that the stakes of such intercultural performances are high: they have the ability to both replicate entrenched power structures and propose alternate modes of collaboration. Or, as Claire Conceison puts it, "Are such projects actually fostering understanding and cultural sharing or are they merely reifying existing hegemonic structures and painful misconceptions?"[28] Karen Shimakawa is even more pointed, cautioning that while "dance can comment upon socially-constructed identities (racial, sexual, able-bodied/disabled) by mining the tension between the body as object/text and body as subject/author[29].... [It] can also reiterate racist stereotypes by un-self-reflexively re-presenting culturally- and racially-marked gestures and images, on the one hand, or on the other hand, by erasing their cultural/racial specificities."[30] What's more, these risks and rewards of making and viewing intercultural dance that Shimakawa enunciates may operate on multiple levels. That is, there may be gaps in knowledge or experience between the performers and the audience that lead to missed signals or unintended interpretations.

The emphasis on relationship and process in *Cambodian Stories* is key in avoiding accusations of appropriation that have been at the center of intense disagreement about the goals and methods of interculturalism over the past three decades. It is not my intention here to rehearse the history of this extensive debate. However, I do want to briefly revisit two series of published exchanges to show how Eiko & Koma's choreography of intercultural alliance engages with ideas central to the discourse while at the same time offering a new model for entering into this kind of work.

One exchange, among Phillip Zarrilli, Avanthi Meduri, and Deborah Neff, centered on the aftermath of Peter Brook's trip to India to conduct research for his 1985 international production of the Indian epic *The Mahabharata*, for which the internationally noted theater director was accused variously of misrepresenting the Indian tale, interpersonal disrespect, and engaging in a one-way relationship.[31] Zarrilli, using the occasion to reflect on intercultural performance more broadly, declared accountability, power, and ethics to be key issues that must be grappled with by anyone working cross-culturally in the arts. I take "power" in this context to refer to issues of imperialism, Orientalism, (post)colonialism, globalization, and sociocultural flows that are necessarily implicated by the historical, political, and economic contexts of individuals and organizations working together across these many ruptures and links. Accountability and ethics point to personal and structural responsibilities that should be implicated with acts of cultural collaboration, appropriation, borrowing, and adaptation. For example, who determines the terms of the collaboration and who has the resources to engage in the work? All of these complex and overlapping issues are inextricably present in intercultural work and must be addressed.

The intercultural alliance between Eiko & Koma and the Reyum Painting Collective built through *Cambodian Stories* has a foundation in commonalities between the dancers and painters, but Eiko cautions, "We are all Asian, we are very strongly connected, but that does not work well unless we also know the differences."[32] Though their identification with each other is deep, it cannot be allowed to gloss over very real cultural and material circumstances that, for example, produce unequal access to resources. Eiko & Koma's years in New York and long-term success as artists gave them access to funders that allowed them to mobilize financial resources to support the project. The pair attempted to foreground these power differentials, normally glossed over or hidden altogether, by incorporating an appeal after the final bows explicitly asking viewers to support the Reyum Art School by purchasing art made by Reyum students and Cambodian crafts after performances or making a donation to Friends of Reyum.[33] Of course there is the danger that audiences will only see this move as a familiar form of arts patronage or support for education. Funding issues, for *Cambodian Stories* and for Reyum, are certainly complex and deserve further examination, although that is not my focus here. I mention the sale of paintings at performances because the way it is incorporated into the staging of the piece furthers the choreography of intercultural alliance.

As the exchange among Zarrilli, Meduri, and Neff reveals, however, approaches like this one are not the norm, nor are accountability, power, and ethics universally accepted terms under which intercultural work is initiated. Another formative printed debate, between Rustom Bharucha and Richard Schechner, lays bare the poles of the intercultural argument.[34] Those like Bharucha, who insist upon a stance much like the one I outlined above, take issue with those like Schechner, who propound theater practices that they believe to be both universalist and humanist and approach different traditions as sources of potential new techniques to add to the performer's toolkit.[35] Critics of the latter practices charge this sort of appropriative interculturalism with treating cultural forms foreign to them as "sources" that may be extracted and applied to a "target" culture, typically Western.

Subsequent scholarship has attempted to move beyond the sort of impasse signaled by the Bharucha-Schechner debate by complicating binaries (e.g., West/East, oppressor/oppressed) and calling for an attention to historical and cultural context. Some argue that a focus on modes of domination to the exclusion of the actions and agency of those considered to be dominated erases a more complicated picture, in the process inadvertently reifying the very dichotomies many scholars seek to undo. Others suggest that easy dichotomies based in geography are no longer tenable in an age of late capitalism and globalization, when power is no longer concentrated in particular locations but rather is distributed across the world (albeit not equally).[36] It seems to me that this so-called dispersal of the West (or perhaps more accurately of capital) could occasion a focus on the specificities of histories and locations, a process not possible under the polarity of a monolithic imaginary of "us versus them" that forecloses the possibility of seeing the particularities of the local.

Yet despite these attempts to construct a more complex framework for intercultural art production, a brand of interculturalism that reinforces a hierarchical relationship between the experimental and abstract West and the traditional East persists, as is evident in Jérôme Bel's internationally successful *Pichet Klunchun and Myself* (2005). In this performance, Bel choreographs an encounter between Thai dancer Klunchun and himself in the form of a staged conversation: laptop in hand, Bel questions Klunchun as he dances, taking notes like an anthropologist. Despite its apparent dialogic format, Bel maintains the (unmarked) position of authority: onstage it is he who holds the laptop, just as it is he who holds the power of self-determination in the title. (The dance is, after all, not called *Pichet Klunchun and Jérôme Bel*.) The dance presumes the possibility of cross-cultural understanding yet buttresses old colonialist and Orientalist assumptions about the Other.

Some see the key to breaking apart these enduring East/West dichotomies as a shift of focus to Asian regionalism, an idea that Bharucha has previously theorized as the intracultural.[37] One example of this is the Asian interculturalism of Ong Keng Sen, who, in his adaptation of *King Lear* for example, brings together the foremost proponents of traditional performance styles from Japan, China, Thailand, and Indonesia to adapt Shakespeare. The hybrid production foregrounds problems of translation and unknowability even as it responds to, reinforces, exceeds, and resists state and regional cultural policies and discourses. At the same time, as a global commodity it veers toward cultural tourism and spectacle. Of course global capital and its attendant implications are often inextricable from intercultural projects; even Eiko & Koma's modest (in comparison to Ong's TheatreWorks) production of *Cambodian Stories* was coproduced by the Asia Society along with Reyum and Inta, Inc., Eiko & Koma's official nonprofit entity. Founded in 1954 by John D. Rockefeller III, the Asia Society's mission demonstrates that the arts are never divisible from the economic interests of nation-states and corporations.[38] Moreover, the mediation of funders and presenters such as the Asia Society between Japanese American choreographers and Cambodian painters has the potential to, as Marta Savigliano describes in the case of the tango, replicate "previous Western mediations among exotics."[39] In other words, there is a danger that the Western discourse of the exoticism of the Other never goes away.

Can the problems raised by interculturalism ever really be solved? Is foregrounding the problems and staging the contradictions the best that can be done? It remains an open question, for example, whether refocusing away from mega-stars such as Brook and Ong and toward more "grassroots" productions might provide alternative ways forward for intercultural performance. This is not to romanticize the local or small-scale, but to admit that collaborations that rely on adaptation of another's culture on the one hand, or bringing together the most accomplished representative of each performance tradition on the other, foreclose the kind of alliances that I am concerned with here.

Intercultural Alliance and Asian American Cultural Politics

My intervention into the ongoing conundrum outlined above is to introduce Asian American cultural politics into the interculturalism debate.[40] In particular, I find it useful to think of the "culture" of interculturalism, in Lisa Lowe's sense, as a site where agency can be exercised and critique can emerge. That is, if we see history and politics and economics, for example, not as the context of cultural products and processes, but as things that are produced and processed by culture itself, we will have a different understanding of what intercultural alliances may contend with and achieve.

The implication of Asian American cultural politics for intercultural cultural productions is to move the consideration away from a product or a production to a process. While the term *intercultural collaboration* gestures to this focus, I invest in the term *alliance* in order to differentiate from earlier debates in which the term "collaboration" was embroiled. I am drawn particularly to the active sense of the word *alliance* in which different parties come together around a common goal. The way I use the term here embeds a politics in it, while also putting that politics in motion over time and in space, as in the emphasis on process I discussed above. Indeed, Karen Shimakawa exhorts scholars to examine the process of intercultural collaboration from inception to presentation alongside an intercultural "product" in order to fully grasp the work of the performance.[41] My notion of intercultural alliance encompasses both of these aspects: the process of coming together alongside the result of the relationship.

Through *Cambodian Stories* Eiko & Koma seek to create something new out of the encounter between Japanese American dancers and Cambodian painters, rather than replicating existing tropes. By choosing to work with painters, Eiko & Koma stage the distinctiveness of the two cultures through the differences between the mediums. In other words, the piece employs interdisciplinarity to demonstrate how artists may collaborate across national and cultural borders to create work that both allows the separate forms to shine while investigating their overlap: How do dancers paint the space? How is painting dance? All of the performers contributed to movement, music, sets, and text to create the collective and multiple stories presented onstage. Furthermore, while Eiko & Koma conceived and directed *Cambodian Stories*, they are "prominent but not dominant"[42] in the performance, in which the voices of the Reyum Painting Collective come through loud and clear, especially through their action paintings and massive sets.

Intercultural alliance, such as what I argue for Eiko & Koma's choreographic project, is a mode of artistic collaboration forged by artists working together across and through difference, in which that difference is neither disavowed nor exaggerated. It acknowledges and addresses the historical, political, and economic contexts of the parties taking part and recognizes that the alliance itself is a condition of and is conditioned by global capital and cultural flows. As a cultural critique, intercultural alliance exceeds the moment of performance with an attention to process that is often, but not always, evidenced in the final product.[43] While this mode of intercultural work aspires to steer clear of the problems that have plagued intercultural performances, it can and will fall short. The kind of work I outline here requires constant practice and reevaluation. When much of this work happens in rehearsal, however, is the audience left out of the alliance? In the next section I consider the relationship of the audience to *Cambodian Stories*, as represented by the writings of dance critics.

Intercultural Alliances with Audiences

Before the 2006 American tour of *Cambodian Stories* began, Reyum Institute founder Ly reflected, "I would be glad if this talk about Cambodia [through *Cambodian Stories*] in the way that it is not showing the flag, or talking about Angkor or the Khmer Rouge, if we achieve that goal—to show that Cambodia is different things and especially is young people's struggle—in a very subtle and emotional way, it would be a great reward."[44] What Ly seeks is a representation of Cambodia that moves beyond fixed historical perceptions or images of disaster to a complex portrayal of what it means to be a young person in that country today. Indeed, the stories told about Cambodia in the performance are ultimately personal and particular, even as they may resonate with larger national implications. The terse sentences of the Reyum Painting Collective's introductions, for example, contain loss and sorrow, especially in noting how many of the students have lost parents. Those deaths, and the historical and national implications thereof, are followed a few breaths later by the painters' aspirations for the future.

While *Cambodian Stories* was presented in several informal showings in Phnom Penh, official performances were only scheduled in the United States, making American audiences a further collaborator in the piece. Given the US role in the Cambodian civil war of the early 1970s and an extensive American bombing campaign, it would follow that American audiences might question their own role in and responsibilities to these *Cambodian Stories*. Many dance critics reviewing the piece mentioned the devastating reign of the Khmer Rouge and subsequent decades of continuing violence, though some only obliquely as "catastrophic destruction"[45] and "tremendous calamity."[46] I only found one review, however, that mentions Americans in relationship to Cambodian history, and that only to identify those who remember the war.[47] Not one of the dance critics considered what these particular *Cambodian Stories* might be saying to or asking of American audiences. Furthermore, the subtitle, *An Offering of Painting and Dance*, begs the question: To whom is the offering being made? The American audience? Cambodia today? Those killed during decades of brutal civil war enabled in some crucial ways by the US bombing of Cambodia? The critics all identified the offering as a type of rebirth or affirmation, but none questioned how or why an American audience might be implicated, revealing the deep-seated assumption in American society that "the world" unproblematically performs for us, as part of a benevolent relationship between the United States and other countries.[48]

Instead, critics lauding the piece focused their attention on the nine novice Cambodian performers who danced alongside the established choreographers. A reviewer for *danceviewtimes* wrote that Eiko & Koma taught dance to the young painters, "these boy-men," "purely, naturally, at the core primitively."[49] The *Chicago Sun Times* wrote that Charian, the young female soloist, "moves like a temple goddess" in this "Asian delicacy,"[50] while the *New York Times* refers to her "wild beauty."[51] Finally, the Asia Society, coproducer of the piece, refers on its Web site to "a forest of beautiful lithe bodies" onstage.[52] The shirtless young, brown, male bodies; the iconic young woman rendered larger than life; and a movement vocabulary full of searching and longing were easily translated by the reviewers — and likely by many audience members — into an objectification of the young performers that easily blended the Orientalist tropes of primitive or natural bodies with the trope of the alien civilization.

Compelled by Yutian Wong's insistence upon a *critical* attention to Orientalism,[53] I seek to acknowledge and challenge Orientalist readings of Eiko & Koma's work. How do Orientalism and its possible alternatives impact works like Eiko & Koma's *Cambodian Stories*? Can distinct and sometimes overlapping practices such as counter-Orientalisms,[54] self-Orientalizing,[55] and autoexoticism and exotic reciprocities[56] be strategic maneuvers of self-representation, or are they only proof of Orientalism as a ubiquitous and totalizing discourse? Returning to the choreography may be helpful to see how an Orientalist reading of *Cambodian Stories* eclipses the labor of the intercultural and intergenerational dance.

As an example, let us look at Eiko & Koma's choice to dress the eight young male Cambodian painters in *Cambodian Stories* in brightly colored, casual sarongs and the one young woman in a more modest and formal outfit. (Eiko and Koma themselves don versions of the latter at the beginning of the piece, but by the middle section they appear in white body makeup and dressed in the type of deconstructed kimonos they commonly wear in their duets.) On the one hand, this costuming decision allowed the young people to be read by critics as exotic, lithe, and ravishing. However, that same choice can also be seen as an attempt to allow the painters control over their self-representation in their first trip to the United States, a country that had bombed their own. Indeed, a careful look at *Cambodian Stories* reveals a number of ways in which the Cambodian artists acted with agency, beginning with naming themselves the Reyum Painting Collective for the purposes of the tour. Their paintings provided not only the sets for the dance, but also movement, as they created the two action paintings during the course of each performance. The painters exhibited agency in their ability to choose and to create how their culture would be represented. Moreover, the choreography places an emphasis on contemporary processes of craft and creation, not on a timeless or fixed tradition. Finally, the recurrence of the Cambodian pop song, "Take Me to Your Heart," the painters' favorite, dislodges the young adults from a fixed and unchanging traditional culture, placing them instead in a vibrant, contemporary, metropolitan Cambodian culture that circulates around Southeast and East Asia and in which they actively take part. This kind of viewing of *Cambodian Stories* takes us beyond the gaze of the reviewers who only saw the surface of the performance — and Said is clear: "Orientalism is premised upon exteriority"[57] — into an engagement with the performance that considers the depth of the intercultural work of the piece.

Choreographing Intercultural Alliances

What was initially imagined as a one-time visit to Cambodia turned into a multiyear collaboration that dominated Eiko & Koma's work for five years. Beginning in 2004, Eiko & Koma took on intercultural alliance as a choreographic concern in a way that represents an intervention into intercultural performance. In their chorography, intercultural alliance is about bringing one's strengths, skills, and experiences to bear in a way that highlights similarities without erasing distinctiveness. Even though the choreographers have engaged in collaborations that could be considered intercultural since as early as 1979, the processes themselves were on the whole not the main focus of the choreography until Eiko & Koma worked with modern and postmodern dance pioneer Anna Halprin (*Be With*, 2001) and with the Reyum students beginning in 2004. With few exceptions, the choreographers stage intercultural alliance as interdisciplinarity. As in *Cambodian Stories*, sometimes this is established as the gradual development of a relationship between painting and dance, while in other pieces the emphasis is on the performers trying out each other's skills. In still other pieces, the focus is instead on the interaction of different generations.

Be With's alliance is choreographed entirely as a relationship among generations, with Eiko & Koma the young ones in relation to Halprin, who is thirty years their senior. Whereas Eiko & Koma operate as a unit with members of the Painting Collective, filling the same roles in relation to the young artists, *Be With* shows the choreographers relating separately to their elder. Koma tends to Halprin as a devoted caretaker or an attentive younger lover, caressing her check and supporting her as she sinks back into a deep pitch. Eiko approaches her rather as a lost or fatigued child, gratefully releasing her small frame head-first into Halprin's welcoming figure. The encounters between first Halprin and Koma

FIGURE 7.2 *Sketches made by Lawrence Halprin during* Be With *rehearsals.*
Courtesy of Anna Halprin.

and later between her and Eiko are tender and tactile. The performers'
faces and hands, their primary points of contact with one another, stand
out against a deep red backdrop and are further emphasized by their
costumes: Halprin in a long, loose salmon robe; Koma in a red, three-
quarter-length kimono; and Eiko in a saffron sarong that brushes the
floor (see figure 7.2).

Much of the dance takes place far upstage in proximity to a striking
red backdrop (later reused for the beginning of *Cambodian Stories*),
giving the whole piece a distant, dreamlike quality, reinforced by Joan
Jeanrenaud's contemplative strains played from her position downstage
left.[58] Late in the dance it is Halprin who finally brings the trio into
community, first in an asymmetrical grouping, then as a small circle of
three. As the lights fade, the elder dancer exits stage left, leaving Eiko and
Koma together for the first time in the piece. It is perhaps with these

final images of *Be With* that Halprin's influence as a community facilitator and leader in expressive therapy resonates most strongly. Until she effects a different structure with which the performers can relate to one another, the dance relies on dyad patterns familiar from Eiko & Koma's other works. While *Be With* does not endeavor to build an intercultural alliance in the way that subsequent works with the Reyum painters do, it does provide an early glimpse into how Eiko & Koma stage interactions among generations.

In 2007 Eiko & Koma continued dancing with Charian and Peace, reworking the original *Cambodian Stories* choreography for a cast of four as *Cambodian Stories Revisited*. *Revisited* was staged in the Saint Mark's graveyard at Danspace Project in New York City, the site of a number of free outdoor performances by Eiko & Koma over the years. The decision to restage the piece with only Charian and Peace was both administrative—two dancers are logistically and financially more practical to work with than nine—and creative: Charian and Peace are the most skilled dancers among the Reyum painters and were already featured in *Cambodian Stories*. *Revisited* effectively strengthens the intercultural and intergenerational work of the original by staging a one-to-one relationship between the Cambodian and Japanese American performers. Whereas Eiko & Koma are only in an elder/teacher role in relationship to the members of Reyum in the original version of the piece, *Revisited* also places them in a student role in relation to Charian and Peace; the painters again perform the dance they learned from Eiko & Koma, while the choreographers paint Cambodian figures for the first time, as Charian and Peace taught them. Moreover, the return to an outdoor setting calls to mind the site of their rehearsals in Phnom Penh when *Cambodian Stories* was first being developed, as seen in the documentary *The Making of Cambodian Stories*. While dirt was brought inside for performances of *Cambodian Stories*, *Revisited* is itself danced in the dirt. What is more, the site of the performance was a graveyard, which only served to underscore the contemporary link between living and dead, past and present that *Cambodian Stories* enacted.

That same year Eiko & Koma choreographed a new work, *Quartet*, with Charian and Peace, which premiered at the American Dance Festival in June 2007. *Quartet* does not involve any live painting, although some of the paintings from *Cambodian Stories* are recycled as a back-drop and ground coverings. Without the dance/painting relationship to concentrate an interdisciplinary/intercultural alliance, the focus is on staging parallels between the elder and younger dancers. At times the Cambodian pair seem to represent the Japanese American couple in their youth, such as when Charian and Peace conclude a duet center stage by parting with Charian's signature *Cambodian Stories* walk, revealing in the process Eiko & Koma slowly stirring on the floor. At other times, the relationship among the four evinces a mutuality of multiple genera-tions living together: Eiko & Koma pull and mold the malleable younger bodies; Charian and Peace lift the elder choreographers to standing; the men struggle with one another, arms raised; the women—chest to chest in an awkward, armless embrace, sharing weight—slowly rise. With a title stripped of all specificities, *Quartet* nonetheless posits an inherent relationship among its four performers, across generations and cultures based in mutual assistance and struggle.

Most significantly, for the first time in their four-decade career Eiko & Koma taught one of their early works to other dancers, reconstructing *Grain* (1983) for Charian and Peace to perform at the American Dance Festival.[59] The grain at issue is rice, a main dietary staple across Asia. At the time of its premiere in 1983, the fifty-five-minute piece was noted for its stark nudity and raw, groping sexuality accompanied by the haphaz-ard scattering of rice grains and desperate consumption thereof. Eiko & Koma were in their early thirties then and were already seasoned per-formers. Charian and Peace, not yet out of their teens in 2007, danced a more modest *Grain*, ceding the glacial nude movements of the opening scene to the choreographers themselves. The reconstruction, while sig-nificant in the arc of Eiko & Koma's career, is also noteworthy for the fact that the dancers they chose were themselves Asian, thereby empha-sizing the cultural overtones of the choreography and the supranational regional affiliations that the choreographers choose to foreground. Some critics questioned the ability of the teenagers to embody the weight and complexity of Eiko & Koma's repertoire,[60] while others hinted at the pos-sibility of passing on other works to them.[61] The reconstruction report-edly came at the prodding of then ADF director Charles Reinhart, who has repeatedly emphasized the need to preserve Eiko & Koma's work in the form of teaching their choreography to others. It is doubtful, however, that the pair would have given into Reinhart's pressure if they had not already been working with Charian and Peace for a number of years.

Entire sections from *Grain* were then incorporated into the third work Eiko & Koma created for themselves and Charian and Peace, *Hunger* (2008). This evening-length piece draws movement from *Rust* (1989) in addition to *Grain*, in a way that underscores the simultaneity of past and present. By incorporating old pieces into new ones, Eiko & Koma put issues of continuity and change in their own work up for consideration and presage their Retrospective Project (2009–2012). The elder dancers echo the 1983 vocabulary briefly when Koma holds a cloth laden with rice in front of Eiko's gaping mouth, but for the most part they leave *Grain*'s movement vocabulary and futon prop for Charian and Peace to continue to inhabit. Eiko & Koma limit themselves instead to the upstage space and the vertical chain-link fence of *Rust*, where they hover like ghosts, their minute movements audible rather than visible. Gone are the vibrant colors of *Cambodian Stories*, replaced here by stark black and white, interrupted only briefly by red tops worn by Charian and Eiko (who later sheds hers in favor of a naked torso). Even the live painting created by Charian and Peace near the end of the evening-length work — covering and perhaps mediating the now empty chain-link fence — lets go of the Cambodian-style paintings they created for previous pieces, opting instead for an abstract display of birds taking flight, black on white canvas. Charian and Peace's action painting continues the interrelationship of painting and dance established in *Cambodian Stories*, but rather than relating kinesthetically to the dancers, the completed canvas gives the impression of a message from the younger performers to the elder ones. The quartet never dance together, but the four are nonetheless meant to be understood as related, perhaps as elders remembering their younger selves.

Conclusion

The process of choreographing and performing *Cambodian Stories* with members of the Reyum Painting Collective represented a new phase of Eiko & Koma's career, characterized by the incorporation of an interdisciplinarity that staged the process of intercultural alliance. As a body of work with Charian and Peace began to accumulate, critics began to see the new and restaged dances as an intergenerational passing on and perhaps even an anointing of a new generation on whom Eiko & Koma's repertory would be bestowed. A careful consideration of the choreography, however, demonstrates that what is occurring is not a passing on, but rather a recognition of affinity across difference and a commitment to building relationships. The intergenerational aspect of the choreographers' alliance with the young painters, moreover, prompted Eiko & Koma to look back over the arc of their career to conceptualize how to move forward into a new phase of dance making.

After investing for half a decade in choreographing intercultural alliance, and restaging *Cambodian Stories* for its Asian premiere in Taiwan in spring 2009, in fall of the same year Eiko & Koma launched their ambitious three-year Retrospective Project. Unlike a typical art retrospective, however, which serves as a capstone on an artist's career, Eiko & Koma conceptualized their project as a midcareer opportunity to look back in order to understand how to move forward. While the Retrospective was proposed by Sam Miller—who has worked with the choreographers over the years through his roles at Jacob's Pillow, the New England Foundation for the Arts, the Center for Creative Research, the Lower Manhattan Cultural Council, and other organizations—it is clear that Eiko & Koma would not have entertained the idea if they had not already begun considering issues of mentorship and legacy, initially with Anna Halprin and later more substantially through their work with the Reyum painters when they had been prompted to reflect on their own beginnings as artists. For example, just as Eiko & Koma performed as untrained dancers with their first teacher, Tatsumi Hijikata, soon after meeting him, so too did they take on nine painters from Reyum who volunteered to participate in the project, whose only prior dance training was a Delicious Movement Workshop with Eiko & Koma the year before. In their acceptance speech at the 2006 Dance Magazine Awards ceremony, Koma said, "It is amazing to realize now that we are at the age of our mentors when we first met them. Now it is our turn to be inspiring, crazy senior artists who encourage the younger generation."[62] When the Retrospective was launched on November 19, 2009, with an exhibition at the Zilkha Gallery at Wesleyan University, where Eiko has been teaching annually since 2007, I was struck by the way the exhibition was deeply tied to her relationship to the Wesleyan students. Not only did the students put in a significant amount of labor in installing (and in some cases creating) the works on display, but they also seemed to be the primary intended audience of the show.

Much in the way that *Cambodian Stories* offers a view into "what we do," so too does the Retrospective Project. The opening exhibition at the Zilkha, in particular, was designed to invite the younger generation into the spaces that Eiko & Koma have created over the years. By asking the audience, and especially the young people, to engage with these spaces and in a sense to populate them, Eiko & Koma demonstrate their continued commitment to generating spaces where they, their collaborators, and their audience may propose and explore alternative ways of being in the world.

*I*N LIEU OF A CONCLUSION
"STEP BACK AND FORWARD, AND BE THERE"

———————————

"Oh my god! They're *naked!*" my friend whispers to me. We are sitting on a low bench in a dimly lit gallery at the Walker Art Center in Minneapolis. Though a hush seems to rest over the cool space, small sounds like my friend's whisper, the careful footsteps of visitors entering or departing the space, and regular drops of water are audible. We are two of perhaps ten people who hover on benches and cushions, barely breathing, mere feet from Eiko & Koma, who lie apparently motionless on an island of black feathers and straw in an expansive sea of dirt. Compared to the feathers, which stir gently in the breeze, and the lights, which subtly phase between twilight and dawn, the performers seem utterly still. Only in hindsight is the turn of a head, the twist of a spine, the extension of a lower leg perceptible. These two apocalyptic newborns move to a time signature altogether disconnected from that of their audience, who come and go, sit, stretch, fidget, and even whisper. Though their eyelids may at times open and blink, these creatures give the impression that they see not through their eyes, but through their skin. Curled less than a foot away from one another, rare moments of contact between the two are exquisite for the amount of information that seems to pass between grazing fingertips or a foot encountering a neighboring leg. There is so much of this intimate experience to take in that it is not surprising that my friend did not notice the bodies she watched were covered only in a layer of white makeup and smudges of dirt. They were not Eiko & Koma in the nude, but previously unknown creatures with whom we could corporeally empathize.

Created for their Retrospective Project (2009–2012), Eiko & Koma performed *Naked* six hours a day for a month at the Walker Art Center in fall 2010 and four hours a day for two weeks in spring 2011 at the Baryshnikov Art Center. Forty years after they first performed together, they are still pushing themselves to create new and challenging works. At the same time, their dances remain connected to what has come before,

FIGURE C.1 Naked, *Walker Art Center, November 23, 2010.*
Photo: Cameron Wittig for Walker Art Center. © *Walker Art Center.*

adapting the scorched landscape that formed the set of their stage work, *Raven*, for example, into an immersive environment for *Naked*. *Raven*'s hard-baked ground is here displaced vertically to envelop the Walker gallery on two sides. Even before stepping through a curtain into the gallery, exhibition visitors could peer through irregular holes the size of a fist burnt into the salt-and-feather-covered, sandstone-colored canvas (see figure c.1). In turn, the live installation's environment was appropriated to create a four-sided "Tea House" that housed a video installation for a number of Eiko & Koma's subsequent Retrospective exhibitions, as well as the environment for the durational collaboration with Kronos Quartet, *Fragile*.

Naked is emblematic of Eiko & Koma's site-adaptive and cyclic choreographic method. As one of the key works created for the Retrospective Project, it is also indicative of how the pair approach retrospecting and archiving. In previous chapters I focused on the ways Eiko & Koma have developed a series of repeating concerns across their body of work by cycling back around to particular themes, movement vocabularies, environments, and so forth. In this concluding chapter I use *Naked* as a point of departure to examine this choreographic practice as a whole and consider the implications of Eiko & Koma's site-adaptive and (re)cycling tactics for choreography and dance archives. I argue that rather than disappearing, dance for Eiko & Koma is something that recurs and is constantly being regenerated under different circumstances and therefore to different effects. This regeneration, I suggest, offers a new approach to dance archives.

Site Adaptivity and (Re)Cycling

At the heart of Eiko & Koma's work is a notion of site adaptivity that extends beyond pieces explicitly designed for multiple outdoor locations to the very idea of choreography itself. This adaptivity is ingrained both in the way Eiko & Koma develop the concepts of their pieces and in their approach to each specific performance. Sets, costumes, and even music may change, or be recycled, according to performance conditions. Even their video archive is site adaptive; Eiko constantly edits raw footage to produce versions of pieces for different platforms (a Retrospective medley, gallery displays, online viewing, etc.).

Even early on, Eiko & Koma were already thinking about their work as site adaptive. Eiko said in a review of their second full-length work, *Fur Seal*, "Our dance changes in small detail according to the theatre. . . . We respect the space we have to work with."[1] In another article, Eiko added, "It's easy to change the dance a little. . . . Changes in detail keep the dance interesting for us. We also find that the length of the piece depends a good deal on the way the audience is responding and on the size of our performing space. It is not an improvisational dance, though; we have a basic style and we always come back to the point of it."[2] As Eiko implies, a mutability directly related to the site of performance is inherent to their work. And yet Eiko & Koma ask their viewers to understand that despite these variations, they are nonetheless dancing the same piece. At the same time, distinctions between pieces with different names, such as the touring version of *Offering* and the subsequent site work, *Tree Song* (2004), can sometimes blur until they seem to be one and the same.

Moreover, pieces not only change from site to site in response to the particulars of sightline, mood, or other specifics, but they may also migrate across formats. Proscenium works become media dances. Site dances are transformed for the stage. Live installations become video installations. Eiko & Koma do not want to make a piece that can only be performed at only one kind of site; for one thing, it is not feasible financially or time-wise, but more important, the piece would be deprived of opportunities to be reexamined and grow. A work can be site specific at the outset (a proscenium is a particular kind of site, after all), but once it is created, Eiko & Koma do not want the concept, structure, and texture of a work to be limited to one place; rather, they are interested to see how it can be translated to new environments, what will survive the transposition, and what can be discarded without the core of the piece being affected. In other words, Eiko & Koma's choreography carries within it an ingrained site adaptivity that suggests that a piece is both contingent — that is, specific to a particular performance at a particular site — and a compilation of possibilities for performance of the piece, both past and future. *Naked* is but one example of the principle of site adaptivity that undergirds Eiko & Koma's body of work. I have already indicated how the installation's environment connects it to previous and subsequent works like *Raven* and the Tea Houses. The idea of choreographing a durational relationship with an environment links *Naked* back to *Breath*, Eiko & Koma's 1998 live installation at the Whitney Museum.

At the same time that specific dances are constantly adapting from site to site and format to format, Eiko & Koma also work with concepts over and over again, revisiting themes, choreographic ideas, costumes, and set pieces to reexamine them for continued or shifting resonances. Sometimes these cycles occur close together, such as the scorched feather and straw landscapes that dominated their work during the Retrospective Project. Sometimes, however, themes like mourning cycle across decades, as demonstrated throughout the book. In fact, dance critic Marcia B. Siegel has observed that Eiko & Koma have occupied themselves with creating what she calls a "lifetime piece,"[3] in which they approach a complex of recurring themes and ongoing questions from a variety of angles. When considered in this way, it makes sense that the pair would reuse sets, costumes, music, and movement phrases as a way of reworking ideas.

The implications of this cyclic pattern across Eiko & Koma's body of work created over more than four decades are significant. Rather than disappearing or being left behind, their themes, movements, and dances are the subject of frequent reconsideration and continual circulation through which contexts and meanings accrue even as they reappear. This cycling keeps their themes and issues always current, always seeking attention from a new audience or reassessment by an experienced one. For example, mourning in *Before the Cock Crows* is an experiment in externalizing an excess of emotion outside the body, whereas in *Elegy* and *Lament* the body becomes a site of grief for friends lost to the early ravages of AIDS and other illnesses. Later, in pieces like *Wind*, *Offering*, *Mourning*, and even *Cambodian Stories*, mourning points to larger historical cycles of violence and calamity. This choreography invites examination of history itself as a cyclical process; history is not only not in the past, but it is being continually re-performed in the present. It is always being created anew. Moreover, this desire to keep history corporeally present, this insistence that we continue to look at it, embody it, experience it, challenges the notion that the past is something we should get over and move on from. On the contrary, Eiko & Koma demonstrate both the impossibility of leaving the past behind and the value in its reexamination.

Choreography/Archives

Eiko & Koma's choreographic process of constantly reexamining older works and bringing elements of those works into new ones indicates a continuous retrospecting that is also an active use of their own archival materials. Archiving is a way of naming the contours of a body of work. According to Eiko, archiving indicates that they care about what they do; working with their own archives is another way to indicate their concerns and spend time realizing something about those concerns. In this way, information and images of past dancers and dances can prompt significant new work, as *Land* provided movement material for *Raven*, which in turn influenced the Retrospective Project dance *Naked*. André Lepecki discusses this relationship between archives and choreography as "a capacity to identify in a past work still non-exhausted creative fields."[4] In other words, the relationship between archives and choreography is not one of simply repeating or reconstructing, but one of new possibilities. It comes as no surprise, then, that Eiko & Koma view their own archives as material for further creation, not objects to be preserved for the sake of legacy. As Palumbo-Liu uses the solidus to indicate the fraught linkages between Asian/American, I employ it here between choreography/

archives to indicate both the tensions between the categories and also the ways that for Eiko & Koma the two are linked and always in process.

Eiko & Koma first explicitly engaged with their own archives through their Retrospective Project. Their Archive Project, an outgrowth of the Retrospective, seeks to create an innovative, artist-led archive in which a collection of files, photographs, press, programs, sets, costumes, videos, and audio material is not only available for specialized study and research, but is also a resource for further artistic production and imagination. The Archive Project questions the artistic possibilities of what a performance archive could be.

One of the central ideas that Eiko & Koma outlined at the Retrospective launch meeting was the way they planned to employ their site-adaptive and cyclic practices to create new Retrospective works; materials from their earlier dances (including costumes, sets, choreography, and photographic and video documentation) would be used to create new installation, video, and choreographic works. In other words, the Retrospective was not just about assembling and displaying or documenting their body of work (although some projects did just that, such as the catalog and the revamped Web site), but also about revisiting and reimagining them. Even the Regeneration tour, featuring the new work, *Raven*, alongside performances of the earlier *Night Tide* and *White Dance*, cannot be said to be a mere performance of repertoire. For example, Eiko & Koma refer to those performances of *White Dance* as a revival and indicate it as a separate piece from the 1976 dance in their official list of dance works. Embedded in this approach is the idea that any new performance of a work is an act of re-creating (or regenerating, as the title suggests) it rather than a restaging. Moreover *Raven*, itself drawing from earlier dances, became a sort of through-line for the Retrospective. The piece was performed extensively, and themes and visual elements from the dance also appeared in *Fragile*, *Naked*, and the exhibition "Tea Houses." Eiko says, "This helped to present the Retrospective not as a collection of unrelated works but as a contiguous exploration with deepening continuity."[5] This idea is indeed a constant across Eiko & Koma's body of work, as they revisit themes and movements to deepen their engagement with them. It makes sense, then, that the choreographers would apply the same approach as they started to think about their own archives. They view their archives as part of their artistic production and make active use of them in exhibitions and installations.

Eiko & Koma's Retrospective and Archive Projects took place in the midst of heightened discussion about dance legacies and preservation, due in part to the death of dance luminaries like Merce Cunningham and Pina Bausch, both in 2009. Beyond those particular losses in the dance community, there was also the context of what scholars have referred to variously as "archive fever,"[6] the "archival impulse,"[7] or the "will to archive."[8] Jacques Derrida, Hal Foster, and Lepecki identify not only an increased attention to archives and archiving, but also a trend for visual and performing artists to use—and perhaps even generate—archival materials as part of their artistic practice. In dance and performance, this heightened attention to the archive as place, thing, and practice[9] is also discussed in terms of reconstruction, restaging, reenactment, re-performance, preservation, legacy, transmission, recovery, continuity, documentation, the score, notation, moving and still images, and so forth. An examination of Eiko & Koma's approach to retrospecting and archiving—a practice consistent with their choreographic method—offers an opportunity to revisit the persistent idea of the ephemerality of dance and the various steps choreographers, dancers, scholars, and historians have taken to challenge the supposed disappearance of dance. I discuss Eiko & Koma's projects in the context of these broader performance practices and lively scholarly discourse in order to highlight their contributions to this archival moment.

The increasing attention to archiving live performance reflects on the one hand a quest for inclusion and officialdom, for the authority and authorization that being part of the official record implies. And yet on the other hand, the attempt to archive live performance, those movements and moments that we are told are defined by their disappearance, necessarily disturbs the foundations of the institution that the archive represents. How is it possible to collect together each shift of weight, each firing of muscle fibers, each interaction of sound and body and objects and audience? And yet we try. We document. We collect documents. Order them. Protect and preserve them. For whom? For what purpose? For legacy? For research? To enter into history? Archiving is both an act of hubris—I know what is important, and I deem it to be this—but also an act of trust, because we cannot yet know what the archive will mean in the future, what inspiration it will spark, or what it will enable. Archiving seems to be a hedge against being forgotten, and yet it is also an urgent action stemming from the understanding of the link between archives and power. Performance archives insist on the persistence of performance, even if only as a trace; if we can only somehow capture, record, document, and collect a past performance, its endurance into the future in some form or another will be assured. The act of archiving is a cry against the disappearance of performance. Of course, if and how performance might remain is the subject of much debate.

Currently this debate seems to be polarized between the legacy preservation approach, on the one hand, which employs archival standards and practices, notation, direct transmission, and reconstruction in order to restage dances and keep them in active circulation, and a postmodern approach, on the other hand, which treats the archive as necessarily in flux, favoring re-performance, reuse, and the performativity of the document. In both cases, however, a binary between liveness and the document is upheld. For example, on the preservation side of things is the emphasis on the live through bodily transmission of choreography from one dancer to another, through *repetiteurs* or otherwise authorized teachers of a dance or a technique, like Yvonne Rainer's certification of five dancers to transmit *Trio A*.[10] On the other hand, preservation is often closely linked to the sort of standard archival processes that value provenance and original order of objects, papers, documentation, and so forth. In "Preserving the Ephemeral," the editors' note to *Dance Chronicle*'s "Preserving Dance as a Living Legacy" special issue, Lynn Matluck Brooks and Joellen A. Meglin accept as a given that dance has a problem of preservation, and that person-to-person transmission of dances is insufficient to protect the legacy of particular choreographers and dancers. In response to this problem, they gather in the special issue "frameworks and guidance for keeping dances, performances, and choreographers' legacies alive today."[11]

Often archives are understood as being simultaneously past- and future-oriented: a collection of items about historical figures and/or events preserved for future audiences. This emphasis on future preservation and legacy often skirts the present time, in consideration of either the assemblage of the archive in the present—the process of archiving—

or the ongoing uses of the archive. Focusing on creative uses of the archive challenges the assumption that archiving and creation are two separate activities. Indeed, Eiko & Koma's insistence on holding onto their archives until they are no longer making and touring dances challenges the typical future-oriented priorities of archives in favor of creation now, sometimes even at the expense of long-term preservation.

At the other end of the spectrum, there is an emphasis on the body and performance as a way to archive dance and for other artists to creatively engage with and reuse another artist's archive. Ramsay Burt and Lepecki have both written about contemporary reenactments/re-performances such as Julie Tolentino's *The Sky Remains the Same*, in which she turns her body into an archive for other artists' work; Martin Nachbar's working through of Dore Hoyer's dances in *Urheben, Aufheben*; and Richard Move's work on Martha Graham. Burt identifies these bodily "re" projects as acts of embodied memory that with their inherent Butlerian failures enable resistance to the society of control.[12] Lepecki prefers to think of these performances as "creative returns" that open up as yet unexplored possibilities in the original work.[13] In either case, Maaike Bleeker points out that "re-enactment thus seems to promise an embodied understanding of the past, while in fact what is experienced is one's own embodied experiences in the here and now, and not those of an historical agent."[14] In the case of Eiko & Koma, however, the point of their "creative return" is precisely the understanding of a previous concern in their current bodies and the current historical moment.

Conversely, others argue that documentation, the score, and even the archive are themselves performative, or perhaps even the performance itself. Philip Auslander, for example, examines photographic documentation of performance art and what he calls "performed photography" to suggest that it is not an audience that makes a performance, but the documentation of such that makes it so.[15] Similarly, Mark Franko, in his editor's note to a special issue on "archival futurity," argues that the recent attention to the score (loosely meaning "notation and/or film, but also as citation, oral transmission, text, and choreographic thought") provides an alternative approach to reconstruction in which the score becomes "the ontological basis of the work's having existed and continuing to exist."[16] In other words, not only does the performance not disappear, the documents *are* the performance.[17]

Eiko & Koma's approach to archiving does not fit comfortably into any of these arguments. Their practice argues for a creative engagement with one's own archive in a manner that is consistent with one's own artistic practice. In this sense they are in line with #JEZ3PREZ & ATCHU, who in writing about the attempt to archive the Occupy Wall Street movement call on archives to reflect the goals and actions of the movement not only in content but in form.[18] In other words, there are choices in how we archive, and those choices are not merely about logistics or best practices, but are fundamentally political. This is a relatively new development in archiving. For Eiko & Koma, this means an acknowledgment that they are always already archiving even as they use old dances, sets, and costumes to reimagine new ones. Their dances are both new creations and an activating of archival memory. For the pair, the question is not so much about liveness, or performance versus document, or future legacy, or even about the "re." The archive is not divided into place, thing, and practice, but rather is all practice. For Eiko, the video documentary *38 Works by Eiko & Koma* that she created (and re-created more than once) for the Retrospective Project was not a document of their performances, but was itself one of her artistic creations (and it is listed as one of their works on their Web site).

Whereas Lepecki argues that it is "clear that dance can only find its proper archival site onto/into a body,"[19] Eiko & Koma show through their archives, as they do in their choreography, that their bodies do not end at their skin, and that their archives, like their choreography, fundamentally involve a relationship among sites, technologies, and bodies that exceeds the body, not reifies it. Thus, dancing bodies (Eiko & Koma's, Charian and Peace's, or other future bodies) are not sufficient to archive Eiko & Koma's body of work. Not only must their archives account for both the corporeal and material aspects of their dances; they actually cannot exist without an attention to the ways the "re-" (recycling, revisiting, reworking) is always already part of the work. Materials matter, not because they are all that is left of performance, but because they are intrinsic to the work. Eiko & Koma's practice suggests that archiving can rest neither solely with the body nor with objects or a place, but must be a combination of all elements.

Sarah Jones, Daisy Abbott, and Seamus Ross get at some of this, but neglect artists who use their own archives in favor of engaging with others' materials.[20] Mathew Reason reveals some of the complications, the ways that performance can make the in-flux state of archives evident, for example, but does not address the active and ongoing relationship between archives and performance.[21] Perhaps returning to a formulation that predates this current archival moment will be helpful. For Michel Foucault, the archive is not a place or object; it is a coherence of ideas, practices, and knowledge that constitute a specific discursive system. It is, quite simply, what can be said, or done, within a particular system, "the rules of a practice that enables statements both to survive and to undergo regular modification. It is *the general system of the formation and transformation of statements*."[22] In addition to an archive being collected and preserved, it must be observed and analyzed, the process of which demonstrates an archive's possibilities and also what lies outside of its boundaries. Through both their Retrospective Project and Archive Project, and indeed throughout their career, Eiko & Koma have been actively constituting, examining, and reconstituting the discourse that is their choreographic process, demonstrating what is possible with their site-adaptive and cyclic practices. They have tested the boundaries with dances like *Nurse's Song*, formed and transformed statements on mourning and alliances with nature and other humans. They have developed a coherent body of work that moves from stage to site to screen to gallery. In doing so, even as they move through their fifth decade of choreography and artistic collaboration, they ask us once again to reconsider our notions of dance, and time, and bodies. Which are their archives. Which are their dance.

Notes

INTRODUCTION

1. In conversation Eiko & Koma sometimes refer to "Neue Tanz" to mean the German modern dance style of artists like Mary Wigman, Harald Kreutzberg, Dore Hoyer, and Manja Chmiel, who influenced them or their teachers. This grammatically incorrect declension of *Neuer Tanz* in spoken English likely comes from the Japanese ノイエダンツ ("noie tantsu"), a phonetic spelling of "neuer Tanz" in the Japanese alphabet *katakana*, reserved for loan words. Takaya Eguchi and Misako Miya, pioneers of Japanese modern dance, studied with Wigman in Dresden in the 1920s. I speculate that "Neue Tanz" was the term Eguchi and Miya encountered in Germany and later promulgated in Japan, although further research would be necessary to confirm this. According to Kate Elswit, "new" was just one of many adjectives used to describe early twentieth-century German dance styles; other words included artistic, free, modern, and expressionistic (personal communication with author, October 27, 2014; see also *Watching Weimar Dance* [New York: Oxford University Press, 2014], xxiv–xxv). Wigman's style, via Eguchi and Miya, influenced the development of modern dance in Japan and across East Asia. Eguchi and Miya also directly influenced the founders of butoh, Hijikata and Ohno. See also Kazuo Ohno Dance Studio, *Kazuo Ohno: Chronicle of a Lifetime 1906–2010* (Tokyo: Canto Co., Ltd., 2010).

2. For a full list of awards Eiko & Koma have won, see http://eikoandkoma.org/index.php?p=ek&id=2666.

3. Eiko Otake, "A Dancer Behind the Lens," in *Envisioning Dance on Film and Video*, ed. Judy Mitoma (New York: Routledge, 2002), 82–88; and "Feeling Wind," in *Site Dance: Choreographers and the Lure of Alternative Spaces*, ed. Melanie Kloetzel and Carolyn Pavlik (Gainesville: University Press of Florida, 2009), 18–198.

4. Nanako Kurihara, "Eiko and Koma: Movement Approach and Works" (master's thesis, New York University, 1988); and Shoko Yamahata Letton, "Eiko and Koma: Dance Philosophy and Aesthetic" (master's thesis, Florida State University, 2009).

5. Rose Eichenbaum and Aron Hirt-Manheimer, "Eiko and Koma," in *The Dancer Within: Intimate Conversations with Great Dancers*, ed. Rose Eichenbaum and Aron Hirt-Manheimer (Middletown, CT: Wesleyan University Press, 2008), 266–71; and

Joyce Morgenroth, "Eiko Otake," in *Speaking of Dance: Twelve Contemporary Choreographers on Their Craft* (New York: Routledge, 2004), 117–36.

6. Joan Rothfuss, ed., *Eiko & Koma: Time Is Not Even, Space Is Not Empty* (Minneapolis, MN: Walker Art Center, 2011).

7. The title is inspired by the Sonic Youth song, "Small Flowers Crack Concrete," on the CD *NYC Ghosts and Flowers* (Geffen Records, 2000, 069490650-2).

8. Slavoj Žižek, *Violence: Six Sideways Reflections* (New York: Picador, 2008).

9. Jack Anderson, "Eiko and Koma Slow Time Down," *New York Times*, December 7, 1986, http://www.nytimes.com/1986/12/07/arts/dance-view-eiko-and-koma -slow-time-down.html?module=Search&mabReward=relbias%3Aw%2C%7B%222 %22%3A%22RI%3A14%22%7D; and Gia Kourlas, "The King and Queen of Slow Get Busy," *New York Times*, May 25, 2010, http://www.nytimes.com/2010/05/26/arts /dance/26eiko.html?module=Search&mabReward=relbias%3Aw%2C%7B%222%2 2%3A%22RI%3A14%22%7D.

10. Rosemary Candelario, "Eiko & Koma: Choreographing Spaces Apart in Asian America" (PhD diss., University of California, Los Angeles, 2011).

11. Žižek employs tempo-related titles from Beethoven's *String Quartet no. 14* ("Adagio ma non troppo e molto espressivo," "Allegro moderato — Adagio," "Presto," etc.) to frame his discussion of subjective and objective violence.

12. Žižek, *Violence*, 7.

13. Paula Josa-Jones, "Delicious Moving," *Contact Quarterly* 30, no. 1 (2005): 57.

14. In an interview with Leslie Windham, Eiko said, "We do not make a piece because we're trying to express something. We make a piece to realize something. That's as selfish as it could ever be. You read a book trying to find out what interests you. That's the same way we make a dance — trying to find out about it. Hopefully, that way we are at least showing our interest, our concern, to the audience" ("A Conversation with Eiko & Koma," *Ballet Review*, Summer 1988, 49).

15. For examples of how other scholars write about the aesthetic of slowness in performance, see Mari Boyd, *The Aesthetics of Quietude: Ota Shogo and the Theatre of Divestiture* (Tokyo: Sophia University Press, 2006); and André Lepecki, "Choreography's 'Slower Ontology': Jérôme Bel's Critique of Representation," in *Exhausting Dance: Performance and the Politics of Movement* (New York: Routledge, 2006), 45–64.

16. Žižek, *Violence*, 207.

17. Ibid., 217.

18. David Palumbo-Liu, *Asian/American: Historical Crossings of a Racial Frontier* (Palo Alto, CA: Stanford University Press, 1999).

19. For more on Asian American theater and performance studies, see James S.

Moy, *Marginal Sights: Staging the Chinese in America* (Iowa City: University of Iowa Press, 1994); Josephine Lee, *Performing Asian America: Race and Ethnicity on the Contemporary Stage* (Philadelphia: Temple University Press, 1997); Dorinne Kondo, *About Face: Performing Race in Fashion and Theater* (New York: Routledge, 1997); Karen Shimakawa, *National Abjection: The Asian American Body Onstage* (Durham, NC: Duke University Press, 2002); Deborah Wong, *Speak It Louder: Asian Americans Making Music* (New York: Routledge, 2004); and Esther Kim Lee, *A History of Asian American Theatre* (New York: Cambridge University Press, 2011).

20. See, for example, SanSan Kwan, "Performing a Geography of Asian America: The Chop Suey Circuit," *The Drama Review: TDR* 55 (2011): 120–36; SanSan Kwan, *Kinesthetic City: Dance and Movement in Chinese Urban Spaces* (New York: Oxford University Press, 2013); Priya Srinivasan, "The Bodies Beneath the Smoke or What's Behind the Cigarette Poster: Unearthing Kinesthetic Connections in American Dance History," *Discourses in Dance* 4, no. 1 (2007): 7–48; and Priya Srinivasan, "The Nautch Women Dancers of the 1880s: Corporeality, US Orientalism, and Anti-Asian Immigration Laws," *Women & Performance: A Journal of Feminist Theory* 19, no. 1 (2009): 3–22.

21. Yutian Wong, "Towards a New Asian American Dance Theory: Locating the Dancing Asian American Body," *Discourses in Dance* 1, no. 1 (2002): 81.

22. Brenda Dixon Gottschild, *Digging the Africanist Presence in American Performance: Dance and Other Contexts* (Santa Barbara, CA: Praeger, 1998).

23. For more on Ruth St. Denis, see Yutian Wong, *Choreographing Asian America* (Middletown, CT: Wesleyan University Press, 2010); Priya Srinivasan, "The Bodies Beneath the Smoke or What's Behind the Cigarette Poster: Unearthing Kinesthetic Connections in American Dance History," *Discourses in Dance* 4, no. 1 (2007): 7–48; and Srinivasan, "Nautch Women Dancers of the 1880s."

24. Yutian Wong, "Artistic Utopias: Michio Ito and the Trope of the International," in *Worlding Dance*, ed. Susan Leigh Foster (New York: Palgrave Macmillan, 2009), 144–62.

25. Karen Shimakawa, *National Abjection: The Asian American Body Onstage* (Durham, NC: Duke University Press, 2002), 3.

26. Wong, *Choreographing Asian America*, 37–38.

27. It would be nearly impossible to include a full listing here. Key early texts include Mark Franko, *Dancing Modernism/Performing Politics* (Bloomington: Indiana University Press, 1995); Susan Leigh Foster, "Choreographies of Gender," *Signs* 24, no. 1 (1998): 1–33; Susan Leigh Foster, "Choreographies of Protest," *Theatre Journal* 55, no. 3 (2003): 395–412; Gottschild, *Digging the Africanist Presence*; and Randy Martin, *Performance as Political Act: The Embodied Self* (New York: Bergin and Garvey, 1990).

28. Thomas DeFrantz, *Dancing Revelations: Alvin Ailey's Embodiment of African American Culture* (New York: Oxford University Press, 2004).

29. Susan Leigh Foster, *Reading Dancing: Bodies and Subjects in Contemporary American Dance* (Berkeley: University of California Press, 1986), 58–59.

30. Eiko & Koma's relationship with the Japan Society and the Asia Society continues to this day.

31. Inta, Inc. (Eiko & Koma), The Retrospective Project, April 12, 2008.

1. FROM UTTER DARKNESS TO *WHITE DANCE*

1. Deborah Jowitt, "In Their Dance No Wind Blows," *Village Voice*, August 9, 1976.

2. Robert Fredericks, "Perspectives: New York," *Dance Magazine*, October 1976, 69.

3. Mona Sulzman, "Moth Comes to Life as Eiko and Koma White Dance," *Soho Weekly News*, July 29, 1976, 13.

4. Quoted in Windham, "Conversation with Eiko & Koma," 59.

5. My use of the conjunction "and" rather than the ampersand in this chapter differentiates the pair's early work together as students and novice performers from their professional artistic identity as Eiko & Koma, which began in earnest upon their arrival in Europe.

6. The time line was displayed during Eiko & Koma's performances at the Yerba Buena Center for the Arts in 2012.

7. Koma took Eiko's surname, Otake, in the 1980s.

8. UCLA course, fall 2006.

9. The postwar Japanese Communist Party was strongly linked with the labor movement and has held seats in the House of Representatives since 1946. The JCP broke with the Soviet Union and China in the 1960s.

10. William Marotti, *Money, Trains, and Guillotines* (Durham, NC: Duke University Press, 2013), 3.

11. Ibid., 3.

12. See also Thomas Havens, *Radicals and Realists in the Japanese Nonverbal Arts: The Avant-Garde Rejection of Modernism* (Honolulu: University of Hawaii Press, 2006); Doryun Chong, ed., *Tokyo 1955–1970: A New Avant-Garde* (New York: The Museum of Modern Art, 2012); and Peter Eckersall, *Performativity and Event in 1960s Japan: City, Body, Memory* (London: Palgrave Macmillan, 2013).

13. Michio Hayashi, "Tracing the Graphic in Postwar Japanese Art," in *Tokyo 1955–1970: A New Avant-Garde*, ed. Doryun Chong (New York: The Museum of Modern Art, 2012), 104.

14. See also Shawn Bender, *Taiko Boom: Japanese Drumming in Place and Mo-*

tion (Berkeley: University of California Press, 2012), especially ch. 2, "Genealogies of Taiko I."

15. Doryun Chong, "Even a Dog That Wanders Will Find a Bone," in *Eiko & Koma: Time Is Not Even, Space Is Not Empty*, ed. Joan Rothfuss (Minneapolis, MN: Walker Art Center, 2011), 59.

16. For more on postwar Japan, see John W. Dower, *Embracing Defeat: Japan in the Wake of World War II* (New York: W. W. Norton & Co., 2000); and Eiji Takemae, *Allied Occupation of Japan*, trans. Robert Ricketts and Sebastian Swan (New York: Continuum, 2003).

17. In 2014 Prime Minister Shinzo Abe bypassed Parliament with a cabinet resolution that allowed Japanese troops to participate in "collective self-defense." The move was seen to gut Article 9. Linda Sieg and Kiyoshi Takenaka, "Japan Takes Historic Step from Post-war Pacifism, OKs Fighting for Allies," *Reuters*, July 1, 2014, http://www.reuters.com/article/2014/07/01/us-japan-defense-idUSKBN0F52S12 0140701.

18. Chong, "Even a Dog That Wanders," 59.

19. Marotti, *Money, Trains, and Guillotines*, 192.

20. Translation by and quoted in Kurihara, "Eiko and Koma," 5.

21. See Alexandra Munroe et al., *Gutai: Splendid Playground* (New York: Guggenheim Museum, 2013).

22. Koma, interview with author, June 15, 2008.

23. As Bruce Baird points out, Hijikata was not alone in pushing the boundaries of modern dance, but he did become a leading representative of dance in the avant-garde. *Hijikata Tatsumi and Butō: Dancing in a Pool of Gray Grits* (New York: Palgrave Macmillan, 2011).

24. In retrospect *Kinjiki* has come to be considered the first butoh performance.

25. Bruce Baird, "Butō: Dance of Difference," in *A Processive Turn: The Video Aesthetics of Edin Vélez*, ed. Jorge Daniel Veneciano (Rutgers, NJ: Paul Robeson Galleries, 2007).

26. Nario Gōda, an eminent Japanese dance critic, has called ankoku butoh the avant-garde of butoh. "On Ankoku Butō," trans. Susan Blakeley Klein, in *Ankoku Butō: The Premodern and Postmodern Influences on the Dance of Utter Darkness*, by Susan Blakeley Klein (Ithaca, NY: Cornell East Asia Series, 1988), 83.

27. See chapter 3 for an analysis of this phenomenon.

28. Eiko & Koma's engagement with nuclear issues is discussed in chapters 2, 5, and 6.

29. William Marotti, "舞踏の問題性と本質主義の罠 'Buto No Mondaisei to Honshitsushugi No Wana'" [The problematics of butoh and the essentialist trap], *Shiataa Aatsu*, no. 8 (May 1997): 88–96.

30. Baird, *Hijikata Tatsumi and Butō*, 2011.

31. Miryam Sas, "Intermedia, 1955–1970," in *Tokyo 1955–1970: A New Avant-Garde*, ed. Doryun Chong (New York: The Museum of Modern Art, 2012), 139.

32. Baird, *Hijikata Tatsumi and Butō*, 2011.

33. Nanako Kurihara, "The Most Remote Thing in the Universe: Critical Analysis of Hijikata Tatsumi's Butoh Dance" (PhD diss., New York University, 1996), 1.

34. Windham, "Conversation with Eiko & Koma," 47.

35. The subtitle can also be translated as "Revolt of the Flesh."

36. I thank Bruce Baird for his insight on these points (e-mail communication with author, January 21, 2015).

37. Bruce Baird, Skype interview with author, October 1, 2013.

38. Caitlin Coker, Skype interview with author, October 1, 2013.

39. I thank Caitlyn Coker for this insight.

40. Coker, Skype interview.

41. I thank Bruce Baird for showing me these photographs.

42. Akiko Motofuji, *Hijikata Tatsumi to Tomo ni* 土方巽と共に [Together with Tatsumi Hijikata] (Tokyo: Chikuma Shobō, 1990).

43. Coker, Skype interview.

44. Baird, Skype interview.

45. I thank Bruce Baird for his insights about Ko, Ikeda, and Yoshioka's initial time in France (personal communication with author, July 7, 2014).

46. The photographer is credited as Mizuho.

47. In fact, Eiko & Koma were part of the impetus for this dance, having sent Ohno a packet of information about La Argentina that they gathered at the New York Public Library for the Performing Arts.

48. *A Portrait of Mr. O* (1969), *Mandala of Mr. O* (1971), and *Mr. O's Book of the Dead* (1972).

49. Eiko, e-mail communication with author, November 26, 2014.

50. Suzanne Carbonneau, "Naked: Eiko & Koma in Art & Life," in *Eiko & Koma: Time Is Not Even, Space Is Not Empty*, ed. Joan Rothfuss (Minneapolis, MN: Walker Art Center, 2011), 27. Brackets in original.

51. Koma, interview with author, June 15, 2008.

52. See Boyd, *Aesthetics of Quietude*.

53. Shoko Yamahata Letton, "Eiko and Koma: Dance Philosophy and Aesthetic" (master's thesis, Florida State University, 2009), 30.

54. Kate Elswit discusses the term "Ausdruckstanz" as a postwar development in *Watching Weimar Dance*.

55. Eiko clarifies: "Cabaret didn't last—we got fired. We were too artistic!" Interview with author, June 15, 2008.

56. Wigman died in 1973.

57. Eiko, interview with author, June 15, 2008.

58. Deborah Jowitt, Interview with Eiko & Koma, Oral History Project, Dance Collection, New York Public Library, January 6, 1998.

59. Carbonneau, "Naked," 27.

60. The title was in English.

61. Carbonneau, "Naked," 27.

62. Western authors influenced by Zeami include W.B. Yeats and Ezra Pound. Makoto Ueda, *Zeami, Basho, Yeats, Pound: A Study in Japanese and English Poetics* (The Hague: Mouton, 1965).

63. Joan Rothfuss, "White Dance," in *Eiko & Koma: Time Is Not Even, Space Is Not Empty*, ed. Joan Rothfuss (Minneapolis, MN: Walker Art Center, 2011), 86.

64. Koma, interview with author, June 15, 2008.

65. Eiko, interview with author, June 15, 2008.

66. Born in 1923 in Austria; died in 2012 in the United States. See Beate Sirota Gordon, *The Only Woman in the Room: A Memoir* (1997; Chicago: University of Chicago Press, 2014). See also Eiko's tribute to Gordon, "Beate: Thank You from Eiko & Koma," http://eikoandkoma.org/index.php?p=ek&id=3754.

67. Beate Sirota Gordon, telephone interview with author, September 2008.

68. The piece was billed variously in 1976 and 1977 as *White Dance*, *White Dance: Moth*, and *The White Moth*.

69. Eiko & Koma, program note for *White Dance Revival*, 2010, http://eiko andkoma.org/notesonwhitedance.

70. Program for *White Dance: Moth* at American Theatre Laboratory, September 15–18, 1977.

71. Eiko, interview with author, June 15, 2008.

72. Irene Oppenheim, interview with author, December 9, 2009.

73. Ibid.

74. Oppenheim clarifies, "I do remember at least two other contemporary Japanese dancers. One performed with Martha Graham; the other was a solo performer whom I saw in San Francisco before Eiko & Koma, Suzushi Hanayagi . . . . She was a radical dancer in the Anna Halprin mode. I say this just to point out I (we) were not totally unfamiliar with Japanese dancers though Eiko & Koma were/are true originals" (e-mail communication with author, November 23, 2014).

75. Janice Ross, "Tension in the Cocoon," *San Francisco Bay Guardian*, October 27, 1977.

76. In retrospect, Eiko questions this one-to-one weighing of their influences from Japan and Germany (interview with author, June 15, 2008).

77. Ibid.

78. *White Dance* program, 1976. An official translation of the full Kaneko poem is not available in English.

79. Other music includes J. S. Bach's *Concerto for Harpsichord* and "Sarabande" from *Suite for Solo Cello no. 5 in C Minor*, as well as Tibetan horn and cymbal.

80. Mitsuharu Kaneko, "Opposition," in *The Penguin Book of Japanese Verse*, trans. and ed. Geoffrey Bownas and Anthony Thwaite (London: Penguin Classics: 2009), 192.

81. Both photos by A. Loffler.

82. According to Oppenheim, the initial San Francisco performance included other images — she remembers one of a Japanese bath — but reviews of subsequent performances only mention projections of moths.

83. Fredericks, "Perspectives," 69.

84. Ibid.

85. Jowitt, "In Their Dance No Wind Blows."

86. Fredericks, "Perspectives," 69.

87. Oppenheim, interview with author, December 9, 2009.

88. Letton, "Eiko and Koma," 2009.

89. Kaneko, "Opposition," 192.

2. "GOOD THINGS UNDER 14TH STREET"

1. Christopher Mele describes these processes in detail in *Selling the Lower East Side: Culture, Real Estate, and Resistance in New York City* (Minneapolis: University of Minnesota Press, 2000). Of particular interest to this time period are chapter 6, "Urban Malaise, Community Abandonment, and Underground Subcultures of Decay," 180–219, and chapter 7, "Developing the East Village: Eighties Counterculture in the Service of Urban Capital," 220–54. See also Julie Ault, ed., *Alternative Art New York, 1965–1985* (Minneapolis: University of Minnesota Press, 2002).

2. Mele, *Selling the Lower East Side*, 217.

3. Chong, "Even a Dog That Wanders," 63.

4. Koma, speech presented to the Lower Manhattan Cultural Council, April 18, 2012. I was working on Eiko & Koma's Archive Project at their apartment at the time. As he was getting ready for the LMCC event, Koma asked me to type as he rehearsed what he wanted to say, and that document became his speech.

5. See Sally Banes, *Democracy's Body: Judson Dance Theater, 1962–1964* (Durham, NC: Duke University Press, 1993).

6. Susan Manning identifies this same transition as one from modernism to postmodernism in "Modernist Dogma and Post-Modern Rhetoric: A Response to Sally Banes' 'Terpsichore in Sneakers,'" *TDR: The Drama Review* 32, no. 4 (1988): 32–39.

7. Marcia B. Siegel, *The Tail of the Dragon: New Dance, 1976–1982* (Durham, NC: Duke University Press, 1991), xiii–xiv.

8. Eiko, interview with author, January 25, 2014.

9. This uncredited text appeared in *Fur Seal* programs under the title "Fur Seal." On Eiko & Koma's Web site, they clarify that the poem was "adapted by Eiko" from Mitsuharu Kaneko's 1937 poem "Seals" ("A Poem from the Program of Fur Seal [1977]," http://eikoandkoma.org/index.php?p=ek&id=3016). The full Japanese poem, accompanied by a 2008 English translation by Hiraoki Sato, is available at http://www.poetryinternationalweb.net/pi/site/poem/item/12103.

10. Daniel Webster, "Eiko and Koma: 'Fur Seal' Explores the Essence of the Animal World," *Philadelphia Inquirer*, February 9, 1978.

11. Eiko & Koma's focus on their own trunks in *Fur Seal* had the added bonus of providing a distinct break from their teachers' movement vocabularies. In a class at UCLA, Eiko said that they made a conscious decision not to use arms for many years, as part of their move away from the influence of Kazuo Ohno. Author's personal notes, November 8, 2006.

12. The set piece bears a striking resemblance to the set for Hijikata's *Hosotan* (1972).

13. Jennifer Dunning, "Flying, Waltzing, Walking and Jogging in Place," *Dance Magazine*, August 1977, 25.

14. *Wallow* is discussed in detail in chapter 4.

15. Jan Halsey, "'Fur Seal' Boring, but Intriguing," *Daily Democrat*, August 11, 1978, 11.

16. K. S. W., "Fur Seal," *Daily Telegraph*, November 6, 1981.

17. Bonnie Sue Stein, "Butoh: 'Twenty Years Ago We Were Crazy, Dirty and Mad,'" *TDR: The Drama Review* 20, no. 2 (1986): 112.

18. Anna Kisselgoff, "Two Dancers from Japan in 'Fur Seal,'" *New York Times*, February 28, 1978, 16.

19. By the fall New York premiere presented by Dance Theater Workshop at American Theatre Laboratory, the title had been shortened to the equally evocative but less directly determined *Before the Cock Crows*. Performances at the San Francisco Museum of Modern Art and the Santa Barbara Museum of Art fit into the pattern Eiko & Koma established in Europe, where they appeared at black box and proscenium theaters, museums and galleries, and universities. As they became more established in the US dance scene, they performed less and less in museums. The past five years have seen them returning to museum and gallery spaces, especially with the Retrospective Project. Mystifyingly, Eiko & Koma accompanied the evening premiere performances of *Before the Cock Crows* with a weekday matinee of *Fur Seal* (described as "a fable for our times") aimed at children. The San Francisco Museum of Modern Art calendar listing described the dance in this way: "Although inspired by biblical quotation, the dance program to be premiered at the Museum is not religious in nature. Instead, the title is used thematically. Eiko and Koma work

with the implied tensions, the time limitation, the suggestion of repetition and the pulse, both physical and emotional, of a contained event, which once started, moves toward an end that is both arbitrary and predestined."

20. Perhaps Kisselgoff's Aesop comment in her *Fur Seal* review influenced their decision to take on this story.

21. Evidently the premiere performances involved three actual chickens, which were fed onstage at the end of the piece. By the time Eiko & Koma performed in Los Angeles the following month, Eiko's pecking solo replaced the live chickens.

22. While it's common for Eiko & Koma to make changes to a dance to relate to its performance space, these changes feel less like the ones that have become part of their performance practice and more like young artists trying out different approaches. "Does this work? How about this?" The version I describe here is from video documentation of the October 28, 1978, performance, during the New York premiere run at American Theatre Laboratory sponsored by DTW.

23. Letton, "Eiko and Koma," 52.

24. Ibid., 58.

25. Janice Ross, "Eiko and Koma in 'Fur Seal,'" *Artweek* 8, no. 41 (1977).

26. Letton, "Eiko and Koma," 57; emphasis in original.

27. In this, Eiko & Koma were aligned with dancers such as Meredith Monk, who also trod the same margins of emotion and nonlinear meaning.

28. Marilyn Tucker, "Avant Garde Dancers to Be Reckoned With," *San Francisco Chronicle*, July 14, 1978, 64.

29. Ibid.

30. Lewis Segal, "Eiko and Koma in 'Cock Crows,'" *Los Angeles Times*, August 29, 1978.

31. Jean Nuchtern, "Tripping," *Soho News*, November 9, 1978.

32. *Fluttering Black* is Eiko & Koma's only piece for which there exists no video documentation. Photographs, reviews, and the performers' recollections are the only remaining traces of the dance.

33. San Francisco Museum of Modern Art program.

34. Carbonneau, "Eiko & Koma in Art & Life," 35.

35. Burt Supree, "Voice Choices: Dance," *Village Voice*, August 6, 1979.

36. Branca's score was later released on the 1981 album *The Ascension*.

37. In fact, Sonic Youth guitarist Lee Ranaldo plays on the 1981 recording of "The Spectacular Commodity."

38. Burt Supree, "Only Disconnect," *Village Voice*, August 27, 1979.

39. Barbara Newman, "Reviews VIII," *Dance Magazine*, October 1979, 110.

40. Eiko & Koma were close friends with Dehn until her death in 1985. She taught them jazz technique and even choreographed a dance for them to Patti Smith's "Be-

cause the Night." She left her papers and the original reels of *The Spirit Moves: A History of Black Social Dance on Film, 1900–1986* to Eiko & Koma when she died.

41. Such a schedule likely offered them the opportunity to try out a new work while meeting the demand for a popular, established one.

42. Kei Takei, to whom Eiko & Koma were often compared at the time despite quite different performance practices, danced in the same space two weeks prior.

43. Tobi Tobias, "Flagging," *Soho Weekly News*, August 16, 1979, 43.

44. Supree, "Only Disconnect."

45. "Review," *Artweek*, September 15, 1979, 3.

46. Ibid.

47. Chong, "Even a Dog That Wanders," 64.

48. Marda Kirn, "Minds Behind the Movement," *Westword*, July 9, 1981, 11.

49. Eiko & Koma press release, March 24, 1981.

50. Jack Anderson, "Dance: Eiko and Koma Under an Umbrella," *New York Times*, November 23, 1979, C17.

51. Eiko & Koma performed "Fission" as part of the Dance '79/80 California Arts Council Dance Touring Program, which also included Margaret Jenkins, Lynn Dally, ODC, Bella Lewitzky Dance Company, Mangrove, Aman Folk Ensemble, and others. Outdoor and site-specific versions of "Fission" were performed at the Battery Park City landfill, the University of California, Berkeley, the University of Hawaii at Manoa's East-West Center, and the San Francisco MoMA using large, white, box platforms as their stage.

52. Deborah Jowitt, "I'll Give You the Answer-If You've Got a Week," *Village Voice*, May 6, 1981, 81.

53. Ariana Burrows, "Dancer's Performance at UB Is Drama on Nuclear Anxieties," *Buffalo News*, July 24, 1983.

54. After 9/11, Eiko became very interested in atomic bomb literature, eventually earning a master's degree on the subject from New York University. This theme in Eiko & Koma's body of work is explored extensively in chapter 6.

55. J. L. Conklin, "Dance Notes: The Wondrous Abstractions of Eiko and Koma," *Reader*, December 18, 1981.

56. Anti-Nuclear Dance Benefit Concert, presented by the People's Anti-Nuclear Information & Cultural Committee, December 14, 1980, at the Larry Richardson Dance Gallery and featuring works by Margaret Beals, Eiko & Koma, June Finch, and Sarah Rudner. Dancers for Disarmament, PS 122, June 3–6, 1982.

57. Eiko & Koma, "Dirt News No. 1," *Contact Quarterly* 7, no. 1 (Fall 1981): 40.

58. *Nurse's Song* program.

59. Naropa residency flyer.

60. Dilley was a noted dancer with the Merce Cunningham Dance Company and The Grand Union.

61. Ivan Sygoda to Barbara Dilley, January 7, 1981 (personal archive, Eiko & Koma).

62. Ginsberg wrote and recorded an album, *William Blake's Songs of Innocence and Experience, Tuned by Allen Ginsberg* (MGM Records/Verve Forecast, 1970). The album featured twenty-one poems set to music with Ginsberg on harmonium and vocals, Peter Orlovsky on vocals, and a band of jazz musicians including Don Cherry.

63. William Blake, *The Project Gutenberg eBook of Songs of Innocence and Songs of Experience, by William Blake*, http://www.gutenberg.org/files/1934/1934-h/1934-h .htm#page25, 2008.

64. Lerner would later create the stage environment for 1991's *Land*.

65. Eiko, interview with author, January 25, 2014.

66. Jennifer Dunning, "Dance: 'Nurse's Song' at the Kitchen," *New York Times*, November 30, 1981, C13.

67. Noted performance artist and member of The Performance Group Leeny Sack was a member of the band. Audience members interested in joining the chorus were directed to the "Dirt Board" in the lobby to sign up to sing in subsequent performances.

68. Dunning, "Dance," C13.

69. Ibid.

70. Nancy Goldner, "Tarzan and Eve," *Soho Weekly News*, December 15, 1981, 25.

71. Ibid.

72. Dunning, "Dance," C13.

73. Deborah Jowitt, "Caught in the Cross-Cultural Riptide," *Village Voice*, December 9, 1981.

74. Chong, "Even a Dog That Wanders," 63.

75. Eiko, interview with author, January 25, 2014.

76. Koma, speech, April 18, 2012.

77. Chong, "Even a Dog That Wanders," 63.

78. Ibid., 64.

3. JAPANESE/AMERICAN

1. Reynaldo Alejandro, "Asian American Dance — A Promising Outlook." *Bridge: An Asian American Perspective*, Summer 1978, 15.

2. Gwin Chin, "Japanese Dancers in America: What Draws Them?," *New York Times*, December 2, 1979, D1, D27.

3. Gloria Strauss, "Roundtable Discussion with Asian American Dance Choreographers," *Bridge: An Asian American Perspective*, Summer 1978, 37.

4. Barbara E. Thornbury, *America's Japan and Japan's Performing Arts: Cultural Mobility and Exchange in New York 1952–2011* (Ann Arbor: University of Michigan Press, 2013).

5. The exhibition ran December 5, 2013, to March 23, 2014, at the Interference Archive, Brooklyn, New York (http://interferencearchive.org/serve-the-people-the-asian-american-movement-in-new-york/).

6. My understanding of the history of *Bridge* in the context of other Asian American movement publications and organizations is informed by William Wei's *The Asian American Movement* (Philadelphia: Temple University Press, 1993).

7. The Asian American Dance Theatre was both a touring company and an arts center. The company toured until 1993, while the arts center continues to exist as the Asian American Arts Centre. "About Us," http://artspiral.org/about.html.

8. New York Public Library Performing Arts Research Collection — Dance.

9. In *America's Japan and Japan's Performing Arts*, Thornbury adapts H. D. Harootunian's concepts of "America's Japan" and "Japan's Japan." For Harootunian, "America's Japan" developed during the occupation and involved an "appeal to fixed cultural values—consensuality—uninterrupted continuity, and an endless present derived from an exceptionalist experience" (2). Thornbury's definition of America's Japan, deriving specifically from the performing arts, "is a complex chronicle of cultural mobility and exchange—one that often reduces Japanese culture to a worn-out set of Orientalist stereotypes, but one that also broadly engages in a dynamic, transnational conversation about artistic production and encounter" (2). Her definition of Japan's Japan is "national culture for the global market" (12); she locates this in particular databases that delineate artists sanctioned by governmental and perigovernmental agencies. See also H. D. Harootunian, "America's Japan/Japan's Japan," in *Japan in the World*, ed. Masao Miyoshi and H. D. Harootunian (Durham, NC: Duke University Press, 1993), 196–221.

10. Thornbury, *America's Japan*, 32.

11. Wei, *Asian American Movement*, 121.

12. "Times Net Down in 4th Quarter," *New York Times*, February 15, 1979, D4.

13. For more on Shuji, the "enfant terrible of Japanese performance," see Carol Fisher Sorgenfrei, *Unspeakable Acts: The Avant-garde Theatre of Terayama Shuji and Postwar Japan* (Honolulu: University of Hawaii Press, 2005).

14. See Nancy Shields, *Fake Fish: The Theater Of Kobo Abe* (Boston: Weatherhill Publishing, 1996).

15. Kazuo Ohno's family name is variously transliterated in English as Ohno, Ōno, or Ono. I prefer "Ohno" because that is the spelling used by the Kazuo Ohno Dance Studio in all its English-language materials.

16. Thornbury, *America's Japan*, 108.

17. Though Beate Gordon told me in a September 2008 interview that she was presenting experimental work before 1976, Thornbury identifies Eiko & Koma as the first time the Japanese avant-garde came uptown.

18. Eiko & Koma press release, 1976.

19. Sulzman, "Moth Comes to Life," 13.

20. Jack Anderson, "New York Newsletter," *Dancing Times*, November 1977, 87.

21. Quoted in Thornbury, *America's Japan*, 114.

22. Letton, "Eiko and Koma," 6.

23. Bert Winther, "Japanese Thematics in Postwar American Art: From Soi-Disant Zen to the Assertion of Asian-American Identity," in *Japanese Art After 1945: Scream Against the Sky*, ed. Alexandra Munroe (New York: Harry N. Abrams/Yokohama Museum of Art, 1996), 55–67.

24. See Wong, "Towards a New Asian American Dance Theory."

25. Deborah Wong, *Speak It Louder: Asian Americans Making Music* (New York: Routledge, 2004), 215.

26. Donna Perlmutter, "Outer Limits of Dance Have Earthly Appeal," *Los Angeles Herald Examiner*, June 30, 1980, B5.

27. Tucker, "Avant Garde Dancers to Be Reckoned With," 64.

28. Though there has been heated debate about the boundaries and definitions of modern and postmodern dance (see especially the exchange between Susan Manning and Sally Banes across three issues of *TDR* in 1988–1989), in the late 1970s and early 1980s there was a fair amount of fluidity among the terms, which also included the short-lived "New Dance." Critics variously labeled Eiko & Koma modern, postmodern, avant-garde, and New Dance, without much specificity.

29. Palumbo-Liu, *Asian/American*, 3.

30. Ibid., 171.

31. For more on the model minority myth, see Victor Bascara, *Model-Minority Imperialism* (Minneapolis: University of Minnesota Press, 2006); Ellen Wu, *The Color of Success: Asian Americans and the Origins of the Model Minority* (Princeton, NJ: Princeton University Press, 2014); Harry Kitano, *Japanese Americans: The Evolution of a Subculture* (Upper Saddle River, NJ: Prentice Hall, 1969); and William Petersen, "Success Story, Japanese-American Style," *New York Times*, January 9, 1966, 21, 33, 36, 38, 41, 43.

32. Palumbo-Liu, *Asian/American*, 172. For an argument that challenges binaries between Asian and African Americans, see Vijay Prasad, *Everybody Was Kung Fu Fighting: Afro-Asian Connections and the Myth of Cultural Purity* (Boston: Beacon Press, 2002).

33. Anna Kisselgoff, "The Dance: Kazuo Ohno's 'Dead Sea,'" *New York Times*,

November 21, 1985, http://www.nytimes.com/1985/11/21/arts/the-dance-kazuo
-ohno-s-dead-sea.html.

34. Yutian Wong insightfully points out that Asians are perceived "as remnants
of a past civilization," with the result that "the Asian body *is* historical rather than
contemporary" (*Choreographing Asian America* [Middletown, CT: Wesleyan, 2010],
12–13).

35. Thornbury, *America's Japan*, 18.

36. Ruby Shang, "A Taste of Japanese Dance." *New York Times*, July 4, 1982, http://
www.nytimes.com/1982/07/04/arts/a-taste-of-japanese-dance.html?module=
Search&mabReward=relbias%3Ar%2C%7B%222%22%3A%22RI%3A12%22%7D.

37. See Marotti, "Buto no mondaisei"; and Baird, *Hijikata Tatsumi and Butoh*.

38. Anna Kisselgoff, "Dance View: Grotesque Imagery Has Come to Dance,"
New York Times, April 15, 1984, http://www.nytimes.com/1984/04/15/arts/dance
-view-grotesque-imagery-has-come-to-dance.html?pagewanted=all.

39. For example, the association of butoh with bald, stark men in white makeup
and *fundoshi* loincloths stems directly from Sankai Juku, not Hijikata or Ohno.

40. Anna Kisselgoff, "Japanese Avant-Garde Dance Is Darkly Erotic," *New York
Times*, July 15, 1984, 1. N.b., the online version of the article is titled "Dance View;
Japan's New Dance Is Darkly Erotic." Baird opens his book with this quotation
(*Hijikata Tatsumi and Butoh*, 1). Even more than direct quotes, however, this sum-
mation of butoh became the basis for the common understanding of the form in
the United States.

41. Kisselgoff, "Japanese Avant-Garde Dance." As I explained in chapter 1, the
association between butoh and the sense of "stamping dance" was not in common
circulation when Hijikata and his collaborators took up the name.

42. Susan Blakeley Klein argues convincingly that butoh has both pre- and postmodern influences, but never calls it prehistorical or primal. *Ankoku Butō: The Premodern and Postmodern Influences on the Dance of Utter Darkness* (Ithaca, NY: Cornell University East Asia Series, 1988).

43. Kisselgoff, "Japanese Avant-Garde Dance."

44. Mindy Aloff, "Dance," *Nation*, June 14, 1986, 835–36.

45. Debra Cash, "The Year of Dance from Japan," *Boston Globe*, June 6, 1986, 66.

46. Granted, butoh was and continues to be a marginal performance practice.
But as Palumbo-Liu points out, Japanese Americans were already both marginal *and*
model.

47. It is worth noting that this narrative remains popular in the United States, as
evidenced by periodic revisiting of the 1954 original Japanese movie, *Gojira*, including the 1998 Roland Emmerich *Godzilla* and the 2014 version by Gareth Edwards.

48. The saying "bomb them into the Stone Age" comes from US Air Force general

Curtis LeMay's ghostwritten autobiography, *Mission with LeMay: My Story* (New York: Doubleday & Co., 1965). In full the quote reads, "My solution to the problem would be to tell [the North Vietnamese Communists] frankly that they've got to draw in their horns and stop their aggression or we're going to bomb them into the Stone Age. And we would shove them back into the Stone Age with Air power or Naval power—not with ground forces" (565). He later claimed the quote was a result of the ghostwriter overwriting. It is significant to this discussion that General LeMay was the architect of the Pacific bombing campaign during World War II, including the firebombing campaign against Japanese cities.

49. See, for example, Aloff, "Dance," 835–36; Marcia B. Siegel, "Japanese Dances: Intriguing Ambiguity," *Christian Science Monitor*, October 21, 1987; and Amanda Smith, "Review," *Dance Magazine*, May 1986.

50. Windham, "Conversation with Eiko and Koma," 52.

51. See Lisa Lowe, *Immigrant Acts: On Asian American Cultural Politics* (Durham, NC: Duke University Press, 1996), especially chapter 4, "Imagining Los Angeles in the Production of Multiculturalism," 84–96.

52. Kisselgoff, "Japanese Avant-Garde Dance."

53. Min did work with Hijikata the year before Hijikata died and was subsequently associated with butoh, although he has long since rejected the term for his own dances.

54. Cash, "The Year of Dance from Japan," 57, 66.

55. Kisselgoff, "Japanese Avant-Garde Dance."

56. Deborah Jowitt, "Dark Art," *Village Voice*, October 11, 1994, 105.

57. My understanding is that the 1985 and 1991 statements are the same; I cite the 1991 version here because it is the one that remains in Eiko & Koma's archives.

58. Bruce Baird, "Killing the Asian Man Twice" (paper presented at the Congress on Research in Dance/American Society for Theater Research joint conference, Seattle, WA, November 7, 2010).

59. Windham, "Conversation with Eiko and Koma," 52; emphasis in original.

60. Gilles Kennedy, "New York-Renowned Butoh Artists Debut in Japan," *Japan Times*, January 22, 1989.

61. Thornbury, *America's Japan*, 20.

62. Ibid., 23.

63. Ibid.; emphasis in original.

64. Wong, "Artistic Utopias," 144–62.

65. See chapter 2 for an extensive discussion of *Fission*. Interestingly, the reception of *Fission* was more directly linked to wanting to do something about the "nuclear anxieties" seen in the dance. Indeed, Eiko & Koma performed the dance at a number of benefits for anti-nuclear organizations. The subsequent nuclear discourse around

butoh was not connected to taking action in the present, but instead fixed the post-nuclear firmly in the past.

66. Rosemary Candelario, "An Asian American *Land*: Eiko & Koma Choreograph Cultural Politics," in *Contemporary Directions in Asian American Dance*, ed. Yutian Wong (Madison: University of Wisconsin Press, forthcoming).

67. Cited in Thornbury, *America's Japan*, 182.

68. Ibid.

69. Jowitt, "Dark Art," 105.

70. A video of the panel discussion is part of the University of Wisconsin–Madison Dance Department archives. Andrea Harris graciously arranged for me to view the footage. All quotes in this paragraph are from the video.

71. Kwan, *Kinesthetic City*; Priya Srinivasan, *Sweating Saris: Indian Dance as Transnational Labor* (Philadelphia: Temple University Press, 2011); and Yutian Wong, "Towards a New Asian American Dance Theory," "Artistic Utopias," and *Choreographing Asian America*.

72. See, for example, Jeffrey Lorenzo Perillo, "Hip-hop, Streetdance, and the Remaking of the Global Filipino" (PhD diss., University of California, Los Angeles, 2013); and Angeline Shaka, "Hula 'Olapa and the Hula Girl': Contemporary Hula Choreographies of the Concert Stage" (PhD diss., University of California, Los Angeles, 2011).

73. I am grateful to Yutian Wong for bringing these blog posts to my attention. Wendy Perron, "Martha Graham and the Asian Connection," *Dance Magazine* (blog), March 24, 2014, http://www.dancemagazine.com/blogs/wendy/5725; and Wendy Perron, "When Martha Got to Be Asian," *Wendy Perron* (blog), March 31, 2014, http://wendyperron.com/when-martha-got-to-be-asian.

74. Douglas McGray, "Japan's Gross National Cool," *Foreign Policy* 130 (May–June 2002): 44–54.

4. DANCING-WITH SITE AND SCREEN

1. Eiko & Koma brochure, http://eikoandkoma.org/sites/ek/files/2PAGER_07 022007.pdf.

2. The collaboration was collected in a book entitled *Kamaitachi*, first published in Japan in a run of one thousand in 1969. Out of print for many years, a limited English edition was published in 2005, and a larger printing was issued in 2009. Eikoh Hosoe, *Kamaitachi* (New York: Aperture, 2009).

3. *Water Lilies* relates to images of flowers in Monet's paintings, and like *White Lotus* it has Buddhist overtones. *Flowers-Birds-Wind-Moon*, or ka cho fuu getsu 花鳥風月, is a compound word meaning "nature" but with strong classical arts overtones. In other words it is more about aesthetics and concepts of beauty than about

those elements themselves. Even *Hana* is more about an artistic blooming rather than flowers. "Hana-gurui," literally translated as "Flower Crazy," refers to a flower that blooms out of season and thus evokes something that is unexpected. In that piece Ohno participated in a performance by ikebana master Yukio Nakagawa. I thank Bruce Baird and Eiko Otake for their insights parsing out these various uses of flowers.

4. For more on these dances see chapters 1 and 2.

5. Deborah Jowitt, "Crawling into a Womb of Rice," *Village Voice*, February 22, 1983; Tobi Tobias, "Food for the Eye," *New York*, March 14, 1983, 68, 71.

6. *Night Tide* initiated a significant body of work performed in the nude, which extends to the recent *Fragile* (2012).

7. Eiko & Koma use the terms "media dance" and "dance for camera" interchangeably to describe their works created collaboratively by their live dancing bodies, a camera, and editing processes, and made to be watched on some sort of screen. I follow their lead and use these terms to describe this work.

8. For more on *Fur Seal*, see chapter 2.

9. Donna Haraway, "The Promises of Monsters: A Regenerative Politics for Inappropriate/d Others," in *Cultural Studies*, ed. L. Grossberg, C. Nelson, and P. A. Treichler (New York: Routledge, 1992), 296.

10. My description and discussion of *River* is based on an amalgamation of documentation of the performance at various sites and times and should be considered my own re-choreography-on-the-page.

11. I use the word *frame* primarily in Susan Foster's sense of a group of devices — including everything from announcements of the performance, the setup of the performance site, program materials, the beginning and ending of a dance, and the dancers' gaze — that establish a set of expectations in the audience about how this performance is set apart from everyday life. *Reading Dancing: Bodies and Subjects in Contemporary American Dance* (Berkeley: University of California Press, 1986). At the same time, I am aware of the filmic sense of the word as a rectangular formatting of what is visible. The stretch of canvas concentrates both of these meanings as a set piece that arouses expectations in the viewers and as a screen on which video frames will be displayed.

12. The sound score included ambient sounds and recorded music by contemporary Japanese composer Ushio Torikai.

13. The inclusion of the media dance in a site-adaptive piece, *River*, may at first appear contradictory, but in fact videos are able to flexibly move — to DVD players, computers, galleries — and in this sense are also site adaptive.

14. Artist Judd Weisberg created the sculpture by using driftwood from Schoharie Creek, the water in which Eiko & Koma developed and premiered *River*. The

sculpture's fan shape evokes Japanese fans that depict a story. *River* program, Art Awareness, 1995.

15. The way that Eiko & Koma engaged with community environmental groups around *River* is admittedly different from recent moves in the visual art world, in which artists actively engage with communities in work that is determined precisely by the nature of the engagement rather than by formalist concerns. In this mode of working, site is defined not as a physical location, but as a relationship and/or community in which the "relationship . . . may *itself* be the artwork" (Suzanne Lacy, quoted in Miwon Kwon, *One Place After Another* [Cambridge, MA: MIT Press, 2002], 105). See also Grant Kester, *Conversation Pieces: Community and Communication in Modern Art* (Berkeley: University of California Press, 2004); and Suzanne Lacy, ed., *Mapping the Terrain: New Genre Public Art* (Seattle: Bay Press, 1994).

16. This description is taken from my own documentation of Eiko & Koma's 2006 course at the University of California, Los Angeles, Making Dance as an Offering, as well as other Delicious Movement workshops I have observed. Rather than direct quotations, these notes should be considered paraphrased statements that attempt to capture Eiko & Koma's style of introducing movement exercises and translate these spoken instructions into written descriptions.

17. Of course, this is a feature of all of Eiko & Koma's performances, whether on proscenium stages or in site-specific locations.

18. Elizabeth Grosz, *Space Time and Perversion: Essays on the Politics of Bodies* (New York: Routledge, 1995), 108.

19. Raymond Williams, "Nature," in *Keywords: A Vocabulary of Culture and Society*, Revised Edition (New York: Oxford University Press, 1985), 219–24.

20. See, for example, Claude Lévi-Strauss, *The Raw and the Cooked*, Mythologiques Volume 1 (Chicago: University of Chicago Press, 1983).

21. More specifically, nature is often linked to the bodies of women, people of color, and cultures of the Southern Hemisphere.

22. A recent example of this recurring trope in literature, television, and film is James Cameron's *Avatar* (2009).

23. Paul Wapner, *Living Through the End of Nature: The Future of American Environmentalism* (Cambridge, MA: MIT Press, 2013).

24. Bill McKibben, *The End of Nature* (New York: Random House, 1989).

25. Paul Crutzen and Eugene Stoermer, "The 'Anthropocene,'" *Global Change Newsletter* 41 (2000): 17–18.

26. Jamie Lorimer, *Wildlife in the Anthropocene: Conservation After Nature* (Minneapolis: University of Minnesota Press, 2015).

27. Other applications of the term *interface*, including "user interface" and "social interface theory" (see especially Norman Long, *Development Sociology: Actor*

Perspectives [New York: Routledge, 2001]), gesture to connections between humans and technology and among humans. The user interface seems to be primarily about increasing ease of operation, however, whereas social interface theory focuses on human interactions that may be difficult because of backgrounds and goals that may be at odds with one another.

28. Donna Haraway, "A Manifesto for Cyborgs: Science, Technology, and Socialist Feminism in the 1980s," *Socialist Review* 15, no. 2 (1985): 65–107.

29. Octavia Butler's science fiction trilogy Lilith's Brood, composed of *Dawn* (1987), *Adulthood Rites* (1988), and *Imago* (1989), explores similar themes among humans and aliens in a postnuclear world.

30. Lorimer, *Wildlife in the Anthropocene*, 5.

31. Ibid.

32. I do not mean to suggest that all of Eiko & Koma's site or screen dances employ methods of dancing-with to generate interface. Some early screen dances, *Tentacle* (1983) and *Undertow* (1988), for example, are abstract explorations of the possibilities of a cinematic choreography, whereas *Wallow* (1984) is a site-specific adaptation of *Fur Seal* (1977), and *Bone Dream* (1985) is a fairly straightforward adaptation of the proscenium dance *Night Tide* (1984) for camera. Site dances such as *Event Fission* (1980) and *Offering* (2002) engage with processes of mourning and reparation. Similarly, not all of Eiko & Koma's dances that take a nature-themed title (e.g., *Land*, *Wind*) generate interface. In pieces such as these, or even in the proscenium version of *River* (1997), nature provides a setting or theme, but the choreography itself has concerns other than the relationship between humans and nature.

33. In a 2006 course at UCLA, Koma taught about eye-angle through the poetry of Masaoka Shiki and photographer Eugene Smith. A noted haiku poet (1867–1902), Shiki spent a number of years bedridden with illness, and many of his haiku deal with things he could see from bed through his window in his bedroom. His eye-angle influenced his art. In Smith's famous photograph *Tomoko Uemura in Her Bath*, Tomoko is very close to her mother. Her eye-angle is perhaps just a foot away. Koma used these works to introduce the idea of dancing and watching from a different angle.

34. See, for example, the lecture and film series *Killing Us Softly* by Jean Kilbourne, http://www.jeankilbourne.com/videos/.

35. The DVD *Media Dance* includes *Lament* (1985), *Husk* (1987), *Undertow* (1988), and *Breath* (1999).

36. In this sense, Eiko & Koma's use of video in this installation reflects Gilles Deleuze's proposition that the postwar "cinematographic image itself 'makes' movement" (*Cinema 1: The Movement-Image* [Minneapolis: University of Minnesota Press, 1986], 156).

37. For more on *Naked*, see the conclusion.

38. In 2013 Eiko & Koma presented a version of *The Caravan Project* in the Museum of Modern Art's lobby as part of the exhibition *Tokyo 1955–1970: A New Avant-Garde*. The six-day durational performance, performed the entire time the museum was open, blurs the distinctions I make between gallery and site-based interfaces.

5. SUSTAINED *MOURNING*

1. In what seems to have been a one-time event, Eiko & Koma performed a version of their 1984 piece *Night Tide* under the title *Mourning* in 2004 as part of the Imagine Festival of Arts, Issues and Ideas at the Asia Society. The 2007 piece, while drawing from a number of pieces from their repertoire, did not reference *Night Tide*.

2. David Eng, "The Value of Silence," *Theatre Journal* 54, no. 1 (2002): 88.

3. Indeed, my use of "intimate" points to the ways that sex and violence are sometimes blurred in the piece.

4. Deborah Jowitt, "Eiko and Koma Pity the Earth: Two Dancers and a Pianist Create a Transcendent Lament," *Village Voice*, October 20, 2007; Thea Singer, "A Primal 'Mourning' and Hope for Rebirth," *Boston Globe*, July 18, 2008.

5. *Mourning* program, May 1, 2007, Santa Barbara, CA.

6. Syllabus for Delicious Movement for Forgetting, Remembering, and Uncovering (DANCE 244/EAST 244, Spring 2007, Wesleyan University).

7. *Offering* was a notable work of mourning in its own right, created by Eiko & Koma in the wake of 9/11 and performed for free in public parks across New York City in 2002 and 2003. See chapter 6 for an extended discussion of this piece.

8. For more on Eiko & Koma's collaboration with Branca, see chapter 2.

9. *Land* and *Raven* are both discussed in chapter 6.

10. Grace Cho, *Haunting the Korean Diaspora: Shame, Secrecy, and the Forgotten War* (Minneapolis: University of Minnesota Press, 2008), 19.

11. Sigmund Freud, "Mourning and Melancholia," in *The Standard Edition of the Complete Psychological Works of Sigmund Freud*, ed. J. Strachey (London: The Hogarth Press and the Institute of Psycho-analysis, 1953), 14:245.

12. Ibid., 256.

13. Alan Tansman, "Catastrophe, Memory, and Narrative: Teaching Japanese and Jewish Responses to Twentieth-Century Atrocity," *Discourse* 25, nos. 1 & 2 (2004): 254.

14. In fact, for Freud melancholia and mourning share all characteristics—"a profoundly painful dejection, cessation of interest in the outside world, loss of the capacity to love, inhibition of all activity" (Freud, "Mourning and Melancholia," 244)—except one, which belongs to melancholia alone: "an extraordinary diminution in . . . self-regard" (246). Freud summarizes this key difference among mourn-

ing and melancholia in the following way: "In mourning it is the world which has become poor and empty; in melancholia it is the ego itself" (ibid). In other words, for the melancholic, the ultimate loss is an ego-loss that may or may not be the result of an actual object-loss.

15. Dominick LaCapra, *History and Memory After Auschwitz* (Ithaca, NY: Cornell University Press, 1998).

16. As a historian writing about Auschwitz, and in particular historiographical, literary, and filmic responses to Auschwitz, LaCapra's central concern is memory. His goal is to find a way to "check acting out through the role of memory and critical perspective" (ibid., 206) and to develop a sort of reflexivity for historians that aims toward an objectivity borne of working through one's own relationship to the historical problem in question, and which helps one avoid what he identifies as a problem of transference. The latter is achieved, he argues, via working through, which becomes "a regulatory ideal whose actual role in history is a matter of inquiry and argument and whose desirability is affirmed but acknowledged as problematic" (ibid., 196).

17. David Eng writes, "If, for instance, there is no public language by which a loss can be recognized, then melancholia assumes a social dimension of contemporary consequence that must be acknowledged and analyzed as a problem of the political" ("Melancholia in the Late Twentieth Century," *Signs* 25, no. 4 [2000]: 1278).

18. Douglas Crimp, *Melancholia and Moralism: Essays on AIDS and Queer Politics* (Cambridge, MA: MIT Press, 2002), 133.

19. Ibid., 147.

20. Ibid., 149.

21. Chungmoo Choi, "The Politics of War Memories toward Healing," in *Perilous Memories: The Asia-Pacific War(s)*, ed. T. Fujitani, Geoffrey M. White, and Lisa Yoneyama (Durham, NC: Duke University Press, 2001), 395–410.

22. This is not to discount the material needs of the former comfort women, nor to deny the satisfaction they may gain from the official acknowledgment of their suffering contained in the reparations.

23. Hyunjung Kim, "Rethinking Korean Subjectivity: Salp'uri and Women in South Korea," *Discourses in Dance* 4, no. 1 (2007): 49–63.

24. Kim claims that the ritual origins of the concert form of *salp'uri* are at best unclear.

25. David Gere, *How to Make Dances in an Epidemic: Tracking Choreography in the Age of AIDS* (Madison: University of Wisconsin Press, 2004), 101.

26. See chapter 3 for an extended discussion of the model minority trope.

27. Anne Anlin Cheng, "The Melancholy of Race," *Kenyon Review* 19, no. 1 (1997): 56.

28. Ibid., 50.

29. Ibid., 52. For Douglas Crimp a similar process plays out in the gay community at the height of the AIDS epidemic, in which gay melancholia is acted out in the policing of the queer.

30. See the introduction for a discussion of abjection.

31. Cheng, "Melancholy of Race," 53.

32. Freud pathologizes repetition as "acting out." See my earlier discussion of LaCapra.

33. Freud, "Mourning and Melancholia," 257.

34. See Gilles Deleuze, *Cinema 2: The Time-Image* (Minneapolis: University of Minnesota Press, 1989).

35. Žižek, *Violence*.

36. Robert Diaz, "Reparative Acts: Redress and the Politics of Queer Undoing in Contemporary Asian/America" (PhD diss., City University of New York, 2007), 15.

37. Eng, "Value of Silence."

38. Miryam Sas, *Experimental Arts in Postwar Japan: Moments of Encounter, Engagement, and Imagined Return* (Cambridge, MA: Harvard University Asia Center, 2011), 20.

39. Eng, "Melancholia in the Late Twentieth Century," 1280.

40. Post-performance talk back, Santa Barbara, CA, May 1, 2007.

41. By 1984 the AIDS crisis was in full swing. Though Eiko & Koma did not intend to make a dance about AIDS, there was an atmosphere of loss in both the dance field and New York. AIDS would have been on the minds of the dancers and many audience members. Eiko, e-mail communication with author, August 8, 2015.

42. Lament was shown as part of the Walker Art Center's collection exhibition *Event Horizon* (2010). Commissioned by the Walker, *Lament* is considered part of their permanent collection.

43. The piece *Offering* premiered in 2002 in response to September 11. In chapter 6 I argue that the piece is a choreography of transformation and reparation, and thus I do not discuss it here.

44. Course titles include Making Dance as an Offering, Delicious Movement for Forgetting, Remembering, and Uncovering, or simply Delicious Movement. Eiko has also taught courses at the University of Minnesota, the New School, Colorado College, and other places.

45. Kyoko Hayashi, *From Trinity to Trinity*, trans. Eiko Otake (Barrytown, NY: Station Hill of Barrytown, 2010).

46. ibid., 50.

47. Ibid., 33.

6. GROUND ZEROES

1. Dancing in the Streets is a New York arts presenter that aims to "illuminate the urban experience with free public performances and site-specific installations that examine the kinetic life and history of natural and architectural public spaces" (http://www.dancinginthestreets.org/about.html). The parks included Battery Park City, Tudor City Park, Bryant Park, Madison Square Park, Clinton Community Garden, and Dag Hammerskjold Plaza. In 2003 Dancing in the Streets once again presented *Offering*, this time at Danspace Project in the cemetery of St. Mark's Church. The dance was also performed across the United States and internationally; I focus here on the seven performances of the piece in New York City in July 2002.

2. The original project, called *Coffin Dance*, was intended to bring death out of the private and into the public realm. When 9/11 made death ubiquitous in New York City, the focus changed to mourning the dead (Eiko, e-mail communication with author, August 20, 2015).

3. Eiko & Koma, *Offering* program notes, http://eikoandkoma.org/index.php?p =ek&id=2282.

4. In *Korematsu v. United States* 323 U.S. 214 (1944), for example, Fred Korematsu, a Japanese American who had attempted to avoid internment, challenged the constitutionality of Executive Order 9066. The Supreme Court upheld the exclusion order in a 6–3 ruling. In 1983 Korematsu's conviction for disobeying 9066 was voided by a US District Court on the basis that the US government knowingly submitted false evidence in support of the necessity of internment. President Gerald Ford issued the first apology in 1976; Ronald Reagan and George H. W. Bush offered subsequent apologies in 1988 and 1992, respectively.

5. Diana Taylor, *The Archive and the Repertoire: Performing Cultural Memory in the Americas* (Durham, NC: Duke University Press, 2003), 243.

6. To my knowledge there is no photographic or video documentation of the first two performances in the series at the Belvedere in Battery Park City. I take my description and analysis of *Offering* at this site from Elizabeth Zimmer, "Sacred Spaces," *Village Voice*, July 23, 2002, http://www.villagevoice.com/2002–07–23/dance /sacred-spaces/; and Jack Anderson, "Images of Devastating Grief and the Courage to Go On," *New York Times*, July 19, 2002, http://www.nytimes.com/2002/07/19 /arts/dance/19EIKO.html?pagewanted=1.

7. Eiko & Koma's performance site is directly across the street from the Japan Society (the documentation shows a close-up of the Society's bright red "Japan" banners), an organization that has presented and supported the choreographers ever since they first came to the United States in 1976.

8. Taylor, *The Archive and the Repertoire*, 264. As a landfill site, Battery Park City is itself a sort of presence (out) of nothing. The development's existence as the rem-

nants of the construction of the World Trade Center seems significant as a site for mourning the WTC's loss.

9. Eiko & Koma's choice of verdant community spaces to make their offering resonates with noted architect Tadao Ando's rejected proposal to mark the 9/11 site with a simple dirt mound from which grass would grow.

10. Interestingly, at Tudor City Park the thrust stage (with the gate directly behind the set piece) became in effect a theater in the round when passersby paused to watch the dance from outside the park through the gates.

11. Aysola performed in the seven 2002 New York performances; other versions of the piece, including the 2003 New York performances at the graveyard of St. Mark's Church, featured Eiko & Koma only. *Be With* is discussed in chapter 7.

12. Preeti Sharma, "The (T)errors of Visibility" (master's Thesis, University of California, Los Angeles, 2008).

13. Diaz, "Reparative Acts," 3.

14. Nicholas Birns, "Ritualizing the Past: Ralph Lemon's Counter-Memorials," *PAJ: A Journal of Performance and Art*, no. 81 (2005): 22.

15. Ibid.

16. Performances at Bryant Park and Madison Square Park happened earlier in the day. All performances were lit with simple par cans.

17. Gere, *How to Make Dances in an Epidemic*, 168.

18. Eiko & Koma, *Offering* program notes, http://eikoandkoma.org/index.php ?p=ek&id=2282.

19. Cheng, "Melancholy of Race," 58.

20. Robert Diaz, "Melancholic Maladies: Paranoid Ethics, Reparative Envy, and Asian American Critique," *Women & Performance: A Journal of Feminist Theory* 16, no. 2 (2006): 204.

21. Diaz, "Reparative Acts," 12.

22. Diaz, "Melancholic Maladies," 216.

23. One could argue that New Yorkers sought to immediately make space for mourning on the streets of Manhattan through impromptu memorials. These personal messages and gestures created quite a different space than those centered on the flag or elected officials. Zipporah Lax Yamamoto has considered these memorials in depth in "After 9/11: Transformations of Memory Into History" (PhD diss., University of California, Los Angeles, 2011). Street performances such as "Our Grief Is Not a Cry for War"—in which groups of more than forty people gathered silently and repeatedly in Times Square, their mouths covered with surgical masks that called to mind the toxic dust that coated the city as well as the silencing of dissent— also attempted to construct an alternative space of mourning in the weeks after 9/11.

24. This wording was used before the memorial opened. The current wording

reads, "a powerful reminder of the largest loss of life resulting from a foreign attack on American soil and the greatest single loss of rescue personnel in American history." It is interesting to notice how the towers have now disappeared from the rhetoric (http://www.911memorial.org/about-memorial).

25. I borrow this phrase from the New Orleans–based organization The People's Institute for Survival and Beyond, which engages in what they call undoing racism training and organizing (http://www.pisab.org/).

26. Saidya Hartman, *Scenes of Subjection: Terror, Slavery, and Self-Making in Nineteenth-Century America* (New York: Oxford University Press, 1997), 77.

27. Joshua Chambers-Letson, "Reparative Feminisms, Repairing Feminism — Reparation, Postcolonial Violence, and Feminism," *Women & Performance: A Journal of Feminist Theory* 16, no. 2 (2006): 170–71; emphasis in original.

28. Ibid., 177.

29. "About Our Work," http://eikoandkoma.org/index.php?p=ek&id=1987.

30. Inderpal Grewal, "Transnational America: Race, Gender and Citizenship after 9/11," *Social Identities* 9, no. 4 (2003): 536.

31. In a speech to a joint session of Congress on September 20, 2001, Bush said that Americans could help through their "continued participation and confidence in the American economy" (http://www.washingtonpost.com/wp-srv/nation/specials/attacked/transcripts/bushaddress_092001.html). One week later, in a speech at Chicago's O'Hare airport, he urged Americans to "do your business around the country. Fly and enjoy America's great destination spots. Go down to Disney World in Florida, take your families and enjoy life the way we want it to be enjoyed" (http://www.washingtonpost.com/wp-srv/nation/specials/attacked/transcripts/bush_092701.html).

32. Doreen Massey, *World City* (Cambridge, UK: Polity Press, 2007), 193.

33. Taylor, *The Archive and the Repertoire*, 46.

34. Joseph Roach, *Cities of the Dead: Circum-Atlantic Performance* (New York: Columbia University Press), 1996.

35. Michel de Certeau, *The Practice of Everyday Life*, trans. Steven Rendall (Berkeley: University of California Press, 1984), 91.

36. In *Kinesthetic City*, SanSan Kwan also uses Certeau's "Walking in the City" essay as a launching point from which to discuss global/local issues in New York City. She is particularly concerned with spatial practices of Chinese transnationalism in that city's Chinatown.

37. Eric Darton, *Divided We Stand: A Biography of New York's World Trade Center* (New York: Basic Books, 1999), 75.

38. The Lower Manhattan Cultural Council offered residency space in the North Tower to artists. Eiko & Koma rehearsed *When Nights Were Dark* (2000) there.

39. Darton, *Divided We Stand*. See also Angus Kress Gillespie, *Twin Towers: The*

Life of New York City's World Trade Center (New Brunswick, NJ: Rutgers University Press, 1999); and James Glanz and Eric Lipton, *City in the Sky: The Rise and Fall of the World Trade Center* (New York: Times Books, 2003).

40. Darton quotes Carl Weisbrod, a longtime public official dealing with planning and economic development and board member of the Lower Manhattan Development Corporation, as calling Lower Manhattan the birthplace of not only New York City, but even the American nation (*Divided We Stand*, 211).

41. The terms "world" and "global" when coupled with city are highly contested. While they have traditionally referred to economically dominant cities (New York, London, Tokyo), they are sometimes used to mean cosmopolitan (itself a contested term). Some scholars argue for alternate definitions that acknowledge the dominance of certain cities in particular spheres (e.g., religion, film). Massey, *World City*, especially 36–42; and Saskia Sassen, *The Global City* (Princeton, NJ: Princeton University Press, 1991).

42. See also David Harvey, *The Condition of Postmodernity* (Malden, MA: Blackwell Publishing, 1990).

43. Massey, *World City*, 207.

44. Ibid., 215.

45. Koma told the story of getting the Art on the Beach gig in his speech at the Lower Manhattan Cultural Council in 2012: "In 1980 we got a phone call from Creative Time. She said, 'We are interested in you dancing at Art on the Beach.' I couldn't believe it that we have a beach in Manhattan! And so the next day we went to the beach. I asked her, 'How much can you pay?' She said, '$750.' I wanted to know, 'Who else is performing?' 'Bill T. Jones.' 'Is he also getting paid $750? OK!'"

46. Darton, *Divided We Stand*, 172.

47. Ibid., 176.

48. Construction was very much ongoing in 1980.

49. SanSan Kwan writes: "De Certeau's essay seems to presage the 11 September 2001 fall of the Twin Towers. It is not so much that he imagines their literal fall, but that he recognizes that the world cannot sustain the totalizing visibility that one has at 1,370 feet up" ("Choreographing Chineseness: Global Cities and the Performance of Ethnicity" [PhD diss., New York University, 2003], 209).

50. Eiko & Koma, "Hunger of the Land," http://www.eikoandkoma.org/sites/eiko /files/HungeroftheLandPR.pdf (link no longer active).

51. *Fragile* was conceived as an extension of *Naked* (2010), a living installation at the Walker Art Center.

52. Eiko, personal communication with author, February 27, 2012.

53. In 2015 and 2016 Eiko continued to perform *A Body in . . .* at numerous locations.

54. Program notes, *Eiko: A Body in Places*, 2014.

7. "TAKE ME TO YOUR HEART"

1. My analysis of the piece is based on two versions: one performed in eleven US cities in 2006, featuring nine members of Reyum, based on an edited video of performances at the Asia Society in New York City, May 19–21, 2006, available at http://www.eikoandkoma.org/index.php?id=1141; the other performed in Taiwan, featuring six members of Reyum, based on my own viewings of rehearsals and performances held at Novell Hall in Taipei, May 11–17, 2009.

2. The one exception was a performance at the Skirball Cultural Center in Los Angeles, where the piece was performed in an outdoor fountain. Eiko & Koma had previously performed *Offering* (2002) in that fountain and suggested to the Cambodian painters that they adapt the normally dirt-grounded *Stories* to water.

3. I use the term "action painting" in the art historical sense, not as a synonym for abstract expressionism, but as a term that calls attention to painting as process rather than a product. This also allows me to focus on the performative aspects of painting that occur during the dance.

4. The 1975 Khmer Rouge communist revolution declared an end to two thousand years of Cambodian history. Anything that was associated with that history—including the traditional arts—was deemed reactionary and was subject to extermination. See Elizabeth Becker, *When The War Was Over: Cambodia and the Khmer Rouge Revolution* (rev. ed., New York: Public Affairs, 1998); David Chandler, *Voices from S-21: Terror and History in Pol Pot's Secret Prison* (Berkeley: University of California Press, 2000); and David Chandler, *A History of Cambodia*, 4th ed. (Boulder, CO: Westview Press, 2007).

5. "About Reyum," http://www.reyum.org/about_reyum.html.

6. Two founding myths conceive of Cambodia as always already intercultural. The first is that of Preah Thaong Neang Neak, in which a foreign Brahmin named Preah Thaong, guided by strange dreams, sails into the domain of a serpent princess named Neang Neak. Their forces engage in battle, but Preah Thaong wins. Neang Neak consequently marries him, and to celebrate this marriage her father, the serpent king, comes from his underwater kingdom and sucks up an ocean to reveal a fertile land in which the two start their kingdom and race. The second recounts the union of Mera, a celestial dancer, with a hermit "born of himself" named Kampu. These two myths have been interwoven at times, but the fact of the matter is, the Khmer race (and therefore Cambodia) has always been a product of the union between native and foreign, feminine and masculine, human and supernatural (Prumsodun Ok, e-mail communication with author, December 12, 2012).

7. Homi Bhabha, *The Location of Culture*, 2nd ed. (New York: Routledge, 2004), 56.

8. The red canvas was originally created for the 2001 collaboration with Anna

Halprin, *Be With*, which I discuss later in the chapter. Eiko reports that the canvas was their attempt to replicate the red earth tones that grace the walls of Halprin's studio (e-mail communication with author, August 8, 2015).

9. Sotha Kun, Sokchanthorn Ngin, Sok Than, and Chivalry Yok performed in 2006 and 2009 in addition to Charian and Peace; Vannak Huoth, Nimit Ouen, and Sophon Phe performed in 2006 only.

10. In the 2009 performances, having entered with the young men at the beginning for the introductions, she moves uninterrupted across the stage.

11. In Khmer the song is called "Sdab Besdong Bong Phaung," or "Listen to My Heart" (Rasmey Hang Meas, audio CD vol. 233, 2006).

12. The 2009 performance of the piece interrupts a reading that sees Charian as an object of painting in that she in fact is the first one to appear with a paint brush in her hand. She literally paints (the backs of) the other Reyum members; they figuratively paint her.

13. Eiko, e-mail communication with author, March 12, 2008.

14. See, for example, Laura Mulvey, *Visual and Other Pleasures* (Bloomington: Indiana University Press, 1989).

15. When *Cambodian Stories* was restaged in 2009 in Taipei, Taiwan, three of the male Reyum Painting Collective members were unable to rejoin the cast due to family or work commitments, necessitating changes to the choreography, most noticeably in the opening sequence. Charian paints the backs of the young men and is first to speak. While she still includes her "when I dance" statement, now she adds a description of the Reyum School, from which at this point they have all graduated. Thus, her role is still differentiated from that of her male collaborators, but she is nonetheless presented as an integrated member of the group.

16. Along these lines, film director Budd Boetticher observes: "What counts is what the heroine provokes, or rather what she represents . . . . In herself the woman has not the slightest importance" (quoted in Mulvey, *Visual and Other Pleasures*, 19).

17. Eiko, e-mail communication with author, March 12, 2008.

18. Susan Leigh Foster, "Choreographies of Gender," *Signs* 24, no. 1 (1998): 8.

19. It is not surprising that one of the first things Cambodians did after the Khmer Rouge was to revive the arts, which were seen as a symbol of the nation's spirit and identity. See Toni Shapiro-Phim, *Dance and the Spirit of Cambodia* (Ithaca, NY: Cornell University Press, 1994).

20. Group interview, May 11, 2009, Taipei, Taiwan.

21. This resonates with Cambodia's animistic and ancestor worship practices. Khmer classical dancer Prumsodun Ok writes, "Before every performance, we stage rituals to appease the gods, deceased teacher and ancestor spirits and offer ourselves in dance and song. By performing choreography passed on to us, we are embodying

the voices, experiences, and visions of our ancestors. Our bodies become a vehicle of their history, and we mark our place within their lineage" (e-mail communication with author, December 12, 2012).

22. It is largely believed that Khmer society, in its earliest days, was matrilineal in nature. See, for example, Trudy Jacobsen, *Lost Goddesses: The Denial of Female Power in Cambodian History* (Copenhagen: Nordic Institute of Asian Studies, 2008).

23. Khmer classical dancers also once painted themselves completely white. This practice was ended with the introduction of modern makeup (Prumsodun Ok, e-mail communication with author, December 12, 2012).

24. Eiko, e-mail communication with author, March 12, 2008.

25. Eiko & Koma, *The Making of Cambodian Stories*, 2005.

26. Nermeen Shaikh, "Cambodian Stories an Offering of Painting and Dance: Interview with Eiko & Koma," 2006, http://www.asiasociety.org/arts/06cambodian interview.html (link no longer active).

27. Cambodia did not suffer the same abuses under Japanese occupation as other countries, largely due to the fact that the French Vichy government remained in nominal control of the country. For more, see Chandler, *History of Cambodia*.

28. Claire Conceison, "Translating Collaboration: *The Joy Luck Club* and Intercultural Theater," *TDR: The Drama Review* 39, no. 3 (1995): 151.

29. Shimakawa is referencing and responding to Ann Cooper Albright's *Choreographing Difference: The Body and Identity in Contemporary Dance* (Middletown, CT: Wesleyan University Press, 1997).

30. Karen Shimakawa, "Loaded Images: Seeing and Being in 'Fan Variations,'" in *Narrative/Performance: Cross-Cultural Encounters at APPEX*, ed. Judy Mitoma, Anoosh Jorjorian, and Richard D. Trimillos (Los Angeles: Center for Intercultural Performance, 2004), http://www.wac.ucla.edu/cip/archive/appexbook/loadedima ges.html, sec. II. N.b., this online publication does not have page numbers. Lacking more specific reference points, I point the reader to sections of the essay.

31. Phillip Zarrilli, "The Aftermath: When Peter Brook Came to India," *TDR: The Drama Review* 30, no. 1 (1986): 92–99; and Avanthi Meduri, Phillip Zarrilli, and Deborah Neff, "More Aftermath after Peter Brook," *TDR: The Drama Review* 32, no. 2 (1988): 14–19.

32. Shaikh, "Cambodian Stories."

33. Eiko & Koma, "Friends of Reyum," http://www.eikoandkoma.org/index .php?id=1289 (link no longer active).

34. Rustom Bharucha, "A Collision of Cultures: Some Western Interpretations of the Indian Theatre," *Asian Theatre Journal* 1, no. 1 (1984): 1–20; Richard Schechner, "A Reply to Rustom Bharucha," *Asian Theatre Journal* 1, no. 2 (1984): 245–53; and Rustom Bharucha, "A Reply to Richard Schechner," *Asian Theatre Journal* 1, no. 2 (1984): 254–60.

35. Bharucha asserts that "intercultural practice is unavoidably subsumed within the inequities of the global economy, but this does not mean it has to submit to the cultural demands of the market. Indeed, there is an oppositional component within interculturalism that cannot be separated from a larger critique of capital" ("Consumed in Singapore: The Intercultural Spectacle of Lear," *Theatre Journal* 31, no. 1 [2001]: 107). In contrast, Schechner believes "as far back as we can look in human history peoples have been deeply, continuously, unashamedly intercultural. Borrowing is natural to our species." He continues: "The more contact among peoples the better. The more we, and everyone else too, can perform our own and other peoples' cultures the better" ("Intercultural Performance: 'An Introduction,'" *TDR: The Drama Review* 26, no. 2 [1982]: 4).

36. Julie Stone Peters, for example, claims that postcolonial theorists have "perpetuated the unnuanced bifurcation of West and East, First and Third Worlds, developed and undeveloped, primitive and civilized" ("Intercultural Performance, Theatre Anthropology, and the Imperialist Critique: Identities, Inheritances and Neo-Orthodoxies," in *Imperialism and Theatre: Essays on World Theatre, Drama and Performance*, ed. J. E. Gainor [London: Routledge, 1995], 199–213). C. J. W.-L. Wee reminds us, furthermore, that in the context of globalization, "economic and political power has shifted away from a geographical location called the 'West' to a less identifiable position in the 'globe'" ("Imagining 'New Asia' in the Theatre: Cosmopolitan East Asia and the Global West," in *Rogue Flows: Trans-Asian Cultural Traffic*, ed. Koichi Iwabuchi, S. Muecke, and M. Thomas [Hong Kong: Hong Kong University Press, 2004], 119–50).

37. For Bharucha, the intracultural is an intervention into multiculturalism that calls attention to diversity within a region that is presumed to be homogeneous, such as India. While multiculturalism is often used to celebrate the nation, intraculturalism challenges the notion of national cohesion. See "Interculturalism and Its Discriminations: Shifting the Agendas of the National, the Multicultural and the Global" *Third Text* 13, no. 46 (1999): 3–23; and *The Politics of Cultural Practice: Thinking Through Theatre in an Age of Globalization* (Middletown, CT: Wesleyan University Press, 2000).

38. The Asia Society's mission statement is as follows: "Asia Society is the leading educational organization dedicated to promoting mutual understanding and strengthening partnerships among peoples, leaders and institutions of Asia and the United States in a global context. Across the fields of arts, business, culture, education, and policy, the Society provides insight, generates ideas, and promotes collaboration to address present challenges and create a shared future" (http://asiasociety .org/about/mission-history).

39. Marta Savigliano, *Tango and the Political Economy of Passion* (Boulder, CO: Westview Press, 1995), 198.

40. For more on Asian American cultural politics, see the introduction.

41. Shimakawa, "Loaded Images."

42. Lewis Segal, "Cambodian Stories Affirms a Lust for Life," *Los Angeles Times*, April 7, 2006, http://articles.latimes.com/2006/apr/07/entertainment/et-stories7.

43. What I am describing here shares some aims with movements such as New Genre Public Art and community-based art, although there are significant differences in scope and intent. See Lacy, *Mapping the Terrain*; Kester, *Conversation Pieces*; and Kwon, *One Place After Another*.

44. Eiko & Koma, *The Making of Cambodian Stories*, 2005.

45. Segal, "Cambodian Stories Affirms a Lust for Life."

46. Hedy Weiss, "Whimsy, Sadness Blend in Asian Delicacy," *Chicago Sun Times*, May 15, 2006, http://findarticles.com/p/articles/mi_qn4155/is_20060515/ai_n163 65902.

47. Lisa Traiger, "After the Killing Fields," April 3, 2006, http://danceviewtimes .com/2006/spring/01/eikoandkoma.html.

48. The critics also accepted unquestioningly the relationship between the Japanese American elders and the Cambodian young people; the history of Japanese occupation of Cambodia was absent from the stories about *Cambodian Stories*.

49. Traiger, "After the Killing Fields."

50. Weiss, "Whimsy, Sadness Blend in Asian Delicacy."

51. Jennifer Dunning, "Grand Themes, Conveyed in Movement and in Paint, in 'Cambodian Stories,'" *New York Times*, May 22, 2006, http://www.nytimes.com /2006/05/22/arts/dance/22stor.html?_r=1&oref=slogin.

52. "Cambodian Stories: An Offering of Painting and Dance," 2006, http://www .asiasociety.org/arts/06cambodianstories.html (link no longer active).

53. Wong, "Towards a New Asian American Dance Theory."

54. Kondo, *About Face*.

55. Aiwah Ong, *Flexible Citizenship: The Cultural Logics of Transnationality* (Durham, NC: Duke University Press, 1999).

56. Savigliano, *Tango*.

57. Edward W. Said, *Orientalism*, 1st Vintage Books ed. (New York: Vintage, 1979), 20.

58. Although the dancers never explicitly interacted with Jeanrenaud, she was visible on stage during the entire piece.

59. Eiko & Koma performed the piece at Reyum during their initial residency there. Thus, it was the first piece of theirs that Charian and Peace saw.

60. Orla Swift, "Handing Down the Dance: Eiko and Koma, Known for Their Impossibly Slow Movement and Exquisite Style, Are Trying to Preserve Their Creations by Teaching Them to Two Teenagers," *The News and Observer*, June 27, 2007, http://www.newsobserver.com/lifestyles/arts_entertainment/adf/story/614914

.html; and Byron Woods, "ADF: Eiko and Koma," *Independent Weekly*, July 4, 2007, http://www.indyweek.com/gyrobase/content?oid=oid%3A156563.

61. Susan Broili, "Eiko & Koma Teams with Cambodian Dancers for First Time," *Herald Sun*, June 20, 2007, http://heraldsun.com/resources/printfriendly.cfm?Story ID=858585.

62. Eiko & Koma, *Dance Magazine* Award acceptance speech, 2006.

IN LIEU OF A CONCLUSION

1. Jim Curran, "Avant-Garde Japaneese [sic] Modern Dance Combines Beatle Music, Whale Wails," *Daily Pennsylvanian*, 1978.

2. Webster, "Eiko and Koma."

3. Marcia B. Siegel, telephone interview with author, July 18, 2008.

4. André Lepecki, "The Body as Archive: Will to Re-Enact and the Afterlives of Dances," *Dance Research Journal* 42, no. 2 (2010): 31.

5. Eiko Otake, "Retrospective Reflections," 2012, 6, http://eikoandkoma.org/sites /ek/files/RetrospectiveProject_Eikoreflections_121017.pdf.

6. Jacques Derrida, *Archive Fever: A Freudian Impression*, trans. Eric Prenowitz (Chicago: University of Chicago Press, 1996).

7. Hal Foster, "An Archival Impulse," *October* 110 (Fall 2004): 3–22.

8. Lepecki, "The Body as Archive."

9. Diana Taylor, "Save As," *Emisferica* 9, nos. 1–2 (Summer 2012), http://hemi sphericinstitute.org/hemi/en/e-misferica-91/taylor.

10. Sara Wookey, e-mail communication with author, March 19, 2014.

11. Lynn Matluck Brooks and Joellen A. Meglin, "Preserving the Ephemeral," *Dance Chronicle* 34, no. 1 (2011): 1.

12. Ramsay Burt, "Memory, Repetition and Critical Intervention: The Politics of Historical Reference in Recent European Dance Performance," *Performance Research* 8, no. 2 (2003): 34–41.

13. Lepecki, "The Body as Archive." For example, it is through Move's drag performance that we learn other things about Graham beyond a reenactment of the choreography.

14. Maaike A. Bleeker, "(Un)Covering Artistic Thought Unfolding," *Dance Research Journal* 44, no. 2 (2012): 14.

15. Philip Auslander, "The Performativity of Performance Documentation," *PAJ: A Journal of Performance and Art* 84 (2006): 1–10.

16. Mark Franko, "Revaluing the Score: Archival Futurity," *Dance Research Journal* 44, no. 2 (2012): 1.

17. For more on this, see the curated discussion on Amelia Jones's "Presence in Absentia" in the *International Journal of Screendance* 2 (2012): 39–55.

18. #JEZ3PREZ & ATCHU, "On the Question of the Anarchives of Occupy Wall

Street," *Emisferica* 9, nos. 1–2 (Summer 2012), http://hemisphericinstitute.org/hemi
/en/e-misferica-91/jez3prezaatchu.

19. Lepecki, "The Body as Archive," 43.

20. Sarah Jones, Daisy Abbott, and Seamus Ross, "Redefining the Performing
Arts Archive," *Archival Science* 9, nos. 3–4 (2009): 165–71.

21. Matthew Reason, "Archive or Memory? The Detritus of Live Performance,"
New Theatre Quarterly 19, no. 1 (2003): 82–89; and Matthew Reason, *Documenta-
tion, Disappearance and the Representation of Live Performance* (New York: Palgrave
Macmillan, 2006).

22. Michel Foucault, *The Archaeology of Knowledge: The Discourse on Language*,
trans. A. M. Sheridan Smith (New York: Pantheon Books, 1972), 130; emphasis in
original.

BIBLIOGRAPHY

Albright, Ann Cooper. *Choreographing Difference: The Body and Identity in Contemporary Dance*. Middletown, CT: Wesleyan University Press, 1997.

Alejandro, Reynaldo. "Asian American Dance — A Promising Outlook." *Bridge: An Asian American Perspective*, Summer 1978, 15.

Aloff, Mindy. "Dance." *The Nation*, June 14, 1986.

Anderson, Jack. "Dance: Eiko and Koma Under an Umbrella." *New York Times*, November 23, 1979, sec. C17.

———. "Eiko and Koma Slow Time Down." *New York Times*, December 7, 1986. http://www.nytimes.com/1986/12/07/arts/dance-view-eiko-and-koma-slow -time-down.html?module=Search&mabReward=relbias%3Aw%2C%7B%222% 22%3A%22RI%3A14%22%7D (accessed January 21, 2011).

———. "Images of Devastating Grief and the Courage to Go On." *New York Times*, July 19, 2002. http://www.nytimes.com/2002/07/19/arts/dance /19EIKO.html?pagewanted=1 (accessed May 12, 2010).

———. "New York Newsletter." *Dancing Times* (November 1977): 87–88.

Apicella-Hitchcock, Stephan, Naomi Ben-Shahar, Monika Bravo, and Patty Chang. *Site Matters: The Lower Manhattan Cultural Council's World Trade Center Artist Residency 1997–2001*. New York: Lower Manhattan Cultural Council, 2004.

apipower. "Art for the Community: A Short History of Basement Workshop in New York." *Azine: Asian American Movement Ezine* (2009). Available from artasiamerica.org.

Appadurai, Arjun. *Modernity at Large: Cultural Dimensions of Globalization*. Minneapolis: University of Minnesota Press, 1996.

Ault, Julie, ed. *Alternative Art New York, 1965–1985*. Minneapolis: University of Minnesota Press, 2002.

Auslander, Philip. "The Performativity of Performance Documentation." *PAJ: A Journal of Performance and Art* 84 (2006): 1–10.

Azuma, Eiichiro. *Between Two Empires: Race, History, and Transnationalism in Japanese America*. New York: Oxford University Press, 2005.

Baird, Bruce. "Butō: Dance of Difference." In *A Processive Turn: The Video*

Aesthetics of Edin Vélez, edited by Veneciano, Jorge Daniel, 42–49. Rutgers, NJ: Paul Robeson Galleries, 2007.

———. *Hijikata Tatsumi and Butō: Dancing in a Pool of Gray Grits*. New York: Palgrave Macmillan, 2012.

Banes, Sally. *Democracy's Body: Judson Dance Theatre, 1962–1964*. Durham, NC: Duke University Press, 1993.

———. "Icon and Images in New Dance." In *New Dance, U.S.A.*, edited by Nigel Redden, 6–21. Minneapolis, MN: Walker Art Center, 1981.

———. "'Terpsichore' Combat Continued." *TDR: The Drama Review* 33, no. 4 (1989): 17–18.

———. *Terpsichore in Sneakers: Post-Modern Dance*. Middletown, CT: Wesleyan, 1987.

Banes, Sally, and Susan Manning. "Terpsichore in Combat Boots." *TDR: The Drama Review* 33, no. 1 (1989): 13–16.

Bascara, Victor. *Model-Minority Imperialism*. Minneapolis: University of Minnesota Press, 2006.

Baxmann, Inge. "The Body as Archive: On the Difficult Relationship between Movement and History." In *Knowledge in Motion: Perspectives of Artistic and Scientific Research in Dance*, edited by Gehm, Sabine, Husemann, Pirkko, and von Wilcke, Katharina, 207–16. TanzScripte. Bielefeld, Germany: Transcript Verlag, 2007.

Becker, Elizabeth. *When the War Was Over: Cambodia and the Khmer Rouge Revolution*. rev. ed. New York: Public Affairs, 1998.

Bender, Shawn. *Taiko Boom: Japanese Drumming in Place and Motion*. Berkeley: University of California Press, 2012.

Bhabha, Homi. *The Location of Culture*. 2nd ed. New York: Routledge, 2004.

Bharucha, Rustom. "A Collision of Cultures: Some Western Interpretations of the Indian Theatre." *Asian Theatre Journal* 1, no. 1 (1984): 1–20.

———. "Consumed in Singapore: The Intercultural Spectacle of Lear." *Theatre Journal* 31, no. 1 (2001): 107–27.

———. "Interculturalism and Its Discriminations: Shifting the Agendas of the National, the Multicultural and the Global." *Third Text* 13, no. 46 (1999): 3–23.

———. *The Politics of Cultural Practice: Thinking Through Theatre in an Age of Globalization*. Middletown, CT: Wesleyan University Press, 2000.

———. "A Reply to Richard Schechner." *Asian Theatre Journal* 1, no. 2 (1984): 254–60.

Birns, Nicholas. "Ritualizing the Past: Ralph Lemon's Counter-Memorials." *PAJ: A Journal of Performance and Art*, no. 81 (2005): 18–22.

Blake, William. *The Project Gutenberg eBook of Songs of Innocence and Songs of Experience, by William Blake*. Project Gutenberg, December 25, 2008. Available from http://www.gutenberg.org/files/1934/1934-h/1934-h .htm#page25 (accessed May 17, 2014).

Bleeker, Maaike A. "(Un)Covering Artistic Thought Unfolding." *Dance Research Journal* 44, no. 2 (Winter 2012): 13–25.

Bownas, Geoffrey, and Thwaite, Anthony, trans. *The Penguin Book of Japanese Verse*. UNESCO Collection of Representative Works: Japanese Series. London: Penguin Classics, 2009.

Boyd, Mari. *The Aesthetics of Quietude: Ota Shogo and the Theatre of Divestiture*. Tokyo: Sophia University Press, 2006.

Broili, Susan. "Eiko & Koma Teams with Cambodian Dancers for First Time." *Herald Sun*, June 20, 2007. http://heraldsun.com/resources/printfriendly .cfm?StoryID=858585 (accessed December 10, 2007).

Brooks, Lynn Matluck, and Joellen A. Meglin. "Preserving the Ephemeral." *Dance Chronicle* 34, no. 1 (2011): 1–4. doi:10.1080/01472526.2011.550170.

Brown, Alan. "A Look at Eiko and Koma." *Berkeley Independent and Gazette*, September 2, 1979.

Burrows, Ariana. "Dancer's Performance at UB Is Drama on Nuclear Anxieties." *Buffalo News*, July 24, 1983.

Burt, Ramsay. "Memory, Repetition and Critical Intervention: The Politics of Historical Reference in Recent European Dance Performance." *Performance Research* 8, no. 2 (2003): 34–41.

Candelario, Rosemary. "An Asian American *Land*: Eiko & Koma Choreograph Cultural Politics." In *Contemporary Directions in Asian American Dance*, edited by Yutian Wong. Studies in Dance History. Madison: University of Wisconsin Press, 2016.

———. "Bodies, Camera, Screen: Eiko & Koma's Immersive Media Dances." *International Journal of Screendance* 4 (2014): 80–92. http://screendance journal.org/article/view/4522#.VIE0YlfF-Q5.

———. "Eiko & Koma: Choreographing Spaces Apart in Asian America." PhD diss., University of California, Los Angeles, 2011.

———. "A Manifesto for Moving: Eiko & Koma's Delicious Movement Workshops." *Journal of Theatre, Dance and Performance Training* 1, no. 1 (2010): 88–100.

Carbonneau, Suzanne. "Naked: Eiko & Koma in Art & Life." In *Eiko & Koma: Time Is Not Even Space, Is Not Empty*, edited by Rothfuss, Joan, 18–43. Minneapolis, MN: Walker Art Center, 2011.

Carstensen, Jeanne. "Spawn On! Bob Carroll and the Art of Dying." Special issue, "After," *ARTicles*, no. 8 (2002): 158–71.

Cash, Debra. "The Year of Dance from Japan." *Boston Globe*, June 6, 1986, 57, 66.

Chambers-Letson, Joshua Takano. *A Race So Different: Performance and Law in Asian America*. New York: New York University Press, 2013.

———. "Reparative Feminisms, Repairing Feminism—Reparation, Postcolonial Violence, and Feminism." *Women & Performance: A Journal of Feminist Theory* 16, no. 2 (2006): 169–89.

Chandler, David. *A History of Cambodia*. 4th ed. Boulder, CO: Westview Press, 2007.

———. *Voices from S-21: Terror and History in Pol Pot's Secret Prison*. Berkeley: University of California Press, 2000.

Cheng, Anne Anlin. "The Melancholy of Race." *Kenyon Review* 19, no. 1 (1997): 49–61.

Cheng, Cindy I-Fen. *Citizens of Asian America: Democracy and Race during the Cold War*. New York: New York University Press, 2013.

Chin, Gwin. "Japanese Dancers in America: What Draws Them?" *New York Times*, December 2, 1979, Arts & Leisure sec.

Cho, Grace. *Haunting the Korean Diaspora: Shame, Secrecy, and the Forgotten War*. Minneapolis: University of Minnesota Press, 2008.

Choi, Chungmoo. "The Politics of War Memories toward Healing." In *Perilous Memories: The Asia-Pacific War(s)*, edited by T. Fujitani, Geoffrey M. White, and Lisa Yoneyama, 395–410. Durham, NC: Duke University Press, 2001.

Chong, Doryun. "Even a Dog That Wanders Will Find a Bone." In *Eiko & Koma: Time Is Not Even, Space Is Not Empty*, edited by Joan Rothfuss, 56–69. Minneapolis, MN: Walker Art Center, 2011.

———, ed. *Tokyo 1955–1970: A New Avant-Garde*. New York: The Museum of Modern Art, 2012.

Chong, Doryun, Michio Hayashi, Fumihiko Sumitomo, and Kenji Kajiya, eds. *From Postwar to Postmodern, Art in Japan, 1945–1989: Primary Documents*. Durham, NC: Duke University Press Books, 2012.

Cocuzza, Ginnine. "Dancers, Eiko and Koma, at Performing Garage." *The Villager*, August 16, 1979, 15.

Commanday, Robert. "Wholly Original and Provocative Dance by Eiko and Koma." *San Francisco Chronicle*, September 6, 1982, 31.

Conceison, Claire. "Translating Collaboration: *The Joy Luck Club* and Intercultural Theater." *TDR: The Drama Review* 39, no. 3 (1995): 151–66.

Conklin, J. L. "Dance Notes: The Wondrous Abstractions of Eiko and Koma." *Reader*, December 18, 1981.

Cook, Terry. "Archival Science and Postmodernism: New Formulations for Old Concepts." *Archival Science* 1, no. 1 (2001): 3–24.

Cook, Terry, and Joan M. Schwartz. "Archives, Records, and Power: From (Postmodern) Theory to (Archival) Performance." *Archival Science* 2, nos. 3–4 (2002): 171–85.

Crimp, Douglas. *Melancholia and Moralism: Essays on AIDS and Queer Politics.* Cambridge, MA: MIT Press, 2002.

Curran, Jim. "Avant-Garde Japaneese [sic] Modern Dance Combines Beatle Music, Whale Wails." *Daily Pennsylvanian*, February 1978.

"Dancers as Toys." *Honolulu Advertiser*, June 20, 1980, sec. A.

Darton, Eric. *Divided We Stand: A Biography of New York's World Trade Center.* New York: Basic Books, 1999.

———. "New York's World Trade Center: A Living Archive." Created in 2000. http://ericdarton.net/a_living_archive/index.html (accessed July 9, 2010).

de Certeau, Michel. *The Practice of Everyday Life.* Translated by Steven Rendall. Berkeley: University of California Press, 1984.

Debord, Guy. *The Society of the Spectacle.* Translated by Donald Nicholson-Smith. Brooklyn, NY: Zone Books, 1995 (1967).

DeFrantz, Thomas. *Dancing Revelations: Alvin Ailey's Embodiment of African American Culture.* New York: Oxford University Press, 2004.

Deleuze, Gilles. *Cinema 1: The Movement-Image.* Minneapolis: University of Minnesota Press, 1986.

———. *Cinema 2: The Time-Image.* Minneapolis: University of Minnesota Press, 1989.

Derrida, Jacques. *Archive Fever: A Freudian Impression.* Translated by Eric Prenowitz. Chicago: University of Chicago Press, 1996.

Diaz, Robert. "Melancholic Maladies: Paranoid Ethics, Reparative Envy, and Asian American Critique." *Women & Performance: A Journal of Feminist Theory* 16, no. 2 (2006): 201–19.

———. "Reparative Acts: Redress and the Politics of Queer Undoing in Contemporary Asian/America." PhD diss., City University of New York, 2007.

Dower, John W. *Embracing Defeat: Japan in the Wake of World War II.* New York: W.W. Norton & Company, 2000.

Dunning, Jennifer. "The Dance: Avant Duo At Garage." *New York Times*, August 5, 1979, 40.

———. "Dance: 'Nurse's Song' at the Kitchen." *New York Times*, November 30, 1981, sec. C 13.

———. "Flying, Waltzing, Walking and Jogging in Place." *Dance Magazine*, August 1977, 22, 24–25, 28.

————. "Grand Themes, Conveyed in Movement and in Paint, in 'Cambodian Stories.'" *New York Times*, May 22, 2006. http://www.nytimes.com/2006/05/22/arts/dance/22stor.html?_r=1&oref=slogin (accessed December 10, 2007).

Eckersall, Peter. *Performativity and Event in 1960s Japan: City, Body, Memory*. London: Palgrave Macmillan, 2013.

Eichenbaum, Rose, and Aron Hirt-Manheimer. "Eiko and Koma." In *The Dancer Within: Intimate Conversations with Great Dancers*, edited by Rose Eichenbaum and Aron Hirt-Manheimer, 266–71. Middletown, CT: Wesleyan University Press, 2008.

Eiko & Koma. "Cubiculo *White Dance* News Release," 1976. Eiko & Koma personal archive.

————. "Dirt News No.1." *Contact Quarterly* 7, no. 1 (1981): 40–41.

————. "A Note to Presenters," 1991. Eiko & Koma, personal archive.

————. "White Dance (Revival) (2010)." http://eikoandkoma.org/notesonwhitedance (accessed November 5, 2015).

Elswit, Kate. *Watching Weimar Dance*. New York: Oxford University Press, 2014.

Eng, David. "Melancholia in the Late Twentieth Century." *Signs* 25, no. 4 (2000): 1275–81.

————. "The Value of Silence." *Theatre Journal* 54, no. 1 (2002): 85–94.

Foster, Hal. "An Archival Impulse." *October* 110 (Fall 2004): 3–22.

Foster, Susan Leigh. "Choreographies of Gender." *Signs* 24, no. 1 (1998): 1–33.

————. "Choreographies of Protest." *Theatre Journal* 55, no. 3 (2003): 395–412.

————. *Reading Dancing: Bodies and Subjects in Contemporary American Dance*. Berkeley: University of California Press, 1986.

Foucault, Michel. *The Archaeology of Knowledge: The Discourse on Language*. Translated by A. M. Sheridan Smith. New York: Pantheon Books, 1972.

Franko, Mark. *Dancing Modernism/Performing Politics*. Bloomington: Indiana University Press, 1995.

————. "Editor's Note: Revaluing the Score: Archival Futurity." *Dance Research Journal* 44, no. 02 (2012): 1–2.

Fredericks, Robert A. "Perspectives: New York." *Dance Magazine*, October 1976.

Freud, Sigmund. "Mourning and Melancholia." In *The Standard Edition of the Complete Psychological Works of Sigmund Freud*, edited by J. Strachey, 14:237–60. London: The Hogarth Press and the Institute of Psycho-analysis, 1953.

Gere, David. *How to Make Dances in an Epidemic: Tracking Choreography in the Age of AIDS*. Madison: University of Wisconsin Press, 2004.

Gillespie, Angus Kress. *Twin Towers: The Life of New York City's World Trade Center*. New Brunswick, NJ: Rutgers University Press, 1999.

Glanz, James, and Eric Lipton. *City in the Sky: The Rise and Fall of the World Trade Center*. New York: Times Books, 2003.

Gōda, Nario. "On Ankoku Butō." In *Ankoku Butō: The Premodern and Postmodern Influences on the Dance of Utter Darkness*, by Susan Blakeley Klein, 79–88. Ithaca, NY: Cornell East Asia Series, 1988.

Goldner, Nancy. "Tarzan and Eve." *Soho Weekly News*, December 15, 1981, 25.

Goodwin, Nöel. "Eiko and Koma." *Dance and Dancers*, no. 385 (1982): 19.

Gordon, Beate Sirota. *The Only Woman in the Room: A Memoir*. Chicago: University of Chicago Press, 2014.

Gottschild, Brenda Dixon. *Digging the Africanist Presence in American Performance: Dance and Other Contexts*. Santa Barbara, CA: Praeger, 1998.

Grewal, Inderpal. "Transnational America: Race, Gender and Citizenship after 9/11." *Social Identities* 9, no. 4 (2003): 535–61.

Grosz, Elizabeth. *Space Time and Perversion: Essays on the Politics of Bodies*. New York: Routledge, 1995.

Halsey, Jan. "'Fur Seal' Boring, but Intriguing." *Daily Democrat*, August 11, 1978, 11.

Haraway, Donna. "A Manifesto for Cyborgs: Science, Technology, and Socialist Feminism in the 1980s." *Socialist Review* 15, no. 2 (1985): 65–107.

———. "The Promises of Monsters: A Regenerative Politics for Inappropriate/d Others." In *Cultural Studies*, edited by L. Grossberg, C. Nelson, and P. A. Treichler, 295–337. New York: Routledge, 1992.

Harootunian, H. D. "America's Japan/Japan's Japan." In *Japan in the World*, edited by Masao Miyoshi and H. D. Harootunian, 196–221. Durham, NC: Duke University Press, 1993.

Hartman, Saidya. *Scenes of Subjection: Terror, Slavery, and Self-Making in Nineteenth-Century America*. New York: Oxford University Press, 1997.

Harvey, David. *The Condition of Postmodernity*. Malden, MA: Blackwell Publishing, 1990.

Havens, Thomas. *Radicals and Realists in the Japanese Nonverbal Arts: The Avant-Garde Rejection of Modernism*. Honolulu: University of Hawaii Press, 2006.

Hayashi, Kyoko. *From Trinity to Trinity*. Translated by Eiko Otake. Barrytown, NY: Station Hill of Barrytown, 2010.

Hayashi, Michio. "Tracing the Graphic in Postwar Japanese Art." In *Tokyo 1955–1970: A New Avant-Garde*, edited by Doryun Chong, 94–119. New York: The Museum of Modern Art, 2012.

Hosoe, Eikoh. *Kamaitachi*. New York: Aperture, 2009.

Iwabuchi, Koichi. *Rogue Flows: Trans-Asian Cultural Traffic*. Hong Kong: Hong Kong University Press, 2004.

Jacobsen, Trudy. *Lost Goddesses: The Denial of Female Power in Cambodian History.* Copenhagen: Nordic Institute of Asian Studies, 2008.

#JEZ3PREZ & ATCHU. "On the Question of the Anarchives of Occupy Wall Street." *Emisférica* 9, nos. 1–2 (Summer 2012). http://hemisphericinstitute .org/hemi/en/e-misferica-91/jez3prezaatchu.

Jones, Sarah, Daisy Abbott, and Seamus Ross. "Redefining the Performing Arts Archive." *Archival Science* 9, nos. 3–4 (2009): 165–71.

Josa-Jones, Paula. "Delicious Moving." *Contact Quarterly* 30, no. 1 (2005): 56–61.

Jowitt, Deborah. "Caught in the Cross-Cultural Riptide." *Village Voice*, December 9, 1981.

———. "Crawling into a Womb of Rice." *Village Voice*, February 22, 1983.

———. "Dark Art." *Village Voice*, October 11, 1994, 105.

———. "Eiko and Koma Pity the Earth: Two Dancers and a Pianist Create a Transcendent Lament." *Village Voice*, October 20, 2007.

———. "Voices Dance: Eiko and Koma." *Village Voice*, 1978.

———. "I'll Give You the Answer — If You've Got a Week." *Village Voice*, May 6, 1981, 81.

———. "In Their Dance No Wind Blows." *Village Voice*, August 9, 1976.

K. S. W. "Fur Seal." *Daily Telegraph*, November 6, 1981.

Kazuo Ohno Dance Studio. *Kazuo Ohno: Chronicle of a Lifetime 1906–2010.* Tokyo: Canta Co., Ltd., 2010.

Kennedy, Gilles. "New York-Renowned Butoh Artists Debut in Japan." *Japan Times*, January 22, 1989.

Kester, Grant H. *Conversation Pieces: Community and Communication in Modern Art.* Berkeley: University of California Press, 2004.

Kim, Hyunjung. "Rethinking Korean Subjectivity: Salp'uri and Women in South Korea." *Discourses in Dance* 4, no. 1 (2007): 49–63.

Kirn, Marda. "Minds Behind the Movement." *Westword*, July 9, 1981, 11.

Kisselgoff, Anna. "The Dance: Kazuo Ohno's 'Dead Sea.'" *New York Times*, November 21, 1985. http://www.nytimes.com/1985/11/21/arts/the-dance -kazuo-ohno-s-dead-sea.html.

———. "Dance View: Grotesque Imagery Has Come to Dance." *New York Times*, April 15, 1984. http://www.nytimes.com/1984/04/15/arts/dance -view-grotesque-imagery-has-come-to-dance.html?pagewanted=all.

———. "Two Dancers from Japan in 'Fur Seal.'" *New York Times*, February 28, 1978, 16.

———. "Japanese Avant-Garde Dance Is Darkly Erotic." *New York Times*, July 15, 1984, 1.

Kitano, Harry. *Japanese Americans: The Evolution of a Subculture*. Upper Saddle River, NJ: Prentice, 1969.

Klein, Christina. *Cold War Orientalism: Asia in the Middlebrow Imagination, 1945–1961*. Berkeley: University of California Press, 2003.

Klein, Susan Blakeley. *Ankoku Butō: The Premodern and Postmodern Influences on the Dance of Utter Darkness*. Ithaca, NY: Cornell East Asia Series, 1988.

Kondo, Dorinne. *About Face: Performing Race in Fashion and Theater*. New York: Routledge, 1997.

Kourlas, Gia. "The King and Queen of Slow Get Busy." *New York Times*, May 25, 2010. http://www.nytimes.com/2010/05/26/arts/dance/26eiko.html?module =Search&mabReward=relbias%3Aw%2C%7B%222%22%3A%22RI%3A14 %22%7D.

Kurihara, Nanako. "Eiko and Koma: Movement Approach and Works." Master's thesis, New York University, 1988.

———. "The Most Remote Thing in the Universe: Critical Analysis of Hijikata Tatsumi's Butoh Dance." PhD diss., New York University, 1996.

Kwan, SanSan. "Choreographing Chineseness: Global Cities and the Performance of Ethnicity." PhD diss., New York University, 2003.

———. *Kinesthetic City: Dance and Movement in Chinese Urban Spaces*. New York: Oxford University Press, 2013.

———. "Performing a Geography of Asian America: The Chop Suey Circuit." *The Drama Review: TDR* 55 (2011): 120–136.

Kwon, Miwon. *One Place After Another*. Cambridge, MA: MIT Press, 2002.

LaCapra, Dominick. *History and Memory After Auschwitz*. Ithaca, NY: Cornell University Press, 1998.

Lacy, Suzanne, ed. *Mapping the Terrain: New Genre Public Art*. Seattle: Bay Press, 1994.

Lee, Esther Kim. *A History of Asian American Theatre*. New York, Cambridge University Press, 2011.

Lee, Josephine. *Performing Asian America: Race and Ethnicity on the Contemporary Stage*. Philadelphia: Temple University Press, 1997.

LeMay, Curtis. *Mission with LeMay: My Story*. New York: Doubleday & Company, 1965.

Lepecki, André. "The Body as Archive: Will to Re-Enact and the Afterlives of Dances." *Dance Research Journal* 42, no. 2 (2010): 28–48.

———. "Choreography's 'Slower Ontology': Jérôme Bel's Critique of Representation." In *Exhausting Dance: Performance and the Politics of Movement*, 45–64. New York: Routledge, 2006.

———. "Reciprocal Topographies—Eiko & Koma's Dancesculptures." In *Eiko &*

Koma: Time Is Not Even, Space Is Not Empty, edited by Joan Rothfuss, 48–55. Minneapolis, MN: Walker Art Center, 2011.

Letton, Shoko Yamahata. "Eiko and Koma: Dance Philosophy and Aesthetic." Master's thesis, Florida State University, 2009.

Levin, Anne. "'Trilogy: Dance with 2 Ghastly Figures.'" *Villager*, April 22, 1981, 11.

Levi-Strauss, Claude. *The Raw and the Cooked*. New York: Harper & Row, 1969.

Long, Norman. *Development Sociology: Actor Perspectives*. New York: Routledge, 2001.

Lorimer, Jamie. *Wildlife in the Anthropocene: Conservation After Nature*. Minneapolis: University of Minnesota Press, 2015.

Lowe, Lisa. *Immigrant Acts: On Asian American Cultural Politics*. Durham, NC: Duke University Press, 1996.

M. G. "Tierliebe Mit Eiko & Koma." *AZ München*, June 1, 1982.

Ma, Sheng-Mei. *The Deathly Embrace: Orientalism and Asian American Identity*. Minneapolis: University of Minnesota Press, 2000.

Manning, Susan. "Modernist Dogma and Post-Modern Rhetoric: A Response to Sally Banes' 'Terpsichore in Sneakers.'" *Drama Review* 32, no. 4 (1988): 32–39.

Marotti, William. "Buto No Mondaisei to Honshitsushugi no Wana" 舞踏の問題性と本質主義の罠" [The problematics of butoh and the essentialist trap]. *Shiataa Aatsu*, no. 8 (May 1997): 88–96.

———. *Money, Trains, and Guillotines: Art and Revolution in 1960s Japan*. Durham, NC: Duke University Press, 2013.

Martin, Randy. *Performance as Political Act: The Embodied Self*. New York: Bergin and Garvey, 1990.

Massey, Doreen. *World Cities*. Cambridge, UK: Polity Press, 2007.

Matsuda, Takeshi. *Soft Power and Its Perils: U.S. Cultural Policy in Early Postwar Japan and Permanent Dependency*. Palo Alto, CA: Stanford University Press, 2007.

McGray, Douglas. "Japan's Gross National Cool." *Foreign Policy*, no. 130 (May–June 2002): 44–54.

McKibben, Bill. *The End of Nature*. New York: Random House, 1989.

Meduri, Avanthi, Phillip Zarrilli, and Deborah Neff. "More Aftermath after Peter Brook." *TDR: The Drama Review* 32, no. 2 (1988): 14–19.

Mele, Christopher. *Selling the Lower East Side: Culture, Real Estate, and Resistance in New York City*. Minneapolis: University of Minnesota Press, 2000.

Mimura, Glen M. *Ghostlife of Third Cinema: Asian American Film and Video*. Minneapolis: University of Minnesota Press, 2009.

Miodoni, Cate. "Placing the Breath within the Body." *The Downtown Review* (Fall 1980): 34–46.

Morgenroth, Joyce. "Eiko Otake." In *Speaking of Dance: Twelve Contemporary Choreographers on Their Craft*, 117–136. New York: Routledge, 2004.

Morris, Gay. "Japanese Dancers Offer Concert Rich in Drama and Color." *Palo Alto Times*, July 13, 1978.

Motofuji, Akiko. Hijikata Tatsumi to Tomo ni 土方巽と共に [Together with Tatsumi Hijikata]. Tokyo: Chikuma Shobō, 1990.

Moy, James S. *Marginal Sights: Staging the Chinese in America*. Iowa City: University of Iowa Press, 1994.

Mulvey, Laura. *Visual and Other Pleasures*. Bloomington: Indiana University Press, 1989.

Munroe, Alexandra. *Japanese Art After 1945: Scream Against the Sky*. New York: Harry N. Abrams/Yokohama Museum of Art, 1996.

Munroe, Alexandra, Ming Tiampo, Yoshihara Jiro, and Gutai. *Gutai: Splendid Playground*. New York: Guggenheim Museum, 2013.

Newman, Barbara. "Reviews VIII." *Dance Magazine*, October 1979, 48, 50, 110.

Nuchtern, Jean. "Tripping." *Soho News*, November 9, 1978.

Ong, Aiwah. *Flexible Citizenship: The Cultural Logics of Transnationality*. Durham, NC: Duke University Press, 1999.

Oppenheim, Irene. "The Stage as a Cutting Board." Unpublished manuscript, 1979.

Otake, Eiko. "A Dancer Behind the Lens." In *Envisioning Dance on Film and Video*, edited by Judy Mitoma, 82–88. New York: Routledge, 2002.

———. "Feeling Wind." In *Site Dance: Choreographers and the Lure of Alternative Spaces*, edited by Melanie Kloetzel and Carolyn Pavlik, 188–98. Gainesville: University Press of Florida, 2009.

Palumbo-Liu, David. *Asian/American: Historical Crossings of a Racial Frontier*. Palo Alto, CA: Stanford University Press, 1999.

Perillo, Jeffrey Lorenzo. "Hip-Hop, Streetdance, and the Remaking of the Global Filipino." PhD diss., University of California, Los Angeles, 2013.

Perlmutter, Donna. "Outer Limits of Dance Have Earthly Appeal." *Los Angeles Herald Examiner*, June 30, 1980, B5.

Perron, Wendy. "Martha Graham and the Asian Connection." *Dance Magazine* (blog), March 24, 2014. (May be available at http://www.dancemagazine.com/blogs/wendy/5725 or http://wendyperron.com/archives/dance-magazine-posts/.)

———. "When Martha Got to Be Asian." *Wendy Perron* (blog), March 31, 2014. http://wendyperron.com/when-martha-got-to-be-asian/.

Peters, Julie Stone. "Intercultural Performance, Theatre Anthropology, and the Imperialist Critique: Identities, Inheritances and Neo-Orthodoxies." In

Imperialism and Theatre: Essays on World Theatre, Drama and Performance, edited by J. E. Gainor, 199–213. London: Routledge, 1995.

Petersen, William. "Success Story, Japanese-American Style." *New York Times*, January 9, 1966, 21, 33, 36, 38, 41, 43.

Prasad, Vijay. *Everybody Was Kung Fu Fighting: Afro-Asian Connections and the Myth of Cultural Purity*. Boston: Beacon Press, 2002.

R. J. "A Gentle Wind Stirs at the Joyce Theater." *Dance Magazine*, December 1993, 30.

Reason, Matthew. "Archive or Memory? The Detritus of Live Performance." *New Theatre Quarterly* 19, no. 01 (2003): 82–89.

———. *Documentation, Disappearance and the Representation of Live Performance*. New York: Palgrave Macmillan, 2006.

"Review." *Artweek*, September 15, 1979, 3.

"Review." *Dance Magazine*, October 1979.

Roach, Joseph. *Cities of the Dead: Circum-Atlantic Performance*. New York: Columbia University Press, 1996.

Ronda, Margaret. "Mourning and Melancholia in the Anthropocene." *Post45* June 10, 2013. http://post45.research.yale.edu/2013/06/mourning-and-melancholia-in-the-anthropocene/.

Ross, Janice. "Eiko and Koma in 'Fur Seal.'" *Artweek*, 8, no. 41 (December 3, 1977).

———. "Tension in the Cocoon." *San Francisco Bay Guardian*, October 27, 1977.

Rothfuss, Joan, ed. *Eiko & Koma: Time Is Not Even, Space Is Not Empty*. Minneapolis, MN: Walker Art Center, 2011.

Said, Edward W. *Orientalism*. New York: Vintage, 1979.

Sas, Miryam. *Experimental Arts in Postwar Japan: Moments of Encounter, Engagement, and Imagined Return*. Cambridge, MA: Harvard University Asia Center, 2011.

———. "Intermedia, 1955–1970." In *Tokyo 1955–1970: A New Avant-Garde*, edited by Doryun Chong, 138–57. New York: Museum of Modern Art, 2012.

Sassen, Saskia. *The Global City*. Princeton, NJ: Princeton University Press, 1991.

Savigliano, Marta. *Tango and the Political Economy of Passion*. Boulder, CO: Westview Press, 1995.

Schechner, Richard. "Intercultural Performance: 'An Introduction.'" *TDR: The Drama Review* 26, no. 2 (1982): 3–4.

———. "A Reply to Rustom Bharucha." *Asian Theatre Journal* 1, no. 2 (1984): 245–53.

Segal, Lewis. "Cambodian Stories Affirms a Lust for Life." *Los Angeles Times*, April 7, 2006, http://articles.latimes.com/2006/apr/07/entertainment/et-stories7 (accessed December 11, 2007).

———. "Eiko and Koma in 'Cock Crows.'" *Los Angeles Times*, August 29, 1978.

Shaka, Angeline. "Hula 'Olapa and the 'Hula Girl': Contemporary Hula Choreographies of the Concert Stage." PhD diss., University of California, Los Angeles, 2011.

Shang, Ruby. "A Taste of Japanese Dance." *New York Times*, July 4, 1982. http://www.nytimes.com/1982/07/04/arts/a-taste-of-japanese-dance.html?module=Search&mabReward=relbias%3Ar%2C%7B%222%22%3A%22RI%3A12%22%7D.

Shapiro-Phim, Toni. *Dance and the Spirit of Cambodia*. Ithaca, NY: Cornell University Press, 1994.

Sharma, Preeti. "The (T)errors of Visibility." Master's thesis, University of California, Los Angeles, 2008.

Shields, Nancy. *Fake Fish: The Theater of Kobo Abe*. Boston: Weatherhill Publishing, 1996.

Shih, Shu-mei, and Francoise Lionnet, eds. *Minor Transnationalism*. Durham, NC: Duke University Press, 2005.

Shimakawa, Karen. "Loaded Images: Seeing and Being in 'Fan Variations.'" In *Narrative/Performance: Cross-Cultural Encounters at APPEX*, edited by Judy Mitoma, Anoosh Jorjorian, and Richard D. Trimillos. Los Angeles: Center for Intercultural Performance, 2004. http://www.wac.ucla.edu/cip/archive/appexbook/loadedimages.html.

———. *National Abjection: The Asian American Body Onstage*. Durham, NC: Duke University Press, 2002.

Shore, Michael. "Punk Rocks the Art World." *ARTnews*, November 1980, 78–85.

Siegel, Marcia B. "Japanese Dances: Intriguing Ambiguity." *Christian Science Monitor*, October 21, 1987.

———. *The Tail of the Dragon: New Dance, 1976–1982*. Durham, NC: Duke University Press, 1991.

Sieg, Linda, and Kiyoshi Takenaka. "'Japan Takes Historic Step from Post-War Pacifism, OKs Fighting for Allies.'" *Reuters*, July 1, 2014. http://www.reuters.com/article/2014/07/01/us-japan-defense-idUSKBN0F52S120140701 (accessed October 11, 2014).

Singer, Thea. "A Primal 'Mourning' and Hope for Rebirth." *Boston Globe*, July 18, 2008.

Small, Linda. "Lord's Aloof/Crow's Minimal." *Other Stages*, November 2, 1978.

Smith, Amanda. "Review." *Dance Magazine*, May 1986.

———. "Reviews." *Dance Magazine*, March 1980, 38–39.

Smith, Imogen. "The Dance Heritage Coalition: Passing on the Vitality of American Dance." *Dance Chronicle* 35, no. 2 (2012): 250–58.

Sorgenfrei, Carol Fisher. *Unspeakable Acts: The Avant-Garde Theatre of Terayama Shuji And Postwar Japan*. Honolulu: University of Hawaii Press, 2005.

Srinivasan, Priya. "The Bodies Beneath the Smoke or What's Behind the Cigarette Poster: Unearthing Kinesthetic Connections in American Dance History." *Discourses in Dance* 4, no. 1 (2007): 7–48.

———. "The Nautch Women Dancers of the 1880s: Corporeality, US Orientalism, and Anti-Asian Immigration Laws." *Women & Performance: A Journal of Feminist Theory* 19, no. 1 (2009): 3–22.

———. *Sweating Saris: Indian Dance as Transnational Labor*. Philadelphia: Temple University Press, 2011.

Stein, Bonnie Sue. "Butoh: 'Twenty Years Ago We Were Crazy, Dirty and Mad.'" *TDR: The Drama Review* 20, no. 2 (1986): 107–26.

Stoermer, Eugene, and Paul Crutzen. "The Anthropocene." *Global Change Newsletter* 41 (2000): 17–18.

Strauss, Gloria. "Roundtable Discussion with Asian American Dance Choreographers." *Bridge: An Asian American Perspective*, Summer 1978, 37–38.

Sulzman, Mona. "Moth Comes to Life as Eiko and Koma White Dance." *Soho Weekly News*, July 29, 1976, 13.

Supree, Burt. "Only Disconnect." *Village Voice*, August 27, 1979.

———. "Voice Choices: Dance." *Village Voice*, August 6, 1979.

Swift, Orla. "Handing down the Dance: Eiko and Koma, Known for Their Impossibly Slow Movement and Exquisite Style, Are Trying to Preserve Their Creations by Teaching Them to Two Teenagers." *News and Observer*, June 27, 2007.

Takemae, Eiji. *Allied Occupation of Japan*. Translated by Robert Ricketts and Sebastian Swan. New York: Continuum, 2003.

Tansman, Alan. "Catastrophe, Memory, and Narrative: Teaching Japanese and Jewish Responses to Twentieth-Century Atrocity." *Discourse* 25, nos. 1 & 2 (2004): 248–71.

Taylor, Diana. *The Archive and the Repertoire: Performing Cultural Memory in the Americas*. Durham, NC: Duke University Press, 2003.

———. "Save As." *Emisferica* 9, nos. 1–2 (Summer 2012). http://hemispheric institute.org/hemi/en/e-misferica-91/taylor.

"Text: President Bush Addresses the Nation." *The Washington Post*, September 20, 2001.

Thornbury, Barbara E. *America's Japan and Japan's Performing Arts: Cultural Mobility and Exchange in New York 1952–2011*. Ann Arbor: University of Michigan Press, 2013.

"Times Net Down in 4th Quarter." *New York Times*, February 15, 1979, sec. D4.

Tobias, Tobi. "Flagging." *Soho Weekly News*, August 16, 1979, 43.

———. "Food for the Eye." *New York*, March 14, 1983, 68, 71.

———. "XII." *Dance Magazine*, January 1979, 115–16.

Traiger, Lisa. "After the Killing Fields." *Danceviewtimes*, April 3, 2006. http://archives.danceviewtimes.com/2006/Spring/01/eikoandkoma.html.

Tseng, Derrick. "Japanese Dance Team." *Orient Times*, August 26, 1979.

Tucker, Marilyn. "Avant Garde Dancers to Be Reckoned With." *San Francisco Chronicle*, July 14, 1978, 64.

Uchino, Tadashi. *Crucible Bodies: Postwar Japanese Performance from Brecht to the New Millennium*. Calcutta, India: Seagull Books, 2009.

Ueda, Makoto. *Zeami, Basho, Yeats, Pound: A Study in Japanese and English Poetics*. The Hague: Mouton, 1965.

Wapner, Paul. *Living Through the End of Nature: The Future of American Environmentalism*. Cambridge, MA: MIT Press, 2013.

Webster, Daniel. "Eiko and Koma: 'Fur Seal' Explores the Essence of the Animal World." *Philadelphia Inquirer*, February 9, 1978.

Wee, C. J. W.-L. "Imagining 'New Asia' in the Theatre: Cosmopolitan East Asia and the Global West." In *Rogue Flows: Trans-Asian Cultural Traffic*, edited by Koichi Iwabuchi, S. Muecke, and M. Thomas, 119–50. Hong Kong: Hong Kong University Press, 2004.

Wei, William. *The Asian American Movement*. Philadelphia: Temple University Press, 1993.

Weisenfeld, Gennifer. *MAVO: Japanese Artists and the Avant-Garde, 1905–1931*. Berkeley: University of California Press, 2001.

Weiss, Hedy. "Whimsy, Sadness Blend in Asian Delicacy." *Chicago Sun Times*, May 15, 2006. http://www.highbeam.com/doc/1P2-1626868.html (accessed October 26, 2015).

Williams, Raymond. "Nature." In *Keywords: A Vocabulary of Culture and Society*, rev. ed., 219–224. New York: Oxford University Press, 1985.

Windham, Leslie. "A Conversation with Eiko and Koma." *Ballet Review*, Summer 1988.

Winther, Bert. "Japanese Thematics in Postwar American Art: From Soi-Disant Zen to the Assertion of Asian-American Identity." In *Japanese Art After 1945: Scream Against the Sky*, edited by Alexandra Munroe, 55–67. New York: Harry N. Abrams, 1996.

Wong, Deborah. *Speak It Louder: Asian Americans Making Music*. New York: Routledge, 2004.

Wong, Yutian. "Artistic Utopias: Michio Ito and the Trope of the International."

In *Worlding Dance*, edited by Foster, Susan Leigh, 144–62. New York: Palgrave Macmillan, 2009.

———. *Choreographing Asian America*. Middletown, CT: Wesleyan, 2010.

———. "Towards a New Asian American Dance Theory: Locating the Dancing Asian American Body." *Discourses in Dance* 1, no. 1 (2002): 69–90.

Woods, Byron. "ADF: Eiko and Koma." *Independent Weekly*, July 4, 2007. http://www.indyweek.com/gyrobase/content?oid=oid%3A156563.

Wu, Ellen. *The Color of Success: Asian Americans and the Origins of the Model Minority*. Princeton, NJ: Princeton University Press, 2014.

Yamamoto, Zipporah Lax. "After 9/11: Transformations of Memory Into History." PhD diss., University of California, Los Angeles, 2011.

Yokobosky, Matthew. "Movement as Installation: Eiko & Koma in Conversation with Matthew Yokobosky." *PAJ: A Journal of Performance and Art*, no. 64 (2000): 26–35.

Yoshihara, Mari. *Embracing the East: White Women and American Orientalism*. New York: Oxford University Press, 2002.

Yoshimoto, Midori. *Into Performance: Japanese Women Artists in New York*. New Brunswick, NJ: Rutgers University Press, 2005.

Zarrilli, Phillip. "The Aftermath: When Peter Brook Came to India." *TDR: The Drama Review* 30, no. 1 (1986): 92–99.

Zimmer, Elizabeth. "Downtown Dance." *Dance Magazine*, 1987, 64–69.

———. "Sacred Spaces." *Village Voice*, July 23, 2002. http://www.villagevoice.com/2002-07-23/dance/sacred-spaces/.

Žižek, Slavoj. *Violence: Six Sideways Reflections*. New York: Picador, 2008.

Index

Page references in *italics* refer to photos.

(273)

ABOUT THE AUTHOR

An emerging scholar in Asian American dance, Rosemary Candelario is assistant professor of Dance at Texas Woman's University. Her publications include an article in the *Journal of Theatre, Dance and Performance Training*, forthcoming pieces in *Asian Theatre Journal*, the *Oxford Handbook of Dance and the Popular Screen*, and *Feminist Scholar Online*. Rosemary holds a MA and PhD in Culture and Performance with a concentration in Dance from the University of California, Los Angeles, and a BA in Anthropology and German Language and Literature from Boston University.